Read
With Me

365 FAMILY READINGS
GIVING AN OVERVIEW OF THE BIBLE

Read With Me

365 FAMILY READINGS
GIVING AN OVERVIEW OF THE BIBLE

Jean Stapleton

CHRISTIAN FOCUS

© Copyright 2006 Jean Stapleton
ISBN 1-84550-148-9
Published in 2006
by
Christian Focus Publications,
Geanies House, Fearn, Tain
Ross-shire, IV20 1TW,
Great Britain

Cover design by Danie van Straaten
Illustrated by Roger de Klerk
Maps and tabernacle pictures by Fred Apps

Printed and Bound by J. H. Haynes & Co. Ltd., Sparkford

BOOKS	DAYS

Mark your progress at the back of the book .... Page 423

INTRODUCTION

This book has been designed for parents to read with children of about five years old and upward. Using daily readings, it introduces that great theme of the Bible, the promise of a Saviour and His coming into the world.

The notes have been written using the New King James Bible. As far as possible the questions that conclude each day's reading have been made compatible with both the New King James and New International Version.

The book is divided up into sections according to the books of the Bible. There are introductory sections which explain the background behind the biblical text and what the main teaching points are. These sections should be read by the adult in the family. However older children may benefit from reading these sections too.

The daily readings encourage you to read the Bible with your family and there are interactive questions as well as a read by myself section for younger children.

THE BOOK OF BEGINNINGS

The importance of the Book of Genesis can hardly be overestimated: it is quoted from or referred to about two hundred times in the New Testament. The first eleven chapters introduce us to the origin of many things, including the universe, man, sin, marriage, languages, nations, and the first promise of redemption. From chapter twelve onwards we learn about the origin of the nation of Israel through which the promised Saviour would come into the world.

Above all else the Bible is God's revelation of Himself. In Genesis we read of the God who brought time, space and all created things into being by His own wisdom and power.

The teaching that because sin results in death, God can only be approached through the death of a substitute, begins in Genesis. Children are able to understand that sin's consequences had been explained to Adam before his disobedience. We can explain the sacrificial death of an animal in terms of both the seriousness of sin and the grace of God in providing a way for sin to be covered until the Lord Jesus Christ came into the world to die in the sinner's place.

Genesis not only lays the foundation of all the great truths of the Bible, it also explains why the world is as it is today.

Day 1: IN THE BEGINNING

Every year our birthday reminds us that there was a day when we were born and our lives began. God is very different: He is eternal. This means that God has no beginning and no end. He is the One who is always there and who never changes. The earth and the sky and all that we see around us had a beginning. We read about this in the first chapter of the Bible.

There were no men or women there to see God making the earth and the sky. But God Himself helped the writer of the Book of Genesis to tell us about this.

The first verse in the Bible says that God created the heavens and the earth. We would call the heavens 'space' and of course the earth is the world in which we live. God also made the light and called it 'day'. He called the darkness 'night'. This was the first day.

When we make something we use things that are already there. When God created the heavens and the earth He did not have things to use: they were created by His own power. On the second day, God made the sky and He made the air we breathe.

We call the space around the earth - atmosphere. It protects the earth, so that it does not become too hot. Some Bibles use the word 'firmament' in verses 6-8. This is an old word which means 'expanse' or 'space'.

Genesis chapter 1 verses 1-8.

The Bible is a very special Book.

The Bible was written by men who lived at different times and in different places. God made sure that the words that these men wrote are true.

What were the first words spoken by God that are in the verses you read today?

Day 2: PLANTS AND STARS

When God first made the earth, it was covered with water. On the third day, God caused the water to form seas, so that dry land appeared. Look at the soil in a garden or field. It does not look interesting, and yet God made the soil so that plants would have all they needed to grow. It was on the third day that God made plants. He made trees and grass and other plants. Each plant had its own seeds so that more plants would grow. Seeds always grow into a plant like the one they have come from.

If you want to grow grass, you plant grass seed. Sunflowers grow from sunflower seeds and acorns can take root in the soil so that more oak trees appear. This is the way that God made the plants, so that as some plants die down, more are always growing.

In daytime we have light and warmth from the sun.

Have you been out when it is dark and seen the stars and the moon? There are many, many stars, more than we can count. The Bible tells us that God made them and set them in space. God placed the sun and moon in just the right place so there would be more light in the day, and less at night. He made the sun, moon and stars on the fourth day.

Genesis chapter 1 verses 9-19.

When God spoke, things happened in a way that we cannot understand. God is much greater than us. He is very wise. God made our wonderful world. He is so powerful: He was able to create all He had planned.

On what day did the dry land appear?
What else did God make on that day?

9

Day 3: FISH AND BIRDS

Have you ever visited an aquarium and seen all the different kinds of fish and sea creatures? The Bible tells us that God made these on the fifth day.

Most fish live and breathe under water. They lay eggs there and the babies grow to look like the parent fish. Whales are different. They come to the surface to breathe and their babies are born underwater. God made tiny fish, brightly coloured fish; dolphins and sharks. He made soft-bodied creatures with shells and the tiny plankton that whales eat.

When you see a ship on the water you can be sure that someone designed it. Someone planned the way it should be made. Fish swim so easily and can live in the water. That is what God designed them to do.

As well as sea creatures, God also created birds on the fifth day. God made the little birds that we see in the garden. He also made larger birds like herons, flamingos and eagles. How is it that birds fly around without any trouble at all? It is because God designed them to fly. Birds have bones that are very light, and strong muscles to move their wings. They also have feathers which are made in such a way that they do not get ruffled when the wind blows.

Genesis chapter 1 verses 20-23.

Baby birds hatch from eggs that the mother bird lays. They become like the parent bird. God made birds like this. What a wonderful God He is.

How many times do we read that God saw that what He had made was good? (Genesis chapter 1 verses 4-23).

Day 4: LAND ANIMALS

On the sixth day, God made the animals that live on the land. He made wild animals like the lions and tigers and dinosaurs. He made farm animals like cows, pigs and sheep. He also made the tiny animals that live on the ground.

GOD'S WORD

Genesis chapter 1 verses 24-25 and 30.

The animals that God made were able to have babies. Lions have cubs, horses have foals, cows have calves. Each baby animal grows up to be like the parent animal.

Each kind of animal that God made may include animals of different sizes and colours. Dogs may be large, like Alsatians, or small like Terriers. We would never mistake a little Shetland pony for a dog: although it is small it belongs to the same family as the big, strong horses that pull carts and carriages.

When God first made the animals their food was the plants that grow on the earth. Plants were for food and no animal had to be killed to provide food for another.

BY MYSELF

God looked at the animals He had made and saw that everything was good.

EXTRA INFO

Animals are wonderful. Camels carry fat in their humps to help them survive for days without drinking. A honey-bee can tell other bees where to find food. Land animals have been designed by God just as birds and fish were.

ASK ABOUT

Which verse that you read today shows us that when God first made the animals they ate plants?

Day 5: THE FIRST MAN

God created a wonderful world. Plants and trees grew on the land; fish swam in the sea; birds flew in the air and animals grazed in the field. The sun shone by day and the moon gave its light at night. All that God had made was good. Then, on the sixth day, after He had made the animals, God created man.

The Bible tells us that men and women were made in the image of God. When a girl is the image of her mother, this means that she looks like her mother. God did not make people to look like Him, but to be like Him. This is quite hard to understand because we know that we are not great and powerful like God is; but we can think and speak and learn. We enjoy looking at things that are beautiful. We are able to feel happy and sad and to explain how we feel. Most of all we can know and love God.

Genesis chapter 1 verses 26-31.

God told Adam that his children were to spread out and fill the world. Men and women were to take charge of the creatures God had made. God gave to the first man the wonderful task of caring for creation.

Some people say that men and women are just another animal. This is not true. God made men and women separately from animals. He made us to live forever, knowing Him as our loving Creator and Friend.

God looked at all He had made and it was very good. The world God had made was beautiful. It was peaceful with no pain, illness or death.

What were men and women put in charge of?

DAY 6: A SPECIAL DAY

God made the earth; sky; sea; dry land; plants; sun, moon and stars; birds and fish; animals, and the first man and woman, in six days. On the seventh day, God rested. He did not rest because He was tired. He rested because His work of creation was finished.

God made the seventh day a special day of rest.

God made us and knows what is best for us. At home or at school, at work or with our friends, life can be very busy. From the beginning God made one day each week to be different from the other days. Some things still need to be done, like getting meals ready and caring for sick people. But as far as possible we should have one day every week free from work. This does not mean that on Sundays we do nothing. This is a day to say thanks God and remember how good He is. It is a day to learn more about Him and if possible to meet with other people who love Him.

Genesis chapter 2 verses 1-7.

From these verses we learn about the way God made the first man. He was made from the dust of the ground. This means that man's body was made from things that God had already created. It was quite different from when the animals were made. God breathed life into man. Only God can give life and only man was given life in this way.

The Bible tells us clearly that we are made in a very special way.

Who decided that each week is made up of seven days?

Day 7: THE FIRST GARDEN

Gardens can be beautiful as well as useful. We enjoy looking at the lovely flowers and trees. We also enjoy eating the vegetables and fruit from the garden. But do you know who planted the first garden?

GOD'S WORD

Genesis chapter 2 verses 8-10 and 15-17.

EXTRA INFO

The first garden was the Garden of Eden and it was planted by God. God gave Adam, the first man, the task of looking after the garden.

There were many trees in the garden with fruit that was good to eat. There were two trees with special names. One was called the tree of life, the other one was called the tree of the knowledge of good and evil.

God told Adam that he could eat fruit from every tree in the garden except one. God explained to Adam that he must not eat the fruit from the tree of the knowledge of good and evil: if he did, he would die.

Adam had work to do and food to eat. But there was something more that he needed. God said that He would make a helper for Adam, so that he would not be alone.

BY MYSELF

God brought the birds and animals to Adam. Adam gave names to them.

As he did this, Adam was learning about the wonderful creatures that God had made. But among all the animals he did not find a real friend, to be with him and to help him.

ASK ABOUT

How was the Garden of Eden watered? From which of the trees was Adam told that he must not eat the fruit?

Day 8: A WIFE FOR ADAM

When God made the world, He made it just right for people to live in. There was air to breathe, food to eat, the day for work and the night for rest. But God knew that Adam needed someone to be with him.

GOD'S WORD

Genesis chapter 2 verses 18-25.

Genesis chapter one tells us that God made the first man and woman on the sixth day. The second chapter explains how the woman was made. None of the other animals could really have helped Adam in the work that God had given him to do. So while Adam was sleeping, God made the woman from a part of his side. Adam was not hurt: God healed him. When he awoke, he saw the woman that God had made. He knew that this was his wife, the friend and helper he needed.

God chose a different and very wonderful way to make the woman. She was actually made from part of the man.

EXTRA INFO

Adam knew what God had done. He felt that his wife was part of himself. This teaches us that when a man and a woman marry, they belong to one another for the rest of their lives.

BY MYSELF

God knows what is best for us. A family where father and mother love one another is a good place for boys and girls to grow up.

Families today are not always like this and in the Old Testament we see that it was the same in Bible times. But God's way is best. He gave us a week made up of seven days and He planned the first marriage.

ASK ABOUT

Which verse tells us that Adam understood the way his wife had been made?

Day 9: A VERY SAD DAY

The first man and his wife had a lovely garden to live in and care for. God gave them everything they needed. But one day Adam's wife heard a voice in the garden. It came from an animal called a serpent, but it was really God's enemy, Satan using an animal to speak to the woman.

Satan does not love God, in fact he hates God and everything that is good.

The serpent asked whether God had really said that they were not to eat fruit from every tree in the garden. The woman explained that they could eat fruit from every tree except one: if they ate from that one tree they would die. The serpent told the woman that she would not die but would become very wise; in fact she would be like God Himself.

Instead of remembering how good God had been the woman listened to what the serpent said. She looked at the fruit of the tree of the knowledge of good and evil, and then put out her hand and took some.

Eve ate the fruit and gave some of it to Adam, who ate it as well.

Until now Adam and his wife had not needed to wear any clothes because they had no wrong thoughts in their minds. Now that they had disobeyed God, they both felt ashamed and sewed some leaves together to cover themselves.

Genesis chapter 3 verses 1-7.

What does it mean to obey? What does it mean to disobey?

Day 10: A SAVIOUR PROMISED

Have you ever tried to hide because you have done something you should not have done? Adam and his wife hid when they heard God's voice in the garden. They had not done this before they disobeyed God, but now they were afraid to meet Him.

God called to Adam and asked him if he had eaten the fruit which he had been told not to eat. Adam blamed the woman, and she blamed the serpent. God said that because Adam and his wife had disobeyed Him, many things would change.

Life became very hard. Thorns and thistles grew. Growing plants for food became very difficult.

Genesis chapter 3 verses 8-13.

Adam gave his wife the name Eve. They were sent away from the Garden of Eden so that they would not be able to eat the fruit of the tree of life. Their bodies began to grow old and one day would die. The Bible teaches that disobeying God is sin. Sin separates us from God so we no longer know Him as our Friend.

After Adam and Eve sinned, God's beautiful world changed. Everyone born into the world would do things that are wrong. Everyone that is, except One.

God promised that one day a Saviour would be born who would defeat Satan and sin.

When we do wrong, we sometimes try to blame someone else.

Who did Adam blame? Who did Eve blame?

Day 11: CAIN AND ABEL

When someone is a hundred years old, we think that they have had a very long life. But long, long ago, people lived a lot longer than they do now. Adam lived for nine hundred and thirty years and during this time his family grew. He probably had many children, but the Bible tells us the names of just three. Cain and Abel were two of Adam and Eve's sons. Cain was the older one and when he grew up he worked in the fields growing crops. When Abel was old enough his work was to look after sheep.

When Adam and Eve disobeyed God, they learned that an animal must die instead of the person who had sinned. Blood had to be shed. We call this a sacrifice or offering. God forgave the sinner because the animal's life had been sacrificed. This happened many times until God sent His own Son to die in the place of sinful people. Adam and Eve must have taught their sons about this.

One day Abel brought a sheep from his flock as an offering to God.

The New Testament tells us that Abel had faith. He believed God and obeyed Him. Cain brought an offering of some crops, but God did not accept this. Cain was angry and hated his brother. When they were in a field together Cain killed Abel. What a terrible thing to do. How sad Adam and Eve must have been when they heard.

Genesis chapter 4 verses 3-8.

Who asked Cain why he was angry? How long did Adam live for?

Day 12: HE WALKED WITH GOD

You may have thought that when Adam and Eve disobeyed God they did not do anything very wrong. Eating some fruit might seem a small thing, but it was disobeying the God who made them. That one sin affected everyone born into the world. Only the Lord Jesus lived without doing or saying or thinking anything that is wrong.

As Adam and Eve watched their children growing up, they saw them choosing to do things that are wrong. Abel knew that the way to be forgiven was to bring the offering that God asked for. Cain thought he could come to God in his own way.

Some time after Abel died, Adam and Eve had a son who they called Seth. From Seth's family, the person who God had promised to send would be born. Of course this would be after many, many years had passed. Seth's great-great-great-grandson, was called Enoch. The Bible says that Enoch walked with God. This means that God was the most important person in Enoch's life.

He loved God and talked with God and wanted to please God in all that he did.

One day God took Enoch out of this world. He did not die: God took him. Enoch's son Methuselah lived longer than anyone else we read about in the Bible. He lived to be nine hundred and sixty-nine years old. Methuselah had a grandson called Noah. In the days that Noah lived, many people lived in the world.

Genesis chapter 5 verses 21-24.

How old was Methuselah when he died? Who was Methuselah's grandson?

Day 13: NOAH

Many years had passed since God made the first man and woman. Many children were born and grew up to have families of their own. God had made a wonderful world for people to live in. But men and women did not love God or want to obey Him. They spent their time thinking of wrong things. Instead of being kind, they took pleasure in hurting one another. God would not let things in His world go on getting worse.

Among the many wicked people living at that time, there was one man who loved God. His name was Noah. God told Noah that He was going to send a great flood which would cover all the earth.

God told Noah to build an ark – a great wooden boat – for himself and his wife, his three sons and their wives. Animals and birds would also be saved from the flood. Two of every kind of animal would come into the ark. Certain animals would come in sevens and there would be seven of every kind of bird. Lots of food would be needed for the animals as well as for Noah and his family. God told Noah exactly how big to make the ark, and Noah did everything God said.

God chose to save Noah and his family from the flood.

There would be one hundred and twenty years before the flood came. God allowed all that time for men and women to change their ways.

Genesis chapter 6 verses 13-22.

Which verse tells us how big the ark was to be? (A cubit is about half a metre).

Day 14: THE GREAT FLOOD

Building the ark was a very big job and must have taken a long time. People saw what Noah was doing, but no one took any notice of his warnings about the coming flood. The day came when God told Noah that it was time to go into the ark.

Of all the people who were living at that time, only Noah's family went into the ark.

Pairs of animals came to Noah: wild animals, farm animals, little creatures that live on the ground, and birds of every kind: they all went into the ark.

When Noah and his family, and the animals, were safely in the ark, God shut them in.

When God shut the door of the ark, Noah and his family were safe. It was now too late for the people outside the ark to escape the flood. Only God knew when He had given them enough time to change their ways. The rain began and continued for forty days and forty nights. All the mountains were covered and the ark floated on the water.

The people who had been so wicked had all been swept away by the great flood. Only Noah and his wife and his three sons Ham, Shem and Japheth and their wives, were kept safe.

Genesis chapter 7 verses 6-16.

How many people were in the ark? Who shut them in? How many days did it go on raining?

Day 15: DRY LAND AGAIN

Ships are designed to be safe even in stormy weather. At the time of the flood there was no dry land anywhere. It was very important for the ark to stay afloat even though it was tossed about. It was God who designed the ark and Noah was careful to follow God's design. As the water rose to cover all the earth, those inside the ark were kept safe.

EXTRA INFO

After one hundred and fifty days the water began to go down. The ark came to rest on a mountain called Mount Ararat.

After waiting many more weeks, Noah sent a raven out of the ark, but it did not come back to him - it kept flying about until the waters dried up. So Noah sent a dove out to see whether the ground was dry yet, but the dove flew back to Noah because the ground was still covered with water. Seven days later Noah sent the dove out again, and this time it returned with an olive leaf in its beak. After another seven days Noah sent the dove out a third time, and this time the dove did not return to the ark.

One year and six days after the flood began, God told Noah that it was time to come out of the ark.

BY MYSELF

The ground was dry when Noah and his family and all the animals at last walked on the land again.

GOD'S WORD

Genesis chapter 8 verses 6-14.

ASK ABOUT

How many times did Noah send the dove out of the ark? How many times did the dove fly back to Noah?

Day 16: THE RAINBOW

Do you know what an altar is? It is like a table and it was used for sacrifices and offerings. When Noah and his family came out of the ark, Noah built an altar. To show his thankfulness to God for saving them, Noah took some of the animals that had gone into the ark in sevens, and sacrificed them. God told Noah and his sons that their families should fill the earth.

It is from Noah's sons that all the nations of the world have come.

At this time God said that as well as crops, animals could also be used for food. God also said that anyone who kills another person should be put to death.

God promised that He would never again send a flood to destroy the earth and those who live there.

Genesis chapter 9 verses 11-17.

Have you seen a rainbow? This is God's sign that He will remember His promise. When we look at a rainbow we can be sure that there will never be another flood that covers the whole of the world.

Noah and his family settled down once more to grow their food and make the things they needed. Noah's sons and their wives had children. As the years went by, there were many people to look after the world that God had made.

Can you remember the colours of the rainbow? What will last as long as the earth? (Genesis chapter 8 verse 22).

Day 17: CONFUSION

Have you ever travelled to a place where you could not understand what people were saying?

When you go to a different country you will probably hear a different language. The book of Genesis tells us why this is so.

God had told Noah and his sons to fill the earth. As more children were born people were to move to different parts of the world to settle down. At that time the people all spoke the same language, and did not want to be scattered all over the earth. They made bricks and began to build a city with a great tower.

They did not want to live as God meant them to: they thought they could manage very well without God.

God saw what they were doing, and He made them speak in different languages. It was impossible to continue building the city when they could not understand each other. To the groups, or families, who spoke the same language, everyone else seemed to be talking nonsense. These groups stayed together and began moving away from the city, to different lands. The city was given the name 'Babel', which means confusion, because it was there that God confused the world's language.

Genesis chapter 11 verses 1-9.

Which verse tells us that the people did not want to fill the earth as God had said?

Day 18: ABRAM LEAVES HOME

Have you ever moved house? If so, I am sure your parents chose a house for you to move into.

Moving house is a busy time. Everything has to be packed and taken to the new house.

Long ago there was a man called Abram who moved away from home. But Abram didn't know where he would be going to live. God told Abram to move to a different land that He would show him. God promised that Abram's family would become a great nation and that from Abram, good would come to all the world.

Abram obeyed God. He and his wife Sarai collected their belongings for the journey. They did not have a removals van, but strong animals would have carried the loads. Abram's nephew whose name was Lot, got ready to move with his uncle.

When Abram set out on his journey, he did not know where he was going but he knew God would bring him to the right place.

As he travelled into the land of Canaan, God told him that this was the land that He would give to Abram's family. Abram built an altar in the place where God had spoken to him. He then travelled and put his tent up near a place that was later called Bethel. Again he built an altar and prayed there.

Genesis chapter 12 verses 1-8.

How old was Abram when he left Haran? Which verses tell us what God said to Abram?

Day 19: LOT'S CHOICE

When we think of what it means to be very rich, we often think of people who have lots of money and live in big houses. Abram lived in a tent and moved from place to place. But he had a lot of gold and silver.

Abram also owned many animals. Animals were considered to be a sign of great riches in Abram's time.

Lot also had large flocks and herds of animals. All these sheep and cattle needed plenty of grass to eat.

Abram and Lot had men who worked for them. They would make sure that there was enough water and grass for the animals. This was not easy. One day Abram heard that there had been quarrelling between his servants and Lot's servants. Abram, as you will remember, was Lot's uncle. He did not want any trouble between them.

Genesis chapter 13 verses 8-13.

Abram allowed Lot to choose the part of the land where he would like to live.

Lot saw how green and well watered the land near the river Jordan was. He saw how good that land would be for his family and all the animals he owned. So Lot moved away from Abram near to a city called Sodom.

After Lot had gone, God spoke to Abram. God promised to give him all the land which he could see, north, south, east and west. God said that this land would always belong to the family of Abram.

What does Genesis chapter 13 verse 13 tell us about the people who lived in Sodom?

Day 20: TAKEN CAPTIVE

Lot chose a place to live in which seemed to be very good. As time went by Lot and his family moved into the city of Sodom. They lived in a house instead of a tent as they had done when they were with Abram. But many wicked people lived in Sodom and in the nearby city of Gomorrah. Lot was very sad to see the people around him who did not love God or obey Him. Living in Sodom brought him great trouble.

It is important to make the right choices. We should ask God to help us make choices that please him.

Many cities in those days had their own Kings. The Kings of Sodom and Gomorrah along with three other Kings led their people into battle against four Kings from other cities. Things did not go well for Sodom. Many were taken captive. Among those who were captured, was Lot.

Genesis chapter 14 verses 14-16.

Abram was able to rescue Lot as well as all the other people from Sodom who had been taken away. Abram had taken a great deal of trouble to bring the captives back. The King of Sodom offered to pay him for what he had done. Abram would not take anything.

Abram trusted in God to give him all he needed.

He did not want anyone to think that the King of Sodom had made him rich.

How many trained men did Abram take with him to rescue Lot?

Day 21: ISHMAEL

God promised Abram that the land of Canaan would belong to his family. Abram moved to that land but ten years later he and Sarai still had no children. God had promised to make a great nation from Abram's family. It was difficult to understand this promise when Abram had no children. Abram talked to God about it. God told Abram that many people would come from his family. Abram believed all that God said to him.

Sarai had a maid whose name was Hagar. Sarai asked Abram to take Hagar as a second wife. She thought that maybe the child God had promised would then be born.

In the Old Testament some men had more than one wife. This was not the way God meant families to be and when it happened, it often brought unhappiness.

Abram did as Sarai suggested. It was not long before Hagar knew that she was going to have a baby. Hagar was still Sarai's maid but she began to behave badly towards her mistress. Sarai complained to Abram about the way Hagar was behaving.

Genesis chapter 16 verses 6-9.

God knew all about what had happened to Hagar.

The angel told her that she must go back to Sarai and be obedient to her. The angel also told Hagar that she would have a son who she must name Ishmael, which means 'God hears'. Hagar did as the angel said. She went back to Sarai. When the baby was born, Abram named him Ishmael.

How old was Abram when Ishmael was born? (Genesis chapter 16 verse 16).

Day 22: VISITORS

Our names are usually chosen by our parents. Perhaps someone else in the family had that name. Maybe it is a name that our parents liked best. Names in the Bible were often chosen because of their meaning.

The name Abram means 'exalted father', but when he was ninety-nine years old God gave him a new name, Abraham, which means 'father of a multitude'. Sarai's new name was Sarah, which means 'princess'.

With his new name God told Abraham once again that many people would come from his family.

At this time Ishmael was about thirteen years old but he was not the son that God had promised. God said that Sarah would have a son who was to be called Isaac. God's promises for the family of Abraham were for Isaac, not Ishmael.

One day three men came to visit Abraham. He asked them to rest while a meal was prepared. These visitors were not ordinary men. One was the Son of God and the others were angels appearing as men. They ate the meal and talked about the son that Sarah would have.

Genesis chapter 18 verses 17-22.

God also spoke about the wickedness of Sodom and Gomorrah. God knew all about it. Abraham realised that this could be the time when Sodom was punished.

Abraham provided a meal for his visitors. What else did he provide for them? (Genesis chapter 18 verse 4.)

Day 23: RESCUED

Abraham knew that Lot and his family were living in Sodom. He knew that the time had probably come when that city would be destroyed. Two of his visitors, the two angels, went on their way towards Sodom. The third, the Son of God, stayed a little longer.

Genesis chapter 18 verses 22-28.

Abraham prayed that God would not destroy Sodom if He found some people there who were living good lives. What if there were forty, thirty, twenty or even only ten good people there? God promised that He would not destroy the city even if there were just ten people there who had not become wicked like those around them.

The two angels came to Sodom and Lot took them into his house to rest. They warned him to take his family out of the city before it was destroyed. Some of Lot's relations would not listen to him. In the morning the angels told him to take his wife and two daughters away. Lot did not hurry, so the angel led him and his wife and daughters out of the city. They were not allowed to look back towards Sodom or the cities around it. Lot pleaded with the angels to allow him to go to the small city of Zoar. They agreed to that, but Lot's wife lagged behind. She turned to look back at Sodom.

Lot's wife was destroyed along with all the people in the city. The Bible says that she became 'a pillar of salt'.

God had not found even ten people in the city of Sodom who were living good lives. But God remembered Abraham's prayer and rescued Lot and his daughters.

How many people were taken out of the city of Sodom? How many came safely to Zoar?

Day 24: A PROMISE

Have you ever waited for someone to keep a promise? Maybe it was a present, or a trip to the seaside. Did it seem a long time to wait? Abraham and Sarah waited twenty-five years for their son to be born. When the baby was born Abraham was one hundred years old and Sarah was ninety years old. People are not usually as old as this when they have children. Yet God kept His promise. When their baby boy was born, they named him Isaac as God had said.

The name Isaac means laughter. Isaac must have brought a lot of joy to Abraham and Sarah. They loved him dearly and taught him to love and trust God.

One day Abraham made a feast for Isaac. Ishmael, who was about sixteen at the time, laughed at the little boy. Sarah saw this and asked Abraham to send Hagar and Ishmael away. Abraham was very unhappy.

But God told Abraham that it would be right for him to do as Sarah had asked.

The next morning Abraham gave food and water to Hagar and sent her away with Ishmael. They wandered about in the desert until the water was used up. Hagar thought that Ishmael would die of thirst.

Genesis chapter 21 verses 16-21.

God did not forget Hagar. A great nation would also come from Ishmael's family. Ishmael married an Egyptian woman and had twelve sons. But Isaac would be the head of the family after Abraham.

What did Hagar see after the angel spoke to her?

Day 25: A JOURNEY

In Old Testament times, God taught His people how they could be forgiven for the wrong things they had done. An animal, such as a lamb, must die instead of the person who had sinned.

One day God asked Abraham to do something which must have seemed very strange. God said that Abraham should take his beloved son Isaac to a mountain in the land of Moriah. There he was to offer Isaac as a sacrifice.

Abraham got up early in the morning. He saddled his donkey and took two of the young men who worked for him. He also took his son Isaac and some wood to make a fire. They set off towards the land of Moriah.

In the New Testament we read that Abraham trusted that God would bring Isaac back to life after he had been offered.

On the third day of their journey, Abraham saw the place that God had spoken to him about. He left the donkey with the servants, and he and Isaac walked on together. Isaac carried the wood. We do not know how old Isaac was at this time. He was certainly old enough to understand that his father was going to make an offering to God. Isaac asked his father where the lamb was for the offering.

Abraham said that God would provide a lamb.

Genesis chapter 22 verses 1-8.

Why do we no longer need to offer sacrifices as people did in the Old Testament times?

Day 26: AN OFFERING

Abraham and Sarah waited a long time for a child of their own. Abraham loved Isaac, and yet he obeyed God and built an altar on which to sacrifice his son. He laid the wood on the altar and then he laid Isaac on the wood. He was willing to offer his own son.

As Abraham picked up his knife an angel called out. The angel told him not to harm Isaac. As he looked up, Abraham saw a sheep caught by its horns in a bush. He took the sheep and sacrificed it instead of Isaac.

God would not allow Abraham to take Isaac's life. But He wanted Abraham to show that he loved and trusted God even more than he loved his own son.

After this, God spoke to Abraham again, telling him that because he had been obedient, all the nations in the world would be blessed through his family.

Reading about Abraham and Isaac helps us to understand what God did when He sent His own Son into the world.

The Lord Jesus was the Son who God loved.

Jesus really did die in the place of men and women and boys and girls who believe in Him. The day that Abraham was willing to offer his son as a sacrifice was like a picture of what God would do many years later.

Genesis chapter 22 verses 9-19; John chapter 3 verse 16.

Who carried the wood up the mountain? (Genesis chapter 22 verse 6). Whose Son was killed for our sins at a place called Calvary?

PRAYER

When Abraham was very old, he sent his most trusted servant on a journey. Abraham gave his servant a very special job. It was time for Isaac to marry.

Abraham did not want Isaac to marry a woman from Canaan who did not love God.

Isaac's wife was to be a woman from among Abraham's relatives. It would be a long journey, so the man took ten of his master's camels and loaded them with all he would need. Then he set off for the city of Nahor where the family of Abraham's brother lived.

Outside the city there was a well where women came to draw water. At the well the servant prayed to God. He prayed that when he asked for water, the woman God had chosen as Isaac's wife would offer to draw water for the camels too. Just then Rebekah, the granddaughter of Abraham's brother, came to the well. Not knowing who she was, the servant asked her for a drink. She drew some water for him and then offered to draw water for the camels.

This showed that she was both kind and hardworking, for ten camels would need a lot of water.

Was this God's answer to the servant's prayer? When Rebekah told him who she was and invited him to stay with her family, the servant thanked God for leading him to his master's relations.

Genesis chapter 24 verses 12-21.

Who did Abraham not want Isaac to marry?
What was the servant's prayer by the well?

Day 28: REBEKAH SAYS YES

Rebekah's brother Laban welcomed Abraham's servant. He provided straw and food for the camels, and prepared a meal for the servant and the men who had travelled with him. But the servant would not eat until he had explained his visit.

He spoke about his master, Abraham, and how God had given him silver, gold, flocks, herds, and servants to work for him. He told of the need to find the right wife for Isaac and how he had prayed at the well, just as Rebekah was coming to draw water. As they listened, Laban and his father Bethuel both realised that God had chosen Rebekah to be Isaac's wife.

The servant gave gifts of gold, silver and clothing to Rebekah. He also gave gifts to Laban and their mother.

The next morning he wanted to start the journey back to Abraham. Rebekah's family would have liked her to wait a few more days, but Rebekah was willing to leave her home and go to Canaan to meet Isaac.

What an exciting journey that must have been. When they reached the end of their journey, Isaac was walking in the field and saw the camels coming. Before very long, Isaac and Rebekah were married.

Abraham had trusted God to find the right person to marry his son, and Isaac loved Rebekah very much.

Genesis chapter 24 verses 50-59.

What did the servant do before he sat down for a meal? What was the name of Rebekah's brother?

Day 29: THE TWINS

When Isaac and Rebekah had been married for twenty years, they had twin boys, who they named Esau and Jacob. Esau was born before his twin brother and so was counted as the older of the two. Usually the oldest son would be the head of the family after the father died. He would be given twice as much of all that had belonged to his father, as any other son. This was called his birthright. In Isaac's family there was something even more important. God's promises to Abraham and Isaac would be given to the next head of the family. Before the twins were born, God had told Rebekah that in this family it would be the younger brother who would have this birthright.

As the two boys grew up, Jacob worked at home but Esau was much more interested in going off into the countryside to hunt.

One day, when Esau came home very hungry after being out in the open air, he saw Jacob cooking a tasty meal. He asked Jacob to give him some of the stew he had made. But Jacob answered that he could only have some, if he paid for it with his birthright. Esau agreed to sell his birthright for just one meal.

Esau did not really care about God's promises to the family of Abraham.

Genesis chapter 25 verses 27-34.

Which grandson of Abraham is named in Matthew chapter 1 verse 2? Who was born into this family long after Abraham, Isaac and Jacob? (Matthew chapter 1 verse 16).

Day 30: THE BLESSING

When Isaac was very old he became blind: he could no longer see. He decided that the time had come for him to give his blessing to his son Esau. Isaac meant to treat Esau as the one who would be the next head of the family. He asked Esau to go hunting, and then prepare a meal with what he brought home from the hunt. After the meal, he would receive his father's blessing.

Rebekah heard what Isaac said to Esau. Isaac and Rebekah both knew that it was Jacob whom God had chosen to become head of the family.

Rebekah made Isaac's favourite food while Esau was out hunting. She told Jacob to pretend he was Esau and take the food to his father. Jacob would then get the blessing instead. But Jacob was not hairy like Esau. If Isaac touched him he would know something was wrong. Rebekah gave Jacob some of Esau's clothes and covered his hands and neck with goatskin.

Jacob did as his mother told him and took the food to Isaac. Isaac didn't realise it was Jacob and not Esau. He blessed his son Jacob, all the time thinking that it was Esau who was with him. As soon as Jacob left his father, Esau arrived.

When Esau found out what had happened he was very sad, and then very angry.

Genesis chapter 27 verses 5-17.

In what ways did Esau and Jacob look and feel different? Who was it that God had chosen to receive Isaac's blessing?

Day 31: BETHEL

Jacob had to get away from Esau so set off to find his mother's family and the home of his Uncle Laban.

Jacob had a long way to go: about five hundred miles.

One night Jacob lay down to sleep. He took a stone for a pillow and dreamed of a ladder that reached heaven. Angels moved up and down the ladder and at the top stood God Himself. God spoke to Jacob, giving him the promises that He had first given to Abraham. God said that the land of Canaan would belong to Jacob's family. Through them good would come to all the peoples of the world. God promised that he would protect Jacob and bring him safely back to Canaan.

God's words came at a very difficult time in Jacob's life. He was leaving his home and the people he knew.

Jacob did not know if his mother's family would welcome him. But he knew God was with him.

When Jacob awoke, he named the place where he had spent the night Bethel. Bethel means house of God. Jacob was sure that God was there and as he remembered God's promises, he made a promise to God. Jacob said that if God really would take care of him and bring him safely back home one day, then the God he had met at Bethel would be his God. Jacob had known the God of his father and his grandfather. Now he began to put his trust in God for his own life.

Genesis chapter 28 verses 10-17.

Why did Jacob go away from home? What does 'Bethel' mean?

Day 32: A LARGE FAMILY

When Jacob reached the end of his journey, he waited by a well. There he met his cousin Rachel, when she came to draw water for her father's sheep. Jacob moved the stone that covered the well and watered the sheep for her. Then he told Rachel who he was.

Rachel's father was Jacob's uncle. She ran to tell him that Jacob had come. Laban hurried out to welcome Jacob to his house. Jacob stayed for a month to help his uncle look after the animals. Laban asked Jacob how he should pay him for his work.

Jacob agreed to work seven years if Laban would allow him to marry Rachel. Laban agreed to this.

Genesis chapter 29 verses 15-20.

The seven years passed quickly for Jacob as he looked forward to marrying his beautiful cousin.

But at the end of the seven years Laban said that his older daughter Leah must be the first to marry. He expected Jacob to marry Leah and take Rachel as a second wife. Jacob did this. He then worked another seven years for Laban. Laban gave each of his daughters a maid to help her. Leah's maid was called Zilpah and Rachel's maid was called Bilhah

While Jacob worked for Laban, he had eleven sons. Here are their names: Reuben, Simeon, Levi, Judah, Dan, Naphtali, Gad, Asher, Issachar, Zebulun, Joseph. He also had a daughter called Dinah.

What relation was Laban to Jacob? What relation were Leah and Rachel to Jacob?

Day 33: BACK TO CANAAN

Jacob had been away from his own country for a long time, but Laban did not want him to leave.

Genesis chapter 30 verses 27-32.

Jacob decided that he would carry on working for Laban. His pay would be animals: all the speckled and spotted sheep and goats and any lambs that were brown. Laban agreed to this and Jacob separated the animals that were now his, from Laban's.

Jacob's flocks did well. He became rich and had servants to work for him.

Laban's sons were not pleased. They complained that Jacob had taken away what should have belonged to their father. Jacob saw that Laban was no longer pleased with him either. Then when Jacob had been with Laban for twenty years, God spoke to him.

God told Jacob that he should go back to Canaan.

Jacob called for Leah and Rachel and told them what God had said. He put his sons and his wives on camels. He took his servants and his flocks of animals and set out on the long journey back to Canaan. When Jacob left, Laban was busy shearing sheep. He was upset when he realised that Jacob had gone. He set out after him. Jacob told Laban that he had been afraid that Leah and Rachel would not have been allowed to leave. Laban felt that Jacob was taking what belonged to him. But they did agree together that in future there would be no trouble between them.

How long did Jacob stay with his uncle Laban? (Genesis chapter 31 verse 38).

Day 34: A NEW NAME

Jacob had been away from home for twenty years. God had promised to bring him back to Canaan, but there was one thing that made him afraid. Can you think what that was? Jacob was afraid that his brother Esau would still be angry with him.

Jacob sent messengers to tell Esau that he was coming. When they returned, the messengers told Jacob that Esau was on his way to meet him and that Esau had four hundred men with him. Jacob then did something that we should do when we are afraid: he prayed. He reminded God of how He had promised to look after him, and he asked God to keep him and his family safe. Then Jacob sent some of his servants on ahead with presents for Esau.

That night Jacob stayed on his own so that he could spend more time praying to God.

He knew that it was a very important time for him. He was coming back to the land which God had promised to his grandfather Abraham's family. He wanted to be sure that God was with him and would help him.

God gave Jacob a new name that night, the name 'Israel' which means 'A prince with God'.

Jacob need not have been afraid of meeting Esau. God had heard his prayer and Esau was overjoyed to see him. They hugged one another and Jacob introduced his family to his brother.

Genesis chapter 32 verses 9-12.

What did Jacob do when he was afraid?
What new name did God give him?

Day 35: THE FAVOURITE SON

After Jacob settled down in Canaan he had one more son, named Benjamin. So Jacob had a total of twelve sons and one daughter.

Jacob loved Joseph more than any other son. He showed this by giving him a very beautiful coat.

Joseph was probably more honest and helpful than his older brothers, but they hated him because he was their father's favourite.

Joseph had two dreams. In the first dream he and his brothers were in a field. They all had sheaves of corn. Joseph's sheaf stood upright while his brother's sheaves bowed down to his. In the second dream, the sun, moon and eleven stars all bowed down to Joseph. Jacob heard about this. He asked Joseph whether he really thought his family would bow down to him. Joseph's brothers hated him even more.

Jacob owned large flocks of animals, so there was always plenty of work for his sons to do. One day, Joseph's ten brothers took the flocks to Shechem which was quite a long way from home. Jacob decided to send Joseph to see whether everything was alright. When Joseph came to Shechem his brothers were not there. He met a man who told him that they had gone to Dothan. This was nearly twenty miles further but Joseph set out again.

He was determined to do as his father had asked and find his brothers.

Genesis chapter 37 verses 1-11.

Why were Joseph's brothers jealous of him? What did Joseph dream?

Day 36: SOLD BY HIS BROTHERS

Joseph's brothers saw him coming. Some of the brothers wanted to kill him and pretend that he had been killed by a wild animal. They were so far away from home no one would ever know. Reuben persuaded them instead to throw Joseph into a pit. Reuben planned to rescue Joseph later and take him home. However, when Reuben did return to the pit, it was empty. The brothers had sold Joseph to some travellers on their way to Egypt.

In those days a person could be bought for money and would then become a slave. He would have to work for his owner whether he was treated kindly or cruelly.

Genesis chapter 37 verses 19-28.

What a day for Joseph! Thrown into a deep, dark pit; sold as a slave; and then the journey along the hot, dusty road to Egypt. He must have wondered whether he would ever see his home and his father again.

Joseph's brothers took his beautiful coat and dipped it into the blood of a goat. They went back to their home and showed the coat to their father. Jacob knew that the coat had belonged to Joseph. He thought that Joseph had been killed by a wild animal.

Jacob was very, very sad. No one could comfort him because he believed that Joseph was dead.

But Joseph was not dead. He had arrived in the land of Egypt, and there he was bought by a man named Potiphar.

**Which brother wanted to rescue Joseph?
Which brother wanted to sell him?**

Day 37: UNFAIR PUNISHMENT

Long ago in the land of Egypt, the ruler was not called 'King': his title was 'Pharaoh'.

EXTRA INFO

Potiphar was the captain of Pharaoh's guard, and it was to his house that Joseph was taken.

We might feel very sorry for Joseph, a slave in a strange land, so suddenly taken away from his home and family. But God had not forgotten Joseph. As he worked hard for his master, God helped him, so that everything he did turned out well. Potiphar came to trust Joseph so much that he put him in charge of everything he had.

One day Potiphar's wife asked Joseph to do something which he knew would be wrong. Joseph explained that he could not sin against God by doing what she asked. Potiphar's wife tried many times to persuade Joseph to do wrong, but each time he refused. At last, she became so angry that she told lies about Joseph to Potiphar. Potiphar listened to his wife and put Joseph into prison, even though he had done nothing to deserve it.

It is not easy to take the punishment for something we have not done. But the Bible tells us that even though he was in prison, God was still with Joseph. The keeper of the prison came to trust Joseph and put him in charge of the other prisoners.

BY MYSELF

If we trust God as Joseph did we will know that God is always with us.

GOD'S WORD

Genesis chapter 39 verses 1-6.

ASK ABOUT

What was the name of Joseph's master?
Who told lies about Joseph?

Pharaoh was angry with his butler and his baker and put them into prison.

The chief butler was in charge of Pharaoh's wine and the chief baker was in charge of Pharaoh's food.

In prison they were looked after by Joseph. One morning Joseph found the butler and the baker looking very sad. They explained that during the night they had each had a dream which troubled them. Joseph told them that God could tell them the meaning of their dreams.

Genesis chapter 40 verses 9-11.

Joseph understood that this dream meant that in three days time, the chief butler would be back serving Pharaoh his wine. When Joseph had told the butler this, he asked him to speak to Pharaoh about him.

Joseph hoped that he might be set free.

When the chief baker heard the meaning of the chief butler's dream, he told Joseph what he had dreamt.

Genesis chapter 40 verses 16-17.

Joseph had to tell the baker that his dream did not have a good meaning. In three days time Pharaoh would have him put to death. Because it was God who helped Joseph to understand the meaning of the dreams, it all happened exactly as he had said. The chief butler was soon back serving Pharaoh but he forgot all about Joseph for two whole years.

What did the chief butler dream about?
What did the chief baker dream about?

Day 39: PHARAOH'S DREAMS

In the days when Joseph lived, people did not have the Bible as we do.

God sometimes used dreams to speak to people. These dreams meant something.

Two years after the butler was freed from prison, Pharaoh was so troubled by two dreams that he sent for all the wise men of Egypt, but no one could help him.

Genesis chapter 41 verses 1-7.

The butler heard about this and remembered Joseph. He told Pharaoh about him.

Joseph was sent for straight away.

Joseph changed his clothes and tidied himself before meeting Pharaoh but soon he was listening as Pharaoh described his dreams.

Joseph explained that God was showing Pharaoh what He was going to do. There would be seven years of plenty of food. After that there would be seven years of famine: the crops would not grow and there would be very little food. Joseph suggested to Pharaoh that he should appoint someone to take charge of storing food during the good years, so that there would be enough to eat when the famine came. Pharaoh chose Joseph to do this. He would be the most important person in the land next to Pharaoh himself!

Genesis chapter 41 verses 41-43.

Can you remember all the different places where Joseph had been?

Day 40: ACCUSED OF SPYING

The seven years of good harvests ended and the seven years of famine began.

Joseph had made sure that a lot of grain had been saved during the years of plenty.

The famine reached other lands besides Egypt, and one day Joseph's ten older brothers came to buy grain.

Genesis chapter 42 verses 1-8.

Joseph accused his brothers of spying. They told him that they had a younger brother in Canaan and a brother who had died. They did not know that the man they were speaking to was their brother Joseph.

Joseph put his brothers in prison for three days. Later he told them that only one need stay in prison.

Nine brothers could return home but they must bring Benjamin with them if they came back to Egypt. The brothers talked about how cruel they had been to Joseph. Even though it had happened twenty years before, they still remembered how Joseph had begged them not to harm him. They believed that they were being punished for what they had done.

The brothers did not know that Joseph understood every word they said. He ordered his servants to fill the sacks with grain and put money that had been paid back in the sacks. The brothers were frightened when they found the money. If they went back to Egypt, they could now be accused of stealing.

Why did Joseph's brothers not recognise him? Were they sorry for what they did to Joseph?

Day 41: THE SILVER CUP

The grain had all been eaten: the time had come for Joseph's brothers to go to Egypt again. Jacob did not want to let Benjamin go, but Judah promised that he would make sure that Benjamin was kept safe.

Jacob sent presents and twice as much money as before, to give to the man his sons were so afraid of.

When Joseph realised that Benjamin had come with his brothers, he told his steward to take them to his house for a meal. Joseph spoke in the Egyptian language which his brothers did not understand: they wondered what was going to happen. They were given a lovely meal but they were suprised to find themselves seated in order of age.

After they had eaten, Joseph told his steward to fill the sacks with grain and put the money back in the sacks again. This time Joseph's silver cup was placed in Benjamin's sack. After his brothers left, Joseph sent his steward after them. They were told that they had stolen Joseph's cup.

The cup was found in Benjamin's sack.

How their hearts sank! Loading everything on their donkeys once more, they returned to Joseph's house. There they bowed down before him, offering to become his slaves. But Joseph assured them that they could all go back to their father, except Benjamin.

Genesis chapter 43 verses 1-10.

Which brother said he would make sure that Benjamin was kept safe? Had Benjamin really stolen the silver cup?

Day 42: GOOD NEWS FOR JACOB

The time had come for Judah to speak to Joseph. He told of Jacob's sorrow when Joseph had, as he thought, been killed by a wild animal. He told of Jacob's love for Benjamin, and how he would die if Benjamin did not return home. Last of all, he asked to be allowed to remain in Egypt as Joseph's slave, in place of Benjamin.

Now Joseph knew that his brothers were truly sorry for their cruelty to him: they really had changed.

Joseph sent everyone out of the room, except his brothers. When he said, 'I am Joseph,' they were frightened. Joseph was powerful and they had treated him cruelly. What would he do? Joseph spoke kindly. He told them not to be afraid or angry with themselves for selling him into Egypt. God had planned it so that He could provide for them during the famine. Now they must bring their wives, their children, and their father to Egypt. Joseph would give them all they needed.

The brothers returned home to tell Jacob that the man they had been so afraid of was really Joseph. Jacob could not believe it. Then he saw the carts which Joseph had sent to carry them to Egypt. It was true. Jacob was overjoyed to know that Joseph was alive.

Jacob's family was given the land of Goshen in Egypt. There they made their home.

Genesis chapter 45 verses 1-11.

What did Judah say that showed he was sorry? What new name did God give Jacob before he returned to the land of Canaan? God named him 'Israel', and because of that his descendants were called 'Israelites'.

DAYS 43-68: Exodus

THE WAY OUT

The Book begins with the Israelites enslaved in Egypt, with the threat of death hanging over their newborn sons. Moses is called by God to lead them out of Egypt and to begin their journey to the land promised to Abraham's descendants. We read of the first Passover and the miraculous crossing of the Red Sea. This is followed by a period of about a year when the people camped at Sinai. Here, through Moses, God gave His law to Israel, and the people promised to obey. In chapter 20 we have the moral law: the ten commandments which set out God's standard for all peoples.

God not only gave the law before the people entered their own land, He also gave instructions for making the tabernacle. God's purpose was to dwell among His people, and the tabernacle was to be the place where He would meet with them. The instructions for the tabernacle are given in great detail because the tabernacle, with its High Priest and its offerings, points us to the Lord Jesus Christ.

In the Book of Exodus we have not only the escape from slavery and death, but also the preparation for new life in a new land.

Day 43: SLAVES IN EGYPT

As time went by, there were many Israelites living in the land of Egypt. Jacob and his sons and their wives died, but the family continued to grow as Jacob's grandchildren and then his great-grandchildren grew up and had children of their own.

The new King did not remember all that Joseph had done for Egypt. He did not like to see so many people who were not Egyptians living in his land. He was afraid that one day they might join Egypt's enemies and fight against them. So Pharaoh gave orders that the Hebrews were to become slaves.

A Hebrew is another name for an Israelite. They were forced to build cities and to work in the fields. They were treated cruelly but the number of Israelites continued to increase.

Pharaoh then said that every Israelite baby boy must be killed. However, the Israelite nurses loved God and would not do this. Then a dreadful command was given that all the Hebrew baby boys must be thrown into the river.

This was a very, very, sad time. But God had not forgotten them.

Exodus chapter 1 verses 6-14.

What is the name of the country that Jacob's family moved to? Who were Jacob's grandparents? (See Day 24).

Day 44: ON THE RIVER

Do you think it would be easy to keep a baby where no one could see or hear him?

Babies may be small, but they can make quite a lot of noise when they cry.

Amram and Jochebed had a son named Aaron and a daughter named Miriam. They also had a baby boy. He was so lovely that Jochebed decided to hide him from the Egyptians. It must have been difficult to keep him out of sight. Jochebed managed it for three months.

Exodus chapter 2 verses 1-10.

When Jochebed had hidden her baby as long as she could, she made a waterproof basket for him. She placed the baby in the basket and put the basket in the reeds by the river. As Miriam kept watch, the baby was found by Pharaoh's daughter. She knew that the baby was a Hebrew. Miriam asked the Princess if she needed someone to help her look after the baby.

The Princess was pleased to pay someone to do this job for her. Miriam ran to fetch her mother.

Jochebed took her baby home, knowing that he would be safe with the protection of Pharaoh's daughter. When he was older Pharaoh's daughter brought him up as if he was her own son. She called him 'Moses', and made sure that he was taught by the very best teachers in Egypt.

Who were Moses' brother and sister? What does Acts chapter 7 verses 20-22 say about Moses?

53

Day 45: THE LAND OF MIDIAN

Moses enjoyed the best that Egypt had to offer, but the Israelites still worked as slaves. They were cruelly treated. Their lives were very hard. When Moses was forty years old, he went to watch the people as they worked. He knew that they were his people and that he was not really the son of Pharoah's daughter. When he saw an Egyptian beating an Israelite he killed the Egyptian and hid his body in the sand.

Moses thought that no-one had seen but the next day he found that people knew about it.

Pharaoh had heard about the killing. Moses was afraid and ran away from Egypt to the land of Midian

Exodus chapter 2 verses 11-15.

As Moses sat by the well the seven daughters of Jethro came to draw water for their father's flocks. Moses helped them. When they were back home much earlier than usual Jethro heard what had happened. He invited Moses to have a meal with the family.

Moses stayed with Jethro. He married one of his daughters whose name was Zipporah.

Moses and Zipporah had two sons: the older one was called Gershom and the younger one Eliezer.
Moses lived in Midian for forty years. During that time the King of Egypt died. The Israelites were still kept in slavery, but God saw their suffering. He remembered His promises to Abraham, Isaac and Jacob.

What did Pharaoh want to do to Moses?

Day 46: A BUSH ON FIRE

One day when Moses was in the desert with Jethro's sheep, he saw an unusual sight.

There was a flame of fire coming from a bush. The bush itself was not being burnt.

Moses went for a closer look. God called him by name. God told him not to come closer and to take off his sandals, because he was on Holy ground.

The place where Moses stood was special because God was there.

God explained that He was the God of Abraham, Isaac and Jacob, and that He knew about the suffering of His people. God was going to send Moses to Pharaoh, to ask him to set the Israelites free. Moses had many questions. How could he do this? Who should he say had sent him? What if no one believed him? God promised that He would be with Moses. Moses must tell the people that the God of Abraham, Isaac and Jacob had sent him. God also showed Moses how to perform three miracles so Pharaoh would believe him.

Exodus chapter 4 verses 1-9.

But Moses still did not want to speak to Pharaoh. He felt that he was not good at speaking. God said that his brother Aaron would speak for him so Moses took his wife and sons and set out for Egypt.

What was unusal about the burning bush?
Did Moses want to do as God asked him?

Day 47: LIFE GETS HARDER

What do you think it would be like to be punished when you have not done anything wrong? This happened to some of the Israelites who were slaves in Egypt.

The leaders of the Israelites were called 'elders'.

Moses and Aaron called the elders together, to tell them all that God had said to Moses. When they saw the miracles Moses performed, they knew that God had sent him.

They thanked God that He cared about them and had seen how hard their lives were.

Moses and Aaron asked Pharaoh to let the Israelites go into the desert, to offer sacrifices to God. Pharaoh would not let the people go. Instead he made their work even harder. Instead of being given straw they had to collect their own and make as many bricks as before. Some men complained that Moses and Aaron had made things worse by speaking to Pharaoh. But God promised Moses that He would free His people and give them the land which He had promised.

God sent Moses and Aaron back to Pharaoh again. This time God said that Aaron should throw his staff down in front of Pharaoh. When he did this, it became a snake, but the Egyptian magicians did the same. However, Aaron's staff swallowed up the others.

Exodus chapter 5 verses 1-9.

In what way did Pharaoh make the work harder for the Israelites?

Day 48: THE PLAGUES BEGIN

In Egypt there is a great river called The Nile.

The Egyptians depended on the river for drinking water, bathing, and to make the crops grow.

One morning when Pharaoh went down to the river, Moses and Aaron met him. God told them what to do and say. Although God had sent them before to ask Pharaoh to let God's people go, he had not listened. They told Pharaoh that now God was going to show His power over the river. When they struck the water with the staff it would change into blood.

As Pharaoh and his servants watched, the water turned into blood. The fish in the river died. Pharaoh still would not listen to Moses and Aaron.

Seven days later God sent Moses and Aaron to Pharaoh again with the same request, 'Let My people go'. Pharaoh was warned that if he refused, there would be a plague of frogs all over the land of Egypt. Aaron stretched out his hand with the staff over all the waters - the streams and canals and ponds. Frogs came up from the water and got into the houses, on people's beds, even into Pharaoh's palace.

Pharaoh asked Moses to pray to God to take the frogs away.

He said he would then let the people go. But when the frogs had gone, Pharaoh hardened his heart and would not let the Israelites go.

Exodus chapter 8 verses 1-8 and 15.

What was Pharaoh's heart like? (Exodus chapter 7 verses 13 and 22 and chapter 8 verse 15).

Day 49: GNATS AND FLIES

God told Moses that Aaron should strike the dust of the ground with his staff. When he did this, the dust became gnats that troubled the people and the animals.

Gnats are small flies that can bite.

Pharaoh's magicians had been able to do some of the things that Moses and Aaron had done, but they could not bring gnats from the dust. They told Pharaoh that only God could do this, but he still would not listen.

Moses and Aaron met Pharaoh again by the river and told him that God had said he must let His people go. This time he was warned that Egypt would have a plague of flies if he would not let the Israelites go. The difference between this and the previous plagues would be that no swarms of flies would be found in the land of Goshen where the Israelites lived. The following day, swarms of flies spread over all the land, except the part of the land called Goshen.

It was dreadful having flies in the houses, on the food and on the people.

Pharaoh sent for Moses and Aaron. First of all he said that they could sacrifice to God in Egypt, but Moses said they must take a three day journey into the desert. Pharaoh agreed to that, and asked Moses to pray for him. When Moses prayed, God took the flies away. Once the flies had gone, Pharaoh hardened his heart and would not let the people go.

Exodus chapter 8 verses 20-28.

So far we have read about four plagues. Can you remember what they were?

Day 50: THREE MORE PLAGUES

The Egyptians had treated the Israelites very cruelly, but God had promised to free His people from slavery and give them their own land. Moses and Aaron continued to warn Pharaoh of the dreadful things that would happen if he did not obey God. They told Pharaoh that if he did not let the people go, a terrible disease would affect the animals.

The next day, the horses, donkeys, camels, cattle, sheep and goats became ill and died.

Pharaoh sent men to find out whether the Israelite's animals had died. None of their animals had been affected. Still Pharaoh's heart was hard.

He would not let the people go.

God told Moses and Aaron to toss soot into the air. The soot became fine dust all over Egypt as God had said it would. Sores, called boils, broke out on the people. Even Pharaoh's magicians could not work because of the boils.

The seventh plague that came upon Egypt was the worst hailstorm that had ever been seen in the land. Some of the Egyptians believed what God said through Moses and Aaron. They brought their workers and animals inside. Those who remained outside were killed by the hail. Crops were destroyed too. Pharaoh told Moses and Aaron that he had sinned. He asked them to pray for him, and then the people could go.

Exodus chapter 9 verses 20-28.

Did Pharaoh let the people go after the hail? (Exodus chapter 9 verses 34 and 35).

Day 51: LOCUSTS AND DARKNESS

Have you ever seen a grasshopper or heard its cheerful song during the summer? In some countries there are creatures like grasshoppers but larger, that are called locusts. Locusts can suddenly appear in great numbers, covering the land, and eating everything that grows.

Moses and Aaron warned Pharaoh that if he didn't allow the Israelites to leave, God would send the worst plague of locusts they had ever seen. Even Pharaoh's advisers asked him to let the people go to worship their God. They were afraid that any crops that had not already been destroyed, would be eaten by the locusts.

To worship God means to love and obey Him because He is great and wonderful. We worship God by praying, singing and listening to what He says in the Bible. For the Israelites, this included bringing offerings.

Pharaoh told Moses that the men could go, but Moses insisted that the women and children should come too. The next day, when the whole land was covered by the locusts, Pharaoh again asked Moses to pray for him. But once the locusts had been removed, he would not let the Israelites leave. The ninth plague that God sent was complete darkness for three days.

The darkness was so thick that the people could not see each other.

They could not go out to work. For three days they stayed inside but in Goshen the Israelites had daylight.

Exodus chapter 10 verses 13-15 and 21-23.

Did Pharaoh let the people go? (Exodus 10 verse 27).

Day 52: PREPARING TO LEAVE

The last night that the Israelites spent in Egypt was a wonderful night for them, but a terrible night for the Egyptians. God gave Moses and Aaron instructions to give to the people. Each man was to take a lamb for his family. Small families could share a lamb with a neighbour. When the lamb was killed, some blood was to be put on the sides and on the top of the doorframe. Then the lamb was to be roasted on the fire. This was to be done in the evening of the fourteenth day of the first month of the year. The meal was to be eaten in a hurry. It was a meal of roast lamb, herbs and bread with no yeast in it.

Yeast is used to make bread rise so that it is quite soft and good to eat. Bread without yeast is called 'unleavened'. It can be made quickly but is flat and harder than our usual bread.

They were not to wait for their bread to rise: they were to be ready for a journey.

The people did as Moses and Aaron told them. The meal of roast lamb, herbs and unleavened bread was prepared. The Israelites had also been told that they must stay in their houses that night. No one must go out until the morning. It was important that each house would have the blood of the lamb on the doorposts and over the door.

Exodus chapter 12 verses 1-8.

What three things did the people prepare for their last meal in the land of Egypt?

Day 53: A NIGHT TO REMEMBER

The time had come for a terrible thing to happen in Egypt. God said that during the night the oldest son in every family would die. But in the houses where the blood of the lamb was on the doorframe, everyone would be safe.

The Israelites stayed in their houses that night as they had been told.

The meal that they ate was called the Passover. This was because God had promised to pass over the houses when He saw the blood of the lamb. No one in those houses would die.

At midnight there was great sadness throughout Egypt. In every family, even Pharaoh's, the eldest son died.

Pharaoh told Moses and Aaron to take the Israelites away. The Egyptians wanted them to leave as quickly as possible, in case more people died. They even gave them gold and silver and clothing to take with them.

It was four hundred and thirty years since Jacob and his family had moved from the land of Canaan to Egypt. Now there were many thousands of Israelites setting out on the journey to their own land.

God said that the people of Israel should eat the Passover meal each year on the fourteenth day of the first month. They would then remember that God had brought them out of Egypt.

The lamb who died instead of the firstborn reminds us of the Lord Jesus. He died in the place of all those who trust in Him.

Exodus chapter 12 verses 29-33.

How many Israelite men left Egypt on Passover night? (Exodus chapter 12 verse 37).

Day 54: TRAPPED

When the Israelites left Egypt, they began a journey towards the land of Canaan. That journey would take them through hot, dry deserts, which the Bible calls the wilderness. How could Moses and Aaron lead thousands of people through the desert?

It was God who led the people. He went ahead of them in a pillar of cloud in the daytime and as a pillar of fire at night.

God led the people towards the Red Sea.

He told Moses that the people should camp near the sea. God warned Moses that Pharaoh would come after them.

Pharaoh and his servants began to feel sorry that they had let the Israelites go. They wanted them to continue working for them. Pharaoh gave orders for his chariot and soldiers to be made ready. Soon the Egyptian army set off after the Israelites.

When the people saw the Egyptian army coming towards them, they were very frightened.

Exodus chapter 14 verses 10-14.

They had the sea in front of them and the Egyptian soldiers coming after them. They even began to think that it would have been better for them to have stayed in the land of Egypt. The Israelites should have remembered all that God had done in Egypt. They should have known that they had a great God who would not leave them.

How did God lead the people? (Exodus chapter 13 verse 21).

Day 55: THROUGH THE SEA

How were the Israelites to get across the Red Sea and escape Pharaoh? God told Moses to hold his rod over the sea. God caused the Pillar of cloud to move, so that instead of being in front of the Israelites, it was behind them. This made everything seem dark to the Egyptians, but it gave light to the Israelites.

That night God sent a strong wind to divide the water. The Israelites walked across on dry ground with the water of the Red Sea like a wall on each side of them.

The Egyptian army followed them, but their chariot wheels came off so that it was hard to keep up. God told Moses to stretch out his hand over the sea again. When he did this, the water flowed back and covered the soldiers and their chariots.

Exodus chapter 14 verses 19-22.

God had done a wonderful thing for his people.

Only a great and powerful God could divide the sea so that they could walk through the sea on dry ground. God had saved His people from the Egyptians. He was also teaching them to know Him better and to trust Him more.

As we read our Bibles each day we are learning more about God. The more we know about God, the more we will want to know Him as our own Saviour and Friend.

What happened to the Egyptians as they followed the people of Israel? (Exodus chapter 14 verse 28).

Day 56: FINDING WATER

God led the Israelites through the Red Sea and saved them from the Egyptians.

The danger had now passed.

They sang a song of praise and thanks to God. Moses' sister, Miriam and some of the women danced for joy as they thanked God for helping them.

It was not easy to begin their journey through the wilderness. For three days they couldn't find any water, and then they found water that was bitter.

Exodus chapter 15 verses 22-27.

We do not know whether there was anything special about the tree that Moses threw into the water. But when he did as God told him, the water became good to drink. Soon the people were able to camp by the wells at Elim.

A place in the desert where there is water and where palm trees grow is called an oasis.

The people began to complain that they had been better off in Egypt. They were afraid that they would die in the desert because they had no food. God knew what the people were saying. He told Moses that He would provide bread for the people to collect on six mornings each week. God did not send this food on the seventh day because when He made the world He rested on the seventh day. Now God was teaching his people to do the same.

How many wells and palm trees were there at Elim?

Day 57: MANNA

God promised food for His people and he provided it. When the Israelites got up in the morning, the ground was covered with something small and round. It was as if frost lay all around them. Moses explained that this was the food that God had provided. They were to collect as much as they needed for each family.

The people called it manna and used it to bake cakes.

Where there is good soil and enough water, crops can be grown for food but the desert is dry and dusty. It is not easy to find food in the desert.

Moses told the people to collect enough for the day: they were not to save any for the next day. Some people did try to save some, but it went bad. Each day, for five days, the Israelites collected enough manna for their families. Then, on the sixth day, they gathered enough for two days. Moses told them that this was what God had said they should do. The seventh day of the week was to be their day for resting from work. It would be called the Sabbath day. There would be no manna on the Sabbath.

On the sixth day of the week the people saved food for the next day. The manna did not go bad that night. They had enough to eat on the Sabbath day.

Exodus chapter 16 verses 27-31.

As long as the Israelites were in the wilderness, God sent the manna for them. They need not have been afraid that God would leave them without food.

What did some of the people do on the seventh day?

Day 58: AMALEKITE BATTLE

God had chosen Moses to be the leader of His people. This was not an easy task. When the people found life difficult they complained about him. There were many times when Moses had to call upon God for help.

The Israelites continued their journey through the desert. They came to a place called Rephidim. Once again there was no water and they were thirsty. The people complained to Moses. They asked him why he had brought them out of Egypt if they were to die of thirst in the desert.

Moses cried out to God. He asked God what he should do with the people who were so angry with him. God told Moses to take some of the leaders with him and to take his rod in his hand. He was to strike the rock with his rod and God promised that water would come from the rock. Moses did as God had said and there was water for the people to drink.

While the people camped at Rephidim, some people called the Amalekites came to fight against them.

Exodus chapter 17 verses 8-13.

The Israelites had not wanted to fight these people. They were weary with their journey and it would be hard for them to fight a battle. But when Moses held up the rod in his hand, they would remember all that God had done for them. It would remind them that God was with them and would help them.

We can be sure that while Moses was on top of the hill, he would have prayed for God's help.

God did help them and the battle was won.

What did Aaron and Hur do when Moses' hands were tired?

Day 59: JETHRO GIVES ADVICE

Do you remember the name of Moses' wife? You will find it in Exodus chapter 18 verse 2. Moses also had two sons called Gershom and Eliezer. Jethro, Moses' father-in-law took his daughter and grandchildren back to his home for a while. But one day, when the people of Israel were camped in the desert, they all came to meet Moses.

Moses told Jethro all that God had done for them.

Jethro gave thanks to God for rescuing His people from Egypt. The next day, many people wanted to speak to Moses, to ask his help and advice.

People waited all day long, because there were so many of them.

When Jethro saw what was happening, he realised that Moses could not deal with all these people on his own. He suggested that Moses should choose men to help him: men who loved God and were honest and trustworthy. When any of the people had a disagreement, they could come to one of these 'judges' who would decide who was in the right. Only the very difficult cases needed to be taken to Moses.

Moses knew that this advice was good, and he did just as Jethro had said. The people would no longer have to wait so long for help with their problems, and Moses would have help in the work of leading God's people.

Exodus chapter 18 verses 13-23.

What was the name of the land where Jethro lived? (Exodus chapter 2 verse 15).

Day 60: AT MOUNT SINAI

In the desert there was a mountain called Mount Sinai. After they left Rephidim, the Israelites camped near there. God told Moses that Israel would be His special people, if they obeyed Him. Moses sent for the leaders of the people and told them what God had said.

They all agreed to obey God.

God spoke to Moses on Mount Sinai, and showed the people some of His power. The people were warned not to touch the mountain. There was thunder and lightning and a thick cloud. The mountain smoked with fire. The people heard a loud trumpet and were afraid. They knew that God was there in all His great power. God then gave Moses laws to teach the people.

The law teaches us what is right and wrong: the things that we should do and the things that we must not do.

The first part of the law that God gave Moses, we call the Ten Commandments. When we command someone, we tell them what they are to do. God does not change: His commandments are still the same today.

Exodus chapter 20 verses 1-8.

These commandments teach us that before we can live in a right way with other people, we must love and obey God. We must not make idols or statues to bow down to. We must be careful to use God's name properly. The fourth commandment tells us that the Sabbath day should be a day to rest from work.

What did God make on each of the six days of Creation? (Genesis chapter 1.) What did God do on the seventh day?

Day 61: SIX MORE COMMANDMENTS

The fifth commandment is about how we should live in our families. God says that we are to 'honour' our parents. This means that we should respect them. Our parents care for us while we are young and we should listen to them and do what they say. Things cannot go well in a country unless people care for their families.

The sixth commandment teaches us not to kill people. Sometimes accidents happen and someone is killed. That is different from deliberately killing someone. The seventh commandment teaches us that when a man and woman get married, they should stay together for life. The eighth commandment is about not taking things that belong to other people.

This is stealing and we must not do it.

The ninth commandment says we must not tell lies. The tenth commandment tells us not to covet.

To covet means to want something that belongs to someone else.

Be content with what you have. It is good to work hard and use your money to buy what you need. To be envious of what others have, leads to unhappiness.

Exodus chapter 20 verses 12-17.

When Jesus lived on earth, He talked to people about God's law. His words teach us that the law is not only about the things we do that everyone can see. God's law is about what we are really like in our hearts.

How many people have broken God's law? (Romans chapter 3 verse 23).

Day 62: A SPECIAL TENT

When people live together they need rules about how to behave. These rules may be quite simple, like being quiet when your teacher is talking in school.

Countries have rules that are called laws.

The Israelites were given their laws by God. He gave them other laws too besides the ten commandments to teach them how they should live.

The people promised that they would obey God.

While the Israelites were living in the desert, they lived in tents which could be carried with them on their journeys. God spoke to Moses on Mount Sinai about a special tent that the people were to make. God wanted His people to know that He was with them. This tent, which we call the tabernacle, would be the place where God would meet His people and speak to them.

This special tent would teach the Israelites how people who are sinful can come to God, who is Holy. When we say that God is Holy, we mean that He is absolutely pure and good in all that He does.

The Israelites were to give everything that was needed to make the tabernacle.

Exodus chapter 25 verses 1-9.

Gold, silver and precious stones; linen and animal skins; bronze and wood; oil and spices, would all be needed to make the tabernacle.

Who would show Moses how to make the tabernacle?

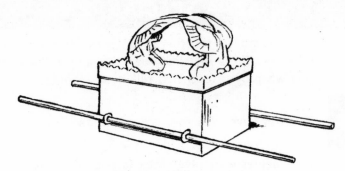

The ark of the covenant

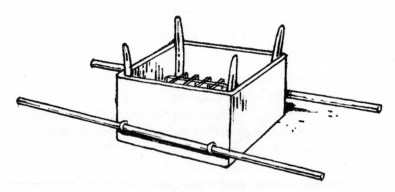

The altar of burnt offering

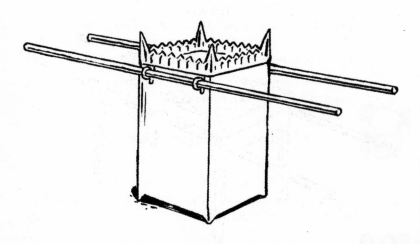

The altar of incense

The lampstand

The laver

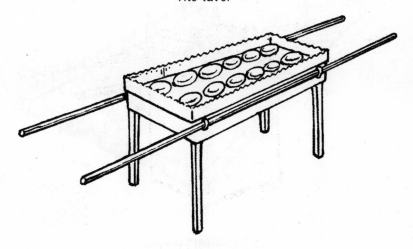

The table

The High Priest

The tabernacle

A view of inside the tabernacle.

Match the numbers to the objects to work out what goes where in the tabernacle:

1. The Ark of the Covenant was situated in the Holy of Holies. The Ark went across the tent from north-south. The wings touched each side of the tabernacle.

2. The Altar of Incense was in front of the veil dividing the Holy of Holies from the Holy place.

3. The golden lamp was on the left-hand side at the south end as you entered the Holy place.

4. The Table of shewbread was on the right-hand side as you entered the Holy place.

5. The laver is generally accepted as having being in line between the brasen altar and the entrance to the Holy place.

6. The Brasen altar was near the entrance to the courtyard.

Day 63: GOLDEN FURNITURE

Before a house is built there has to be a plan. The plan for the tabernacle came from God. God explained how everything was to be made. He described the furniture which would be placed inside the tabernacle.

Exodus chapter 25 verse 10-16.

You often read of different sorts of measurements in the Bible. For example a cubit is almost half a metre.

The lid of the chest was called the mercy seat and was to be made of pure gold.

At each end of the lid was a golden figure called a cherub. God told Moses to put the stones on which He had written the Ten Commandments into the chest. The full name for this chest was 'The Ark of the Covenant'. A covenant is an agreement. God promised to speak to His people from above the mercy seat. God's people were to remember to obey His commandments.

A wooden table was to be made for the tabernacle. It would be covered with gold and have rings and poles for carrying it, like the ark. Every Sabbath day twelve loaves of bread were to be placed on this table. As well as this, special dishes and plates were to be made and a golden lampstand. The lampstand would hold seven lamps. Olive oil would keep them burning.

God told Moses to make sure that everything was made exactly as He said. The New Testament helps us to understand that this was important because everything in the tabernacle teaches us about Jesus.

Which words of The Lord Jesus do the bread and the lamp remind us of? (John chapter 6 verse 35; John chapter 8 verse 12).

Day 64: BOARDS AND CURTAINS

How strange to have a house you could take to pieces and carry on a journey, but this was how the tabernacle was planned. It was made from wooden boards covered with gold. The boards fitted into silver bases to help them stand. Wooden bars covered with gold fitted across the boards to hold them together.

One end of the tabernacle was the door. A curtain hung across this end instead of wooden boards. Another curtain divided the tabernacle into two rooms, one twice as long as the other. The roof of the tabernacle was made of four curtains. The outer curtains were made of animal skins and the inner one was made of embroidered linen. Around the tabernacle was a courtyard and around that was a fence of linen curtains.

The entrance was easy to find because it had a curtain of blue, purple and scarlet. It was different to the plain linen of the fence.

Between the entrance to the courtyard and the door of the tabernacle would stand the altar for the sacrifices and offerings. It was made of wood covered with bronze. It would be one and a half metres high, two and a half metres long and two and a half metres wide. It had rings and poles to carry it, like the other furniture.

Exodus chapter 26 verses 30-37.

There was only one way into the tabernacle. This helps us to understand that there is only one way to God. Read John chapter 14 verse 6.

What stood between the entrance and the door of the tabernacle?

Day 65: PRIESTS AND LEVITES

The families of Jacob's sons grew bigger and then they were called tribes. Jacob's third son was called Levi. God chose the tribe of Levi to look after the tabernacle. Moses and Aaron belonged to that tribe. God chose Aaron and his family to be priests.

The men in the tribe of Levi were allowed to go into the tabernacle courtyard. It was their job to look after the tabernacle and its furniture and carry it when it was time for the Israelites to move. Aaron's sons, who were priests, were allowed to go into the larger of the two rooms in the tabernacle.

The priests offered sacrifices so that God would forgive His people for their sins.

Every morning and evening the priests burned incense on an altar made of wood and covered with gold.

Incense is a mixture of beautiful smelling spices.

The altar of incense stood in front of the curtain that separated the two rooms. It was smaller than the bronze altar that stood in the courtyard. Once a year, Aaron, the High Priest, was allowed to go into the smaller room. This was called 'the Most Holy Place'.

Read about the priest's beautiful clothing: Exodus chapter 28 verses 1-4.

In the courtyard was a bronze basin, called the laver, for the priests to wash their hands and feet.

What did Aaron do every morning and evening, besides burning the incense? (Exodus chapter 30 verses 7-8).

Day 66: DISO.BEDIENCE

Have you had to wait a long time for someone - so long that you grew tired of waiting? Moses stayed on the mountain for forty days while God spoke to him.

The Israelites became impatient. Although they had promised to obey God, they began to think about the idols worshipped in Egypt. They gave their gold earrings to Aaron to make an idol with. The idol was in the shape of a calf but the people pretended that they were worshipping God. God knew what they were doing. He told Moses that he must go back to them.

Moses prayed to God for the people.

God listened to Moses and did not destroy the people. When Moses came down the mountain, he broke the two stones on which God had written the Ten Commandments. He also destroyed the golden calf. Moses saw that the people were doing the wrong things that other nations did. He called for all who were true to God to come to him. The Levites came and Moses told them what to do. They went through the camp and killed some of those who had worshipped the idol. Moses prayed that God would forgive His people. God then called Moses up the mountain and told him to bring two more stone tablets.

On these two stones God Himself wrote the words of the Ten Commandments.

Exodus chapter 32 verses 1-8.

What does the second commandment say we must not do? (Exodus chapter 20 verses 4 and 5).

Day 67: SKILLED WORKERS

The Israelites made all the beautiful things for the tabernacle because God gave certain people just the skills that were needed for the work.

Exodus chapter 35 verse 30 to chapter 36 verse 1.

Moses told the people that they needed gold, silver, bronze; blue, purple and scarlet yarn, linen, animal skins, wood, oil, spices and precious stones. No one was forced to bring anything.

The people were glad to give what they could. Moses had to tell them not to bring any more as enough had been given.

Everything was made exactly as God had instructed Moses. This was very important because the New Testament tells us that in the tabernacle we have a picture of what the Lord Jesus would do.

Just as the High Priest went into the Most Holy place once a year after offering sacrifices, so Jesus would enter Heaven after He had offered His own life on the Cross.

When the tabernacle was finished, and the clothing for the priests had been made, everything was brought to Moses for him to see. He inspected the work and saw that it had all been done as God had commanded.

Who were the two men who God put in charge of making the tabernacle?

Day 68: CLOUD AND FIRE

On the first day of the first month of the second year after the Israelites left Egypt, the tabernacle was set up. God again spoke to Moses, telling him the order in which everything was to be done. Aaron and his sons were dressed in the priests' clothing. Moses anointed them by pouring some oil on their heads. This meant that God had chosen them for the work that only the priests could do.

It was important that everyone understood that Aaron and his family had not made themselves priests. God had given them this special job to do.

Do you remember the pillar of cloud and fire by which God led His people? Now the cloud appeared over the tabernacle. It stayed there when God wanted the people to remain where they were. It lifted from the tabernacle when the Israelites were to set out on their journeys. At night, fire could be seen in the cloud.

Whenever the Israelites camped, the tabernacle was in the middle of the camp. The tribe of Levi pitched their tents around the tabernacle and all the other tribes camped at a distance from it. God gave instructions so that everyone knew where they should be: three tribes on the north side, three on the south, three on the east and three on the west. When the people looked from their tents towards the tabernacle, they could see the cloud over it.

The people knew that God was with them.

Exodus chapter 40 verses 18-30.

How many times do we read that Moses did 'as the Lord commanded him'?

DAYS 69-75: Leviticus

THE WAY INTO GOD'S PRESENCE.

God's purpose was to dwell among His people, and in this Book
we learn how it could be possible for people who are sinful to have
fellowship with a God who is Holy. We read in chapter 17 that blood
had to be shed to make atonement for sin. Through the offerings
detailed in the Book of Leviticus, sin was covered until the coming of
the promised Saviour, who would be for His people both Priest and
Sacrifice.

Day 69: FINDING FORGIVENESS

For many years the Israelites had been slaves who could not choose they way they lived. They had to obey the Egyptians. When God brought them out of Egypt, He began to teach them how they were to live as His people.

God gave them His commandments and instructions for making the tabernacle.

The nations living around the people of Israel worshipped idols. They made offerings that they thought would please these false gods. God taught His people that they needed to bring offerings to the tabernacle. But these offerings were not like giving God a present to please him. God gave instructions about the offerings that should be brought.

In the Book of Leviticus the Bible teaches us that we can only come to God in God's way. We are too sinful to know God as our Friend, until our sin is forgiven.

God taught His people that the life of an animal must be given instead of the person who had sinned. If God's instructions were carried out, then the sinner would be forgiven.

Sacrificing a lamb or a goat could not pay for the wrong things people did, but this was God's way of covering sin, until the time when He sent His own Son to die in place of sinful people. Those who obeyed God's instructions trusted Him for the forgiveness that they knew they needed.

Leviticus chapter 6 verses 1-7.

Can you find two things that must be done?

Day 70: BEING THANKFUL

Did you find an answer to yesterday's question? The person who had stolen from his neighbour had to give back what he had taken, and then bring his offering to the tabernacle. God wanted His people to know that it was no use bringing their offering, if they were not truly sorry for their sin. A man who kept what he had stolen was only pretending to be sorry.

The Book of Leviticus shows us that God knows all about us. Sometimes we do something wrong without meaning to. Sometimes we say wrong things without thinking. God taught His people what they must do when these things happened.

There were two offerings that were not brought because the person had sinned. One was the Peace Offering and the other was called the Grain Offering.

The Peace Offering and the Grain Offering were brought by people who were thankful to God for His goodness to them. They already knew that God had forgiven their sins. Now they could come to Him as Saviour and Friend, to say thank-you.

God's people were thankful.

God had made it possible for them to come to Him for forgiveness. Since the Lord Jesus came, there is no need for any more offerings to be made because of the wrong things we do. How thankful we should be that God loved the world so much that He sent His Son.

Leviticus chapter 5 verses 17-19.

Whose family did God choose to become priests, to offer the people's sacrifices? (Exodus chapter 28 verse 1).

Day 71: LIVING TO PLEASE GOD

When we are with people who do wrong things, it is not easy to do what is right. The people of Israel had seen the Egyptians do many wrong things. When the day came for them to go into the land that God had promised, they would also see people worshipping idols and doing wicked things. God told his people how to behave.

He wanted everything in their lives to show that they were His people.

Leviticus chapter 18 verses 1-5.

It is not surprising then, that in the Book of Leviticus we find God's instructions about many things. The people were taught which animals to use for food and which ones they must not eat. They were told what to do when someone caught a bad illness called leprosy. God explained to Moses and Aaron how to tell if someone had the illness and how to tell if he was better. Nowadays there are medicines for this illness.

God also taught His people to care for one another.

When they brought in crops at harvest time, they were to leave the corners of the field for the poor people to gather. They were to be kind to those who were deaf or blind. They were not to 'tell tales' about anyone. God also taught His people to respect older people and to be kind to people from other lands.

All these things remind us that if we love the Lord Jesus, we will show that we do by the way we live.

Some fruit was to be left for the poor. What was it? (Leviticus chapter 19 verse 10).

Day 72: THREE CELEBRATIONS

Do you look forward to special days such as Christmas or your Birthday? The people of Israel had special days that were chosen for them by God.

On the fourteenth day of the first month they were to keep the Feast of the Passover.

The Feast of the Passover was to celebrate the night when they came out of Egypt. As they offered the Passover lamb, they remembered the lambs that died so that the oldest son in each family would be safe.

The day after the Passover, the Feast of Unleavened Bread began. This lasted for seven days. During this time they ate bread that had not risen: it had no yeast in it. This reminded them of the night when they began their journey out of Egypt. There had been no time to wait for bread to rise.

The Feast of First Fruits took place on the day following the Sabbath Day after the Feast of the Passover. This was the first day of the week. Before the people ate any of their crops, at the beginning of the harvest, they were to bring a sheaf to the priest. This was to thank God for giving them food to eat.

Remember that every good thing comes from God.

These Old Testament Feasts look forward to what Jesus would do. In the New Testament He is called 'The Lamb of God'. He was crucified during the Passover. On the first day of the week, He rose from the dead.

Leviticus chapter 23 verses 5-6, 10-11, 14.

What were the people to do before they ate their crops?

Day 73: TWO FEASTS

Another celebration was the Feast of Weeks, called later on the Feast of Pentecost. This was on the fiftieth day after the Feast of Firstfruits, so it was also held on the first day of the week. On this occasion the people brought two loaves that they had baked. In the New Testament we read that God sent His Holy Spirit to the followers of Jesus, on the Day of Pentecost. We will find out about this when we read the Book of Acts.

Leviticus chapter 23 verses 15-17.

In the seventh month of the year, there were two special days and a special week. The first day of the seventh month was the Feast of Trumpets. God told Moses to make two silver trumpets. These were used to call the people together, to tell them to move, or in time of war. This feast reminds us that one day God will call His people together.

All who love and obey God will be with Him forever.

The tenth day of the seventh month was The Day of Atonement. God is so pure and sinless that sinful people cannot come to Him, unless their sin is forgiven.

'Atonement' means something God has done about our sin so that we can know Him as our friend.

The Day of Atonement was special. No one was to work on that day except for one man. We will learn why, tomorrow. The Israelites brought the offerings God asked for and received forgiveness.

How many days were there from the Feast of Firstfruits to the Feast of Pentecost?

Day 74: THE HIGH PRIEST

God's special Tent, the tabernacle, was divided into two rooms. Between the rooms hung a curtain that was called the veil. The priests had duties to do in the larger room, called the Holy place. But the smaller room, the Most Holy place, could only be entered by one man once a year.

On the Day of Atonement, the High Priest made certain offerings to God and then went into the Most Holy place. He was not dressed in his beautiful robes. Instead he wore plain linen clothes. No one else was allowed in the tabernacle while he made offerings for his own sin and the sins of the people.

The people were told not to do any work on the Day of Atonement. They were to be truly sorry for the wrong things they had done. The Day of Atonement is about what the Lord Jesus would do when He died on the cross. The offerings reminded them that they were sinful people needing God's forgiveness.

We cannot do anything to make ourselves good enough for God, however hard we try.

The work of taking away sin was done by the Lord Jesus for all who trust in Him.

Just as the High Priest took off his beautiful clothes, so the Lord Jesus left the splendour of heaven.

He came to earth as a man so that He could do what all the Old Testament offerings could never do: take away our sin.

Leviticus chapter 23 verses 26-31.

How often did the High Priest go into the Most Holy place?

Day 75: A JOYFUL WEEK

At harvest time it is good to see the crops that have grown well.

We can thank God for fruit and vegetables, corn, wheat and barley. There are so many things that are good to eat.

Some people go to a harvest thanksgiving service to thank God for making the crops grow.

In the land of Israel, on the fifteenth day of the seventh month, when the harvest was gathered in, the Feast of Tabernacles began. This feast lasted seven days and it was a very joyful time. The people gathered branches from the trees and built shelters for themselves. For a week they lived in these leafy shelters. When they came into their own land, this feast would remind them of when they had lived in tents in the desert. As they thanked God for the harvest, God wanted them to have a happy time enjoying the good things He had provided. The Feast of Tabernacles reminds us that there will be a time of great joy, when all God's people are together with Him.

All the special occasions that the Israelite people celebrated remind us of what God has done so that our sin can be forgiven and we can know Him as our Saviour and Friend.

Leviticus chapter 23 verses 39-44.

How many of the special feasts can you remember?

DAYS 76-86: Numbers

THE WAY THROUGH THE WILDERNESS

We learn from this Book that God's people were to be a disciplined people. They were given instructions as to their places when in camp or on a journey. The duties of the Levites, the tribe chosen by God for the work of the tabernacle, were clearly laid down. We read of the failure of the Israelites to enter Canaan, which resulted in forty years living in the wilderness. In spite of this and other failures, we see God's unfailing provision for His people.

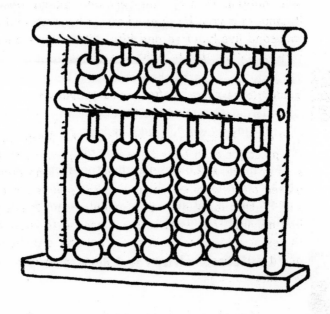

Day 76: COUNTING

The people of Israel had been living in the desert near Mount Sinai for about ten months. God told Moses that he and Aaron must do some counting. They were to count all the men of twenty years old and over from each tribe except the tribe of Levi. God gave to Moses the names of twelve men who were leaders of each tribe. They were to help Moses and Aaron as they gathered the men together to count them.

There were still twelve leaders of the tribes even though the tribe of Levi was not counted because Joseph's two sons became the heads of two tribes: Ephraim and Manasseh.

The number of men from twenty years old in each tribe was counted. Then the numbers were added together. It came to a very large number: six hundred and three thousand five hundred and fifty. All these were men who would be able to fight in a battle.

Each tribe had a banner to camp beside.

God gave the instructions to Moses and Aaron about the place for each tribe to camp. They were also to stay in order whenever they packed up camp and moved on. It was important that the people did as God said. Such a large number of people living together and moving from place to place needed to know these things. It also meant that there were no arguments about someone taking the best place or always wanting to be first.

Numbers chapter 1 verses 1-4.

Who did Moses and Aaron have to count?

Day 77: MOVING

Jacob's son Levi had three sons, Gershon, Kohath and Merari. It was their job to look after the tabernacle. They did this work from the age of thirty to fifty years old. They did not choose what work they did: God told Moses exactly how it must be done.

The sons of Kohath looked after the tabernacle furniture when the people moved from place to place.

First of all the priests had to put covers over the ark, the table, the lamp stand, the golden altar and the bronze altar. All the smaller things that were used in the tabernacle had to be covered as well. The priests put carrying poles through the rings that were on the corners of the furniture. When everything was ready, the men from Kohath's family used the poles to carry the furniture on their shoulders.

They did not see the furniture or touch it.

The sons of Gershon were responsible for moving all the coverings and curtains from the tabernacle. Four curtains made up the tabernacle roof and curtains also made the fence around the courtyard. Two carts with four oxen were provided to carry them.

The boards, bars, pillars, sockets and cords of the tabernacle were moved by the men from the family of Merari. They were provided with four carts and eight oxen to carry all these things.

Numbers chapter 7 verses 1-9.

How many men were there in the tribe of Levi from twenty to fifty years old? (Numbers chapter 4 verses 46-48).

Day 78: SILVER TRUMPETS

Some things have instructions to tell us how to use them. If the instructions are not good, we may not understand what to do.

When God gave instructions to Moses for His people, everyone knew exactly what they should do.

When God told Moses to make two silver trumpets, He explained how and when they were to be used.

Numbers chapter 10 verses 1-9.

The trumpets were to be used on special feast days, and when the people went out to fight their enemies.

We have seen that the priests and Levites had their duties to do. Each tribe knew where it was to camp and who its leader was. Everyone knew where they should be when they were travelling. God did not want His people to live in a muddled way. He was teaching them to live in an orderly way. The way in which God's people live should show others something about what God is like.

The people of Israel stayed near Mount Sinai for nearly a year. Then the cloud moved from the tabernacle and they set out on their journey once again. They knew that God was with them, because they could see the cloud going on ahead to show them the way. They travelled for three days and then camped again. Moses asked Jethro, his wife's father, to stay with them. He would be a help to them, as he knew a lot about the land that they were travelling through.

Which tribe set out first when the people went on their journey? (Numbers chapter 10 verse 14).

Day 79: GRUMBLING

The food that God provided for the people was called Manna. It appeared on the ground each morning except the Sabbath day. Some people from Egypt had joined the Israelites on their journey. They longed for different food. Soon many people became discontented.

GOD'S WORD

Numbers chapter 11 verses 4-10.

It seems as if the people had forgotten that they were travelling to a land that God had promised them. In Canaan they would be able to grow all sorts of food. God had given them enough for their journey, but they were not satisfied.

Moses was very troubled by the complaints. He told God that caring for all these people was too hard. He could not provide meat for so many people. God told Moses to choose seventy men who were leaders among the people. They would be called elders. God promised to give His Spirit to them so that they would be able to help Moses deal with all the people. God also said that He would provide enough meat for the people for a whole month. God sent a wind that brought lots of quails near the Israelite camp.

EXTRA INFO

Quails are small birds that are good to eat.

BY MYSELF

The people were rather greedy, collecting as many birds as they could.

God was not pleased with the way some of the people behaved. Some of them became ill while they were eating and some of them died.

ASK ABOUT

What did the people remember eating when they were in Egypt?

Day 80: EXPLORING

Would you like to be an explorer who travels to other lands and finds out about faraway places? The day came when God told Moses to send twelve men to explore the land of Canaan. One man was chosen from each tribe. They were told to find out if the land was a good land to grow food and if the people there were strong or weak.

The twelve men spent forty days exploring the land.

When they came back they told the people what a good land it was. They brought back a large bunch of grapes to show how well the fruit grew. But they said that the people of the land were powerful, and lived in towns with strong walls around them.

Ten of the men said that the Israelites would not be able to fight against the people of Canaan. Only two men, Joshua and Caleb, believed that God would give them the land as He had promised.

The people did not listen to Joshua and Caleb.

The people grumbled at Moses and Aaron, and even talked about going back to Egypt. God told Moses that because the people were not willing to go into Canaan, they would have to stay in the desert for forty years - one year for every day the twelve men had explored the land. No one over twenty years old would live long enough to enter the land of Canaan except for two men.

Numbers chapter 13 verses 26-33.

What were the names of the two men? (Numbers chapter 14 verse 30).

Day 81: REBELLION

God chose Moses to lead His people, Aaron and his sons to be priests, and the tribe of Levi to look after the tabernacle. So when the people grumbled about Moses and Aaron, they were really grumbling about God's choice.

One day a man named Korah from the tribe of Levi, and two men from the tribe of Reuben called Dathan and Abiram, rebelled against Moses and Aaron. Two hundred and fifty men were with them. They said they did not see why Moses should be their leader. Moses knew that they were really rebelling against God. This was a very serious thing to do. Moses prayed for the people and then he told them to move away from the tents of Korah, Dathan and Abiram.

Moses explained that God would show whether he had been sent by God to lead them.

As soon as he had spoken, the ground split open and Korah, Dathan and Abiram were swallowed up. The men who had followed them also died. The next day the people grumbled against Moses and Aaron because of what had happened.

Numbers chapter 17 verses 1-11.

Moses placed twelve rods in the tabernacle: one from the leader of each tribe. God caused Aaron's rod to have buds, blossom and almonds on it.

In this way God showed the people that He had chosen Aaron to be the High Priest.

How many rods were placed in the tabernacle? What happened to Aaron's rod?

Day 82: WATER

Have you ever felt really thirsty and longed for a drink?

In hot countries people need lots to drink.

The Israelites would have been anxious when they travelled through the desert and could not find water. There were thousands of men, women, children and animals. Sometimes, instead of remembering that God would help them, the people grumbled and blamed Moses and Aaron.

One day, when there was no water to be found, Moses and Aaron went to the tabernacle to ask for God's help. God told Moses to take his staff and to take Aaron with him. In front of all the people, Moses was to speak to a rock. God promised that water would come pouring out for them. Moses and Aaron called the people together in front of the rock.

Moses took his staff and struck the rock twice.

Water poured out just as God had said. The people and their animals were able to drink. But God had not told Moses to strike the rock, only that he should speak to it. God told Moses and Aaron that they would not lead the Israelites into their land when the years in the desert were ended. Even though Moses was the leader God had chosen, it was still important for him to obey God.

Numbers chapter 20 verses 2-11.

Whenever the people grumbled, where did they say they would rather be? Did the Israelites really have a happy life there? (Exodus chapter 3 verse 7).

Day 83: POISONOUS SNAKES

Do you know anyone who is eighty years old? When God told Moses that he would lead the Israelites out of Egypt, Moses was already eighty years old, and his brother Aaron and his sister Miriam were older than he was. In the Book of Numbers chapter 20 we read that first Miriam and then Aaron, died.

Aaron's place as the High Priest was taken by his son Eleazar.

After the death of Aaron, the Israelites were attacked by a Canaanite king. They asked God to help them and they won the battle. But after this, they began to grumble again. They said wrong things about God and about Moses, and even complained about the food that God provided for them. God sent poisonous snakes among the people and many were bitten and died. Then the people told Moses that they knew they had been wrong to speak against God and against him.

They asked Moses to pray that God would take the snakes away.

When Moses prayed, God told him to make a snake and put it on a pole. Anyone who was bitten by a snake could look at the snake on the pole, and live. Moses made a bronze snake and put it on a pole. As God had promised, anyone who had been bitten by a snake and who looked at the bronze snake, did not die. As the people believed and obeyed what God told them to do, He made them well.

Numbers chapter 21 verses 4-9.

Read what the Lord Jesus said about this in John chapter 3 verses 14 and 15.

Day 84: BALAAM'S DONKEY

Balak King of Moab was afraid when the Israelites came near to his land. They had won battles against other people and he was frightened of what they would do to his country. Twice Balak sent messengers to a man named Balaam. He offered him money to put a curse on the people of Israel.

To bless someone means to ask God to be good to them. To curse someone means to want very bad things to happen to them.

At first Balaam said that he could not go with the messengers because God would not allow him to put a curse on His people. However he did eventually saddle his donkey and set out for Moab.

God sent an angel to stop Balaam.

The donkey saw the angel and turned into a field to get away. Balaam beat the donkey to make her get back on the road. The angel then stood in a narrow place and the donkey pressed against the wall, hurting Balaam's foot so that he beat her again. After that the angel stood in a place so narrow that the donkey just lay down. Balaam was angry and beat his poor donkey a third time. God made Balaam's donkey able to speak. She asked him why he had beaten her when he knew she did not usually behave like this. Then Balaam saw the angel and bowed down on the road. The angel told Balaam that he could go with the messengers, but he must only say what God told him.

Numbers chapter 22 verses 14-21.

**Why was Balak afraid of the Israelites?
What did he want Balaam to do?**

Day 85: BALAAM AND BALAK

Do you remember what an idol is? It is like a statue, and can be made of stone, wood, gold or silver. It is a false god that people bow down and pray to.

An idol is something that people love more than the one true God.

The people that the Israelites met on their journeys worshipped idols, and did many things that were wrong.

King Balak and Balaam looked down on the Israelite camp. Balaam asked for seven altars to be built and offerings made. But God would only allow Balaam to bless Israel. Balak was not satisfied and so another seven altars were built in a different place. God still did not allow Balaam to speak against His people. For the third time Balak had seven altars built but Balaam was unable to speak as Balak wanted him to. Balak became very angry.

Balak told Balaam to go back home.

But even though Balaam could not speak against God's people, he did give Balak some advice. He could see that the people of Israel were strong because God protected them. So he said that the women of Moab should invite the men of Israel to come and worship their idols. Some of them did. This brought great trouble on Israel because they had disobeyed God.

Numbers chapter 24 verses 10-14.

Did the Israelites know that it was wrong to worship idols? (Exodus chapter 20 verse 4).

Day 86: A NEW LEADER

Can you remember the names of the two men who brought a good report about the land of Canaan? You will find their names in Numbers chapter 14 verse 30.

One day God told Moses to climb up a mountain so that he could see the land of Canaan.

Moses knew that he would not live to lead the people into their land.

He asked God to give the people a new leader, so that they would not be like a flock of sheep without a shepherd. God told Moses to bring Joshua to Eleazar the priest, and let all the Israelites see that he was the man God had chosen to lead them into Canaan. Joshua and Caleb had been willing to obey God and enter the land of Canaan when the rest of the people were too afraid to do so.

Now God was going to be with Joshua, just as He had been with Moses.

Moses had led the people of Israel out of Egypt: Joshua would lead them into Canaan. God gave Moses instructions about the land of Canaan, so that the people would know how much land was to be theirs. God said that Joshua and Eleazar would give land to each tribe. One leader from each tribe was to help them do this. After living in tents for forty years, it was time to prepare the people for settling down in their own land.

Numbers chapter 27 verses 12-23.

What did Moses ask God to do for the people? What was God's answer? (Deuteronomy chapter 28 verse 1).

DAYS 87-89: Deuteronomy

THE SECOND READING OF THE LAW

Moses knew that he would not lead the Israelites into their promised land: God would give that task to his successor. Apart from two men, Caleb and Joshua, all those who had been twenty years old or over when the people refused to enter Canaan, had died in the wilderness. Faithfully, Moses ensured that the new generation were instructed in the Law given at Sinai. He told them of the blessings God would send if they were obedient. He also warned them of the awful consequences of disobedience.

Day 87: GOD'S GOODNESS

The Israelites had been afraid to go into Canaan even though God was with them. As a punishment God said they would have to stay in the wilderness for forty years. When the forty years were over all the people who had refused to go into Canaan had died. Only Caleb and Joshua were still alive. They had told the people that God would help them.

Moses knew that his life would soon end. He wanted to make sure that the Israelites knew all that God had done for them since they left Egypt. Those who would go into the promised land had either been born in the wilderness or had been under twenty years old when their parents refused to go into the land of Canaan.

Moses also wanted to make sure that they knew God's laws and commandments. So Moses spoke to the people.

Moses' words are written in the Book of Deuteronomy.

Deuteronomy chapter 8 verses 11-18.

Moses looked forward to when the Israelites would be in their own land. He knew that they might forget that God had helped them. He reminded them of the years in the desert when God gave them food and water.

Moses knew that sometimes men, women, boys and girls forget God. We need to remember that it is God who gives us all that we have. We should have thankful hearts.

What were the Israelites told not to do? (Deuteronomy 8:11). For how long did the people of Israel live in tents in the wilderness?

Day 88: WORDS OF WARNING

Some old people can remember things that happened years and years ago. Do you have a good memory?

Moses wanted the people to remember all that God had done for them, so that they would trust Him always. He reminded them of when they had disobeyed God, so that they would not do so again. Moses made sure that the people who would go into Canaan knew God's commands. When they were in their own land they were to take some large stones and write God's law on them. Moses knew that if the people of Israel obeyed God, then God would keep them safe. If they disobeyed God, they would have great trouble and would even be taken away from their land.

Deuteronomy chapter 28 verses 1-6; 15-19.

Moses told the people about the good things that would happen if they obeyed God's commands. Their enemies would run away from them. There would be plenty of rain for the crops. The people living in other countries would see that God was with them.

Moses told the Israelites about the bad things that would happen if they disobeyed God's commands. God would not send rain. Their crops would not grow. Their enemies would take them captive to a strange land.

Moses loved his people.

He wanted them to live safely in their own land. He wanted them to love and obey God.

What did Moses tell the people to do if they wanted God to give them good things? (Deuteronomy chapter 28 verse 1).

Day 89: ON MOUNT NEBO

Moses knew that he would not go with the Israelites into the land of Canaan. When he had struck the rock, instead of speaking to it, God had said that he would not enter the land.

Although he was a hundred and twenty years old, Moses continued to teach the people about how they should live.

Moses knew that when the people settled down in their own land, they would begin to worship the idols of the nations around them. There would also be a time when God would take them away to other lands. Moses told them that even then, if they began to obey God's commands, God would bring them back again.

Deuteronomy chapter 31 verses 9-13.

For many years Moses had led the people and taught them God's laws. He even told them how to teach their children. Moses had told the Israelites all the words that God had spoken to him. Then God told him to climb up into the mountains. From Mount Nebo he would be able to see all the land of Canaan. Moses spoke for the last time to the people of Israel. Then he climbed the mountain and looked at the land that he could not enter. God told him that this was the land He had promised to the family of Abraham, Isaac and Jacob. There on the mountain, Moses died.

The people spent thirty days crying because Moses was no longer with them.

Who did the people obey after Moses died? (Deuteronomy chapter 34 verse 9).

VICTORY THROUGH OBEDIENCE

Joshua was chosen by God to lead the people into Canaan. The book which bears his name begins with preparations to cross the River Jordan. After the miraculous crossing of the River, there follows the account of how the land was occupied, showing how God gave victory when the people were obedient, defeat when they disobeyed Him. God's judgement on the wickedness of the people of Canaan had waited four centuries, reminding us of His forbearance towards sinful people (see His words to Abraham in Genesis chapter 15). The division of the land between the tribes of Israel is also given in great detail.

Day 90: GETTING READY

Have you ever seen anyone who is more than a hundred years old? When people reach that age, they are not usually as strong as they were when they were younger. Sometimes they cannot see or hear very well.

Moses lived to be one hundred and twenty years old. The Bible says that he had not lost his strength, and his eyesight was still good.

The Israelites were sad when Moses died.

He had led the people for many years. Before he died, Moses had asked God to give the people a new leader. God chose Joshua to lead the people into their own land.

Joshua chapter 1 verses 1-7.

God promised to be with Joshua, just as He had been with Moses. Joshua sent a message to all the people. They were to be ready in three days time to cross the River Jordan. Then they would be in the land of Canaan.

Some of the people had already settled down on the eastern side of the River Jordan. They had asked Moses if they could stay there and he had agreed. They were the people who belonged to the Tribe of Reuben, the Tribe of Gad, and half the Tribe of Manasseh. They had promised Moses that they would help the other tribes, when the time came to cross the river. Joshua reminded them of their promise, and they replied that they would do as they had said. They told Joshua that they would obey him just as they had obeyed Moses.

What did God tell Joshua to be? (Joshua chapter 1 verse 7).

Day 91: GOD IS PATIENT

Do you know what it means to be patient? It means waiting calmly and quietly for something, without getting upset. We can also be patient with other people, not getting angry when someone treats us unkindly.

The Bible teaches us that God is patient.

We disobey God and do wrong things. But God is willing to forgive us, if only we will change our minds.

Stop doing wrong and start doing what is right.

The people, who lived in the land of Canaan before the Israelites, worshipped idols. They were wicked and cruel. But God was patient. Abraham's descendants lived in a land that was not their own for four hundred years. The Canaanites had all that time to change their ways. But they did not change. God said that the time had come to destroy them. The Israelites were to fight against them. God would be with them and give the land of Canaan to them. Because God is patient, we must never think that He will not punish those who do wrong. God's commands are good. When we disobey God, we are disobeying the One who created us and who knows what is best for us.

Joshua made sure that the people were ready to go into Canaan. Moses had already spoken to them about living in their own land.

Deuteronomy chapter 6 verses 10-12 and chapter 8 verses 6-10.

Find seven things that would be food for the people when they came into their own land. (Deuteronomy chapter 8 verse 8).

Day 92: THE TWO SPIES

Does the place where you live have a high wall around it? Some places have the remains of walls that were built hundreds of years ago. But we do not build walls around towns nowadays. There were walled cities in the land of Canaan. One of these was called Jericho.

Joshua sent two men to Canaan. They were to spy out the land, especially the city of Jericho. A woman named Rahab lived there in a house built on the city wall. The two spies went to her house. The king heard that they were there. He sent a message to Rahab that she must hand the men over. Rahab hid the two spies on the roof of her house underneath some flax.

Joshua chapter 2 verses 4-11.

Flax is a plant used for making cloth. It would have been laid on the roof to dry in the sun.

Rahab knew that God would help the Israelites win. She asked the spies to keep her family safe. They told her to take her family to her house. She was to tie a red cord in her window and she was not to tell anyone about the men she had hidden. She agreed and lowered the spies out of her window with a rope.

The men hid in the hills for three days, until everyone had given up searching.

The spies crossed the River Jordan and told Joshua what had happened. They told him that the people were afraid of the Israelites. They were sure that God would give the land of Canaan to them.

What was the name of the woman who hid the spies? Where did she hide them?

Day 93: CROSSING THE RIVER

The Israelites camped by the River Jordan for three days. Then they were told what they must do.

GOD'S WORD

Joshua chapter 3 verses 2-4; 14-17.

The ark was the gold-covered box that was kept in the tabernacle. It reminded the people that God was with them. Inside the ark were the two stone tablets with the Ten Commandments written on them. This reminded the people that in their new land, they must live as God had told them to.

EXTRA INFO

God made a path through the river, just as He had through the Red Sea years before.

Now the people were sure that God was with Joshua, just as He had been with Moses. God had told Joshua to choose twelve men, one from each tribe. Each man was to take a stone from where the priests stood in the middle of the riverbed. The priests who carried the ark stayed in the middle of the river until all the people were safely on the other side. Then God told Joshua that the priests could come up from the river. As soon as they had done this, the water flowed back and the river was as it had been before.

BY MYSELF

Joshua set up the twelve stones at Gilgal.

He told the people that their children would want to know why the stones were there. Then they could tell them about how God had brought them across the river on dry ground.

ASK ABOUT

Who went ahead when the Israelites crossed the river? What happened when the priests reached the water's edge?

Day 94: JERICHO

The people in Jericho were frightened. They knew that God had helped the Israelites to win their battles. They closed the gates in the city walls. No one went out of the city and no one came in. The people waited to see what would happen. Then one day, they heard the sound of trumpets. People were marching around the walls. Then everything went quiet again. This happened every day for six days. On the seventh day the trumpets sounded and the marching began again.

Joshua chapter 6 verses 1-7.

The Israelites did this because it was what God had told them to do.

For six days they marched around Jericho once each day. On the seventh day they marched around the city seven times. They did not speak at all as they marched. Then, on the last day as the priests blew the trumpets, Joshua told the people to shout. When they did, the walls of Jericho fell down. The people in the city were killed except for one family. Rahab had tied the red cord in the window just as she had been told.

Rahab and her family were brought to safety. After this, the city was burnt down.

Joshua told the Israelites not to take anything from Jericho for themselves. Only the gold, silver, bronze and iron were saved: they would be placed in the tabernacle. The people of Jericho had been so wicked that everything else had to be destroyed.

How many times did the Israelites march around Jericho? Whose family was saved?

Day 95: TROUBLE

In the tenth commandment, God says that we must not covet things that belong to other people. A man named Achan coveted some things he saw in Jericho and brought great trouble on Israel.

To covet means to want something that does not belong to us.

Joshua chapter 7 verses 2-5.

The Israelites lost the battle at Ai. Joshua was sad. He asked God why it had happened. God told him that things had been stolen from Jericho. The guilty person must be found. So early in the morning the Israelites gathered together. God showed Joshua that the thief belonged to the tribe of Judah. The family of a man called Zabdi had to come forward. A man named Achan, from that family, had disobeyed God.

Joshua chapter 7 verses 19-21.

Achan had coveted the clothing, and the gold and silver. This led to stealing and then lying. He was put to death for what he had done. The place where he died was called the Valley of Achor, which means valley of trouble. Achan's sin brought trouble to Israel. He could not hide his sin from God, neither can we.

When we do wrong we need to ask God to forgive us. He will forgive us if we know the Lord Jesus as our Saviour and Friend.

What happened to the Israelites who went to fight the people of Ai? Why had God not helped them to win the battle?

Day 96: VICTORY AT AI

It would not have been easy for Joshua to lead the people against Ai a second time. The Israelites might have felt afraid.

God told Joshua not to be afraid. He also told him how to win the battle against Ai.

Joshua did exactly as God had said. He gave orders for some soldiers to hide behind the city. Then Joshua led the others towards Ai. The King of Ai led his men out to fight them. Joshua let the soldiers from Ai chase them away towards the desert. The soldiers behind the city moved in quickly and captured it. Then Joshua and the others turned around and fought against the men from Ai. The soldiers who had captured the city also came towards them.

Israel won the battle that day.

God punished the people of Ai for their wickedness. He also taught the Israelites that when they obeyed Him, He would be with them and help them. When they disobeyed Him then he would not help them. After this battle, God allowed the Israelites to keep the animals and other things in the city of Ai.

Joshua remembered what Moses had told the people they should do when they entered the land of Canaan. He took large stones and wrote the words of the law on them. The people saw this being done and listened as the words were read to them.

Joshua chapter 8 verses 30-35.

Did the children hear God's law being read?

Day 97: OLD CLOTHES

Do you like dressing up? Some children have a box of clothes to dress up in. It can be great fun pretending to be all sorts of different people. One day some people dressed up in old clothes. Joshua and the leaders of Israel did not realise who they were.

GOD'S WORD

Joshua chapter 9 verses 3-9.

The people of Gibeon knew that God was helping the Israelites. They pretended that they had come from a long way away. They wanted a peace agreement with Israel.

BY MYSELF

Joshua should have asked God what to do but he did not.

He believed the people of Gibeon, although they were really telling lies. Joshua and the leading men of Israel promised that they would not fight against the Gibeonites. Then, just three days later, they heard that the Gibeonites lived near them. The Israelites grumbled about what their leaders had done, but the leaders would not break their promise. When Joshua asked the men from Gibeon why they had told lies, they told him what they had heard about Israel. They knew God would give the land to the Israelites. They were afraid that they would be killed. Joshua kept his promise and would not let anyone kill them.

EXTRA INFO

From that time on, the Gibeonites had to work for the Israelites, carrying water and cutting wood.

ASK ABOUT

How did the people from Gibeon make it look as if they had come a long way? What did Joshua not do, that he should have done? (Joshua chapter 9 verse 14).

Day 98: KEEPING THE PROMISE

Have you ever made a promise? If so, I hope that you keep your promise. The city of Jerusalem had a king whose name was Adoni-Zedek. When he heard of the agreement between Joshua and the people of Gibeon, he was very frightened. So he asked four other kings to help him fight against Gibeon.

In those days many of the cities in Canaan had their own king.

When the five kings attacked Gibeon, the Gibeonites sent a message to Joshua asking for help. Helping them fight against their enemies must have been part of the promise Joshua had made. He kept this promise. All the Israelite soldiers fought against the five kings.

Once again God told Joshua not to be afraid.

Joshua marched all night. He took the enemy by surprise. As they began to run away from the Israelites, God sent a great hailstorm which killed many of them.

Joshua chapter 10 verses 12-18.

The five kings and their people were all 'Amorites'. In a way which we cannot understand, God made the day longer so that Joshua could finish the battle. All five kings were captured and shut up in a cave. Later, they were all put to death. After this the Israelite army won many battles because God was with them.

How many kings attacked the people of Gibeon? Where were they put when they were captured?

Day 99: DIVIDING THE LAND

The Israelites fought many battles with Joshua as their leader. Now the time had come to divide the land, so that each tribe would have its own land to settle in. This was an important job and God had told Moses who would do it. They were Eleazar the priest, Joshua, and one man from each of the nine and a half tribes.

The list of names is in Numbers chapter 34.

The other two and a half tribes had already been given land on the other side of the River Jordan. The tribe of Levi was not given a large part of the land as the other tribes were.

The Levites were given forty-eight cities to live in.

These cities were in different parts of the land. Each city had fields round it that were also given to the Levites. One man from the tribe of Judah said that Moses had promised him some land. His name was Caleb. Do you remember what Caleb had done many years before? He was one of the twelve men Moses had sent to explore the land of Canaan. Only Joshua and Caleb brought back a good report and told the people that God would help them to take over the land. The people listened to the other ten men and were afraid to enter the land. It was because of this that they had stayed in the desert for forty years.

Joshua chapter 14 verses 6-14.

How old was Caleb when he first explored the land of Canaan? How old was he when he asked Joshua to give him the land that was promised to him?

Day 100: THE SIX CITIES

If we do something wrong, like hurting another person or stealing, then we expect to be punished. But sometimes things happen by accident. If something slips out of our hand and falls on someone's foot, we will be very sorry that we have hurt them. But it was an accident. We would not usually be punished for that sort of thing.

EXTRA INFO

God's law says that we must not kill anyone.

If one person takes away someone's life, then their life should be taken from them.

BY MYSELF

God teaches us to be careful not to take life.

But sometimes accidents happen. No one should be put to death when a person has been killed in an accident.

GOD'S WORD

Joshua chapter 20 verses 1-6.

If a person is killed, the family are upset and may feel angry. They might blame someone and try to kill them. God said that there should be places where someone who has caused an accident would be safe. These places were called 'cities of refuge' and there were six of them. These cities were chosen from the cities where the Levites lived. A person could be safe in a city of refuge until a trial could be held. At the trial, anyone who knew anything about what had happened could tell what they had seen. If it was an accident, then the one who had caused it could live in the city until the high priest died. After that, he could go home.

ASK ABOUT

How many cities of refuge were there? What were the cities of refuge for?

Day 101: TIME TO GO HOME

Most people enjoy being away on holiday. But when it is over, it is always good to be back in your own home. Some of the people we have been reading about were away from their homes for quite a long time. They had not been on holiday though. They had been helping to fight the Canaanites, as they had promised.

Joshua chapter 22 verses 1-8.

The men from the two and a half tribes must have been glad to be on the way home. When they came to the River Jordan, they built a large altar.

There already was an altar in the tabernacle and that was the only altar where the Israelites were told to bring offerings to God.

The nine and a half tribes who lived on the western side of the Jordan got ready to fight against the other two and a half tribes because they were afraid that these tribes were going to stop bringing their offerings to the tabernacle. Phinehas, the son of Eleazar the priest, went to talk to the people of Reuben, Gad and the half tribe of Manasseh. He took ten men with him, one from each of the nine and a half tribes. They soon found that the people were not going to use the altar for offerings. They had built it to remind the Israelites that the two and a half tribes still belonged to them. They would still come to the tabernacle, even though the river was between them and the rest of the people.

Everyone was glad that these men were not going to disobey God.

How were the people told to serve the Lord God? (Joshua chapter 22 verse 5).

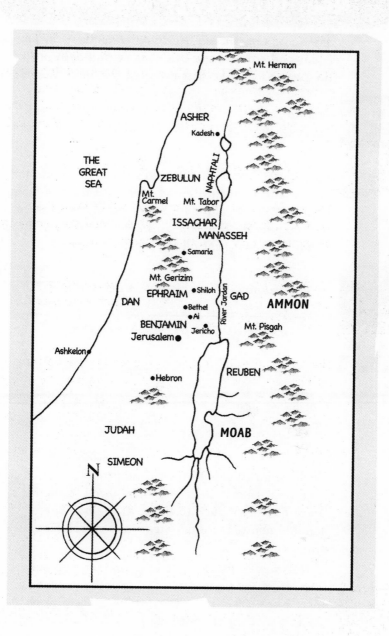

A map of Israel in Old Testament times

Day 102: A LAST WARNING

Joshua had grown old. He could remember leaving Egypt and crossing the Red Sea. He had been one of the twelve men who first explored the land of Canaan.

Joshua had been a helper to Moses during the years in the desert.

After Moses' death, he had led the people across the Jordan into Canaan. He had been with them in many battles. Now, an old man, he reminded the Israelites that they must obey God's law. He also reminded them of how God had kept all His promises to them.

Joshua warned the people not to worship idols.

Joshua chapter 24 verses 1-7.

Joshua wanted the people to remember that the God of Abraham, Isaac and Jacob, was their God. He knew that he would not be with them much longer. He wanted to make sure that they understood that God would be with them if they obeyed Him. But if they disobeyed God and began to worship idols, then God would bring trouble to them. The people promised to obey God. Then Joshua sent them away to the land which had been given to them. At the age of one hundred and ten, Joshua died. Aaron's son Eleazar also died.

Not every part of the land of Canaan had been taken from the Canaanites during Joshua's lifetime. There were still more battles to fight. There were some places that they did not take from the Canaanites, even though God had told them to.

How old was Joshua when he died? (Joshua chapter 24 verse 29).

LEADERS IN BATTLE AND RULERS IN PEACE

The times of the Judges were characterised by a repeated cycle of events. The people sinned and God allowed their enemies to oppress them. When they called on God in their distress, He raised up men to lead them. Through these leaders, known as Judges, God saved His people from those who ruled over them. Four of the Judges are named in the letter to the Hebrews as men of faith, reminding us that in spite of certain weaknesses, they exercised faith in very difficult circumstances.

Day 103: NEW LEADERS

For about two hundred years after Joshua died, God gave Israel leaders who were called Judges. We will read about some of them in the Book of Judges. The people who lived in the time of Joshua had seen many wonderful things. They had seen God make a path through the River Jordan. They had seen the walls of Jericho fall down. They knew that God had helped them to fight against the Canaanites. But as the years went by, the people who had come into the land of Canaan with Joshua, died. Their children had grown up, but they had forgotten all that God had done for Israel.

Judges chapter 2 verses 10-12 and 18-19.

The Baals were idols that the Canaanites worshipped. To bow down to a statue that cannot see or hear or speak, is foolish and wrong.

People who worshipped idols also did cruel and wicked things. The people of Israel should not have copied the Canaanites. They should have shown other nations how good it is to obey God's law. Instead, many married idol-worshippers and began to bow down to idols themselves. When the Israelites forgot God and worshipped idols, their enemies made their lives hard.

When they were sorry for doing wrong and asked God for help, God answered their call. God gave them leaders to free them from their enemies.

What peoples lived in the land of Canaan? (Judges chapter 3 verse 5).

Day 104: OTHNIEL AND EHUD

Each country in the world has its own laws, so that people can live safely and happily.

However, when there is a war, the country that loses the war will have to do what it is told.

When the Israelites disobeyed God and worshipped idols, God caused them to lose the battles against their enemies. Then they were treated cruelly, until they asked God to help them.

The first time this happened, Israel came under a king called Cushan-Rishathaim. This lasted for eight years until they called to God for help and he gave them a leader called Othniel. The Israelites were free again. This lasted for forty years. After Othniel died, the people disobeyed God again. This time they were attacked by the King of Moab and had to serve him for eighteen years. Once again their lives were unhappy.

The people of Israel called to God to help them.

God gave the Israelite people another Judge called Ehud. The Israelites had to pay money to the King of Moab. Ehud took this money to him. But then he told the king that he had a secret message. The king sent everyone out of the room so that Ehud could tell him the secret. But Ehud took his sword and killed the King of Moab. Then he blew a trumpet to call the men of Israel to come and fight against the people of Moab. Israel won the battle that day and lived in peace for eighty years.

Judges chapter 3 verses 12-15.

When the Israelites called out to God for help what did he give them?

Day 105: JAEL AND SISERA

Has anyone ever said to you, 'you will never learn'? Perhaps you made a mistake. Instead of doing it right the next time, you make the same mistake again. This is what happened to the Israelites in the time of the Judges. After Ehud died, the people disobeyed God again and did many wrong things. They had to serve King Jabin, a Canaanite king, for twenty years.

Judges chapter 4 verses 4-10.

The man in charge of King Jabin's army was called Sisera. He got all his soldiers and his chariots together to fight against the Israelites. But God helped the Israelites to win the battle. Sisera ran away, and a lady named Jael brought him into her tent to rest. Jael was not an Israelite, and Sisera thought that he was safe in her tent.

Jael gave him a drink because he was thirsty after the battle.

Sisera lay down and fell fast asleep, he was so tired. While he was asleep, Jael came up to him very quietly, and killed him.

When Barak came looking for Sisera, Jael showed him what she had done. It had all happened as Deborah had said it would (see verse 9). After this, there was peace for forty years.

In Judges chapter 5 we have the words of a song that Deborah and Barak sang. They thanked God for helping them to fight against King Jabin's army.

Which verse tells us that the people came to Deborah to sort out their quarrels? How many men followed Barak?

124

Day 106: GIDEON

Have you ever seen a camel? Camels are wonderfully made so that they can live in the hot, dry desert. The Midianites and Amalakites owned many camels. They came and destroyed Israel's crops and animals. This went on for seven years. The Israelites were ready to go and hide in the caves. They asked God to help them. God sent a prophet to speak to them.

A prophet is someone who tells the people what God says: he is God's messenger.

Judges chapter 6 verses 7-10; 27-29.

Israel once again disobeyed God and worshipped idols. But the Angel of the Lord spoke to a man named Gideon. Gideon belonged to the tribe of Manasseh. The Angel said that God was going to send Gideon to save Israel from the Midianites. That night, God told Gideon that he must break down the altar of Baal and the idol that his father had. He was also to build an altar and make an offering to God. The people would have attacked Gideon because of what he had done, but his father was able to stop them.

God had promised to be with His people while they obeyed Him. But they quickly joined in the idol-worship of the Canaanites. If we belong to the Lord Jesus, we should ask God every day to help us to live as He wants us to.

Our lives should show that we are people who love and obey God.

What did the Midianites ride on? Why did Gideon break down the altar of Baal at night?

Day 107: A SMALL ARMY

A trumpet can sound very loud. When Gideon was preparing to fight the Midianites he used a trumpet to call the people together. He also sent messengers to those who were further away. But Gideon wanted to be sure that this was what God wanted. If he was obeying God, then he knew that God would help him.

Judges chapter 6 verses 36-40.

God answered Gideon's prayer. Gideon was sure that God would help Israel to win the battle. But God told Gideon that he had too many soldiers. God knew that if Gideon led a big army into battle, the Israelites would think that they had won because they were so strong. So anyone who was afraid was allowed to go home. Twenty-two thousand men left but God said that there were still too many. Gideon was told to take the men down to the water. Most of them knelt down and lapped the water with their tongues.

Three hundred men cupped their hands and drank the water from their hands.

God told Gideon that He would save Israel with the three hundred men who drank from their hands. The rest were told to go home. Three hundred men do not make a very big army, but God was teaching the Israelites to trust Him. It was when the Israelites trusted God and obeyed Him, that they were able to fight against their enemies.

If we trust the Lord Jesus and obey Him, then He will be with us and help us to live for Him.

What happened the first night when Gideon put the woollen fleece on the ground?

Thousands of Midianites and Amalakites were camped in a valley. Gideon and his servant Purah, went to the camp. God had told Gideon to do this so that he would hear what the people were saying.

GOD'S WORD

Judges chapter 7 verses 13-18.

When Gideon heard the men talking, he knew that it was the right time to attack. Each of the three hundred men with Gideon carried a trumpet, a jar and a torch.

EXTRA INFO

The jars may have been made of clay. The torches were probably long poles with oil-soaked material on the end that was set alight.

Gideon told the men what to do. There was the sound of trumpets and breaking jars, and suddenly the torches appeared. The enemy began to fight against each other and then they ran away. Gideon, with his three hundred men, went after them. Gideon captured Zebah and Zalmunna, the two kings of Midian. He won a great victory over the army of the Midianites and the Amalakites. But he knew that it was God who had helped him win. Once again there was peace in the land, this time for forty years.

When we feel afraid, it is good to remember Gideon and his small army. You may think that you cannot tell others about Jesus. But the God who helped Gideon will help us if we trust Him and obey Him.

BY MYSELF

The Bible says that the Lord Jesus is the same yesterday, today and forever.

ASK ABOUT

How many men went with Gideon to attack the Midianites? What did each man have with him?

Day 109: JEPHTHAH

God has given us families, so we can grow up being loved and cared for. But we are sinful, so families are not always happy. Jephthah was a brave soldier whose brothers did not want him to be part of the family. So he left his home and lived away from them.

At that time, the Israelites had been cruelly treated by the Ammonites for eighteen years. This was because they had been worshipping idols again. At last they called on God for help, and got rid of their idols. The Ammonites camped at Gilead, where Jephthah's family lived. The leading men of Gilead went to Jephthah to ask for help against the Ammonites.

They promised that if he helped them he would be their leader.

Jephthah sent messengers to the Ammonites, giving them a chance to make peace. But they would not.

Judges chapter 11 verses 30-36.

A vow means a promise, and the word vow is often used for a promise made to God.

God did not allow the Israelites to sacrifice children. (Idol worshippers sometimes did so). Jephthah kept his promise, but it does not say that this was right. The Judges were sinful like you and me. But they fought against the enemies of Israel because they had faith in God: they believed that God would be with his people as He had promised.

What was Jephthah's vow? Who came out to meet him?

Day 110: SAMSON

The Philistines lived in the southern part of the land of Canaan, near to the Mediterranean Sea. For forty years they brought trouble to the Israelites, because the Israelites were doing wrong again. Then one day, the Angel of the Lord spoke to the wife of a man named Manoah. The angel told her that she was going to have a son, and that her son would be a Nazirite.

We can find out what that word means from the Book of Numbers chapter 6.

A man or woman who made a special promise to God, called a Nazirite vow were not allowed to eat or drink anything made from grapes during the time of their promise. They were not allowed to cut their hair or go near a dead body. Manoah's son was to be a Nazirite from the beginning of his life. He would fight against the Philistines. Manoah's wife was also not allowed to drink any wine. When she told her husband what the angel had said, he prayed that the angel might speak to them again.

Judges chapter 13 verses 8-14.

Manoah made an offering to God while the angel was there.

As he and his wife watched, the angel went up towards Heaven in the flame from the altar. Manoah and his wife had a son, as the angel had promised. Their son was given the name Samson. As he grew up God was with him, and he became very strong.

What was the name of Samson's father?
Who were the enemies of Israel at that time?

Day 111: LOST STRENGTH

One day a lion attacked Samson. God made Samson strong and he was able to kill it. He did not tell anyone what he had done.

Lions are strong, fierce animals. In some countries, you only see lions in a zoo. In some parts of the world lions are part of the local wildlife.

It was at the same time as he killed the lion that Samson began to fight the Philistines. The Israelites did not help him: they were too afraid. However, Samson fell in love with a woman named Delilah and when the Philistine leaders knew this, they went to see her. They offered her a lot of money, if she could find out what made Samson so strong. They wanted to tie him up, so that he would stop fighting them.

Judges chapter 16 verses 6-14.

Three times Samson teased Delilah with answers that were not true. Every day she continued asking him for the secret of his strength. Finally he told her that if his head was shaved, he would become as weak as any other man. While Samson slept, Delilah had a man come and shave off his hair. When he awoke, Samson could not escape as he had before. God no longer helped him: his great strength had gone. When his hair was cut, his Nazirite promise was broken. Delilah was not a true friend to Samson. She helped the Philistines to capture him, so that she could have a lot of money.

Samson should have cared more about his promise to God than he cared for Delilah.

What three things did Samson tell Delilah that were not really true?

Day 112: THE PRISONER

Samson could no longer fight the Philistines. They captured him, and made him blind. They took him to prison and chained him up. Samson was made to work, turning the stones that were used to grind the corn.

The Philistines worshipped an idol called Dagon. Some time later they held a big celebration and praised their idol for helping them to capture Samson. Samson was sent for, so that they could make fun of him. Now Samson's hair had begun to grow again, and it may be that he was sorry for the foolish things he had done.

Judges chapter 16 verses 26-31.

When Samson prayed, God heard him and made him strong again.

Samson had been chosen by God to do a special job. The angel had told his mother that he would begin to save Israel from the Philistines. He did do this and even died doing it.

We can see that Samson did things that were foolish. He lived at a time when the Israelites were afraid of the Philistines. They did not help Samson. In fact one day they tied him up and took him to the Philistines. This was so that the Philistines would not be angry with them. But God had helped Samson.

Samson fought bravely when no one else would.

But he did not choose friends who loved God as he did and that was what brought him trouble in the end.

What was the name of the idol that the Philistines worshipped? Did their idol really help them? (Psalm 115 verses 4-7).

A FAMILY IN THE DAYS OF THE JUDGES

It would be easy to love this Book just for the beauty of the story it tells, and the love and loyalty displayed by its main characters. But, though short, it is an important book which explains the ancestry of king David, through whose descendants the Messiah was born. The Book of Ruth also explains the work of the Kinsman Redeemer, who had to be qualified, able and willing to redeem. In this way the work of the Lord Jesus Christ as Redeemer of His people is pictured.

Day 113: A FAMILY MOVE

Sometimes we hear in the news that there is a famine in some part of the world.

EXTRA INFO

A famine is when people do not have enough food to eat, because the crops have not grown.

We read about a time of famine in the Book of Genesis, when Joseph's brothers went to Egypt to buy corn. There was also a famine during the time of the Judges. The Book of Ruth tells us about a family who lived at that time. Elimelech and his wife Naomi lived in the town of Bethlehem. They had two sons called Mahlon and Chilion. To escape the famine, Elimelech took his family to the land of Moab on the other side of the River Jordan. But the people of Moab did not love God: they worshipped idols.

GOD'S WORD

Ruth chapter 1 verses 1-7.

The years that followed were sad years. Elimelech died, so Naomi became a widow. Mahlon and Chilion both married women from Moab. Mahlon's wife was called Ruth and Chilion married Orpah. Mahlon and Chilion died, so there were now three widows in one family. Life would have been very hard for them. But some good news reached Naomi. She heard that there was no longer a famine in the land of Israel.

BY MYSELF

The journey back would not be easy, but Naomi decided to return to Bethlehem.

Ruth and Orpah went with her, as she set out on the road home.

ASK ABOUT

What was the name of Elimelech's wife?
Why did Naomi's life seem bitter?

133

Day 114: BACK TO BETHLEHEM

As they walked towards Israel, Naomi thought about Ruth and Orpah. If they came with her, they would leave friends and relations behind. Israel would be a strange land to them. How would they marry again and have their own homes? Naomi told them that it would be best for them to go back to Moab.

To be selfish means to think about yourself more than others. To be unselfish means caring about others more than yourself. Naomi was unselfish.

Ruth and Orpah did not want Naomi to go on alone. They cried and said that they would go with her. But eventually Orpah decided to go back. She kissed Naomi goodbye.

Ruth chapter 1 verses 15-22.

Ruth had made up her mind to stay with Naomi. She did not want to go back to the idols of Moab, because she had learned to trust in God. When the people of Bethlehem saw Naomi, the women wondered at first if it could really be her. She had been away a long time. No doubt she looked very different from the Naomi they remembered. But after all the sadness of life in Moab, we notice two good things.

Naomi was not alone: Ruth would not leave her.

It was also a good time to be back in Israel: harvest time, when food would be plentiful.

'Naomi' means pleasant, but 'Mara' means bitter. Why did Naomi's life seem bitter?

Day 115: GLEANING

God taught the people of Israel to be kind to the poor. When it was harvest time, the farmer was to leave the crops growing in the corners of his fields. If a sheaf of corn was dropped, he was not to pick it up.

The poor people were allowed to take what was left in the field. This was called 'gleaning'.

Naomi had a relation whose name was Boaz. He was quite important in Bethlehem, and owned some land. Ruth went out to glean in the fields, so that she and Naomi would have enough to eat. She began gleaning in a field belonging to Boaz, but she did not know that he belonged to the same family as Elimelech. When Boaz came to his field, he asked the man in charge who Ruth was. The man explained that she was the woman who had come from Moab with Naomi.

Ruth chapter 2 verses 8-16.

Boaz spoke kindly to Ruth and she was grateful for his kindness. She worked all day, and when she went home, Naomi saw how much she had gathered. Ruth gave Naomi some of the food she had saved that day.

Naomi realised that someone had been very kind to Ruth.

When she found out about Boaz, Naomi explained that he was their relation. Boaz had said that Ruth should continue to glean in his fields. She did this during the barley harvest and the wheat harvest.

Why was Boaz so kind to Ruth? What did he tell his workers to do to help her?

Family life was very important in Israel. God had taught His people how to care for one another. Naomi knew this. She knew that Ruth should marry again and have a husband to care for her. God's law said that a widow should marry someone belonging to her husband's family. Naomi believed that Boaz would be willing to marry Ruth and buy back Elimelech's land. Naomi told Ruth to visit Boaz at the winnowing floor - the place where the barley was separated from the chaff. Naomi knew that Boaz would understand that Ruth was asking him to obey God's law.

Someone who did this was called a Kinsman Redeemer. The word kinsman is another word for relation. To redeem means to buy back.

Ruth chapter 3 verses 1-9.

Boaz had seen Ruth's kindness to Naomi. Boaz was willing to care for Ruth. But when she spoke to him about it he had to tell her that there was a nearer relation. He must be given the chance to act as kinsman-redeemer if he wanted to. Boaz gave Ruth some of his barley to take to Naomi. When Naomi heard all that Boaz had said, she was sure that he would speak to the other relation as soon as possible.

Naomi told Ruth to do something which is quite hard to do: just wait.

Read chapter 3 verse 1 again. Was Naomi being selfish or unselfish? Was Ruth obedient to Naomi?

Day 117: A VERY HAPPY FAMILY

Sometimes we need a witness to something important in our lives, such as getting married.

A witness is someone who has seen something happen and can tell other people about it.

Boaz needed witnesses when he met his relation to talk about Ruth. With others to see what happened, there need be no family quarrels about it in the future.

Ruth chapter 4 verses 1-8.

Boaz did what was right. He explained to Naomi's nearest relation that he could marry Ruth and buy Elimelech's land if he wished. But the relation refused. So there was nothing to stop Boaz and Ruth being married. Ruth now had Boaz to care for her. Naomi knew that as she grew older, Ruth and Boaz would be there to help her. In time, a baby boy was born. Ruth and Boaz called him Obed.

Naomi loved her little grandson. Her friends were glad to see her happiness.

Do you remember the long, sad journey back to Bethlehem that Naomi and Ruth took? But God was looking after them even through the sad days. God has never promised us an easy life. But if we know the Lord Jesus as our Friend and Saviour, He has promised that He will always be with us.

Find a promise in Deuteronomy chapter 31 verse 6 and Hebrews chapter 13 verse 5. What will God never do?

Day 118: A FAMILY TREE

Do you know what a 'family tree' is? It is not a tree growing in your garden! It is a way of writing down the different parts of a family - boys and girls, mothers and fathers, grandparents and great-grandparents. The last verses of the Book of Ruth are a family tree. There you will find the names of Boaz, his son Obed and his great-grandson David.

GOD'S WORD

Ruth chapter 4:18-22.

EXTRA INFO

We read about David in the two books called 'Samuel' that come after the Book of Ruth. He became a great king of Israel.

When Ruth travelled with Naomi to Bethlehem, she did not know what good things lay ahead of her. She did not know that she would marry Boaz and have a little boy to care for. She certainly could not know that one day her great-grandson would be a king.

BY MYSELF

Ruth trusted in God, and God brought great happiness into her life.

Now look at the much longer family tree in the first chapter of Matthew's Gospel from verse 3 to verse 6. This is another family tree like Ruth chapter 4 verses 18-22. Can you find two names in Matthew's list that are not in Ruth? Rahab, the mother of Boaz and Ruth are two of just four women whose names are included in this wonderful family tree. This long list of names ends with the Lord Jesus.

ASK ABOUT

Where did Rahab live before the Israelites came to Canaan? (Joshua chapter 6 verse 1. Where did Ruth live before she travelled to Bethlehem? (Ruth chapter 1 verse 6).

DAYS 119-135: First Samuel

THEOCRACY TO MONARCHY

The people of Israel were ruled by their God through leaders who He appointed. The first book of Samuel begins in the days of Eli, a priest who judged Israel for forty years. Samuel followed Eli and was both judge and prophet. He was faithful in calling the people away from idolatry, and led them to victory over the Philistines. However, as he grew old the people demanded a king so that they could be like the nations around them. Their request was granted and Saul became their first king and reigned for forty years. His reign was characterised by several acts of disobedience to the known will of God. Samuel grieved over Saul's failure, but God sent him to anoint David as Israel's next king. There follows the account of Saul's jealousy and David's many escapes from the danger this caused. The book ends with Saul's death in battle.

DAYS 136-145: Second Samuel

THE REIGN OF KING DAVID

The first ten chapters of this book tell us of David's consolidation of the Kingdom. For seven years he reigned over Judah and then for thirty-three years he reigned over a Kingdom which again united all the tribes of Israel. David brought the Ark of God to Jerusalem, although God did not allow him to build the temple there. God's promise that David's Kingdom would be established forever is clearly an indication that the Messiah would come through his descendants.

In chapters eleven and twelve we read about David's sin with Bathsheba which led to murder and deceit. The Bible, because it is the Word of God, is always truthful and does not gloss over the sin of this great king.

Much of the remainder of the book concerns the result of David's sin: he found forgiveness but God did not allow him to escape the consequences of his actions.

Day 119: HANNAH'S PRAYER

In the Bible names often had a meaning. There are two books in the Old Testament called 'Samuel', which means 'heard by God'. As we read about Samuel, we will discover why he was given that name.

A man named Elkanah had two wives, Hannah and Peninnah. As so often happened in families where a man had more than one wife, someone became unhappy. Peninnah had children to care for. Hannah had no children and Peninnah treated her unkindly.

Every year Elkanah took his family to Shiloh where the tabernacle was.

EXTRA INFO

The tabernacle no longer had to be moved from place to place. It was sometimes called the temple.

Once, when the family was in Shiloh, Peninnah was so unkind to Hannah that Hannah cried and could not eat her food. Elkanah loved Hannah and did not like to see her so sad.

GOD'S WORD

1 Samuel chapter 1 verses 9-18.

BY MYSELF

Hannah told God all about her sorrow.

She also promised that if God gave her a baby boy, she would give him to God, to serve Him all his life. When she went back to her family, Hannah did not look sad any more. She trusted God and believed that He would answer her prayer. The next day, Elkanah took his family home to Ramah. After some time had passed, Hannah had a baby boy. She named him Samuel, because God had heard her prayer.

ASK ABOUT

What was the name of the priest at the temple? What did the priest think about Hannah at first?

Day 120: ELI'S HELPER

While Samuel was very small, Hannah did not go on the yearly visit to Shiloh with Elkanah. She stayed at home to care for the baby. Hannah had promised to give her son back to God. Hannah told Elkanah that when Samuel had been weaned, she would take him to Shiloh and he would stay there. Elkanah agreed that Hannah should do this.

For little babies to grow strong they need to drink their mother's milk. They can't eat grown-up food. As babies grow they have to get used to less milk and more solid food. We call this 'weaning'.

1 Samuel chapter 1 verses 21-28.

Hannah kept her promise.

She went to Shiloh with Elkanah after Samuel had been weaned. Samuel was still very young, but he stayed at the temple to help Eli the priest. Hannah did not forget Samuel. Every year she made new clothes for him. As she sat sewing she must have wondered how much Samuel had grown since her last visit. Each year Hannah took Samuel's new clothes with her when she went to Shiloh with Elkanah.

Eli's sons were priests, but they did not love God. They did many things that were wrong. They would not listen when Eli spoke to them about the wrong things they did. But as Samuel grew up, he helped Eli in the temple.

What did Hannah pray for? What promise had she made to God?

When we have good news for someone we look forward to telling them. They will be pleased. When we have bad news to tell it can be very difficult.

One day, God gave Samuel some bad news for Eli. Samuel did not want to tell Eli the bad news.

1 Samuel chapter 3 verses 1-10.

It was wonderful for Samuel to hear God speaking to him. But the message was about Eli and his sons.

God knew all about the wrong things that Eli's sons had done.

Eli's sons were priests, and they should have helped the people to know and love God.

The people actually cared more about pleasing God than they did. God said that Eli had done wrong as well. He had not stopped his sons bad behaviour. God told Samuel that Eli's family would be punished.

In the morning, Samuel got up and opened the doors of the temple. He was afraid to tell Eli what God had said. But Eli asked Samuel to tell him everything. Eli knew that whatever God chose to do would be right. As Samuel grew up, God continued to speak to him. The people of Israel realised that God had chosen Samuel to be a prophet. Samuel told the people the things that God wanted them to know and they listened to him.

Who did Samuel think was calling him? What did he say when he realised that God was speaking to him?

Day 122: A LOST BATTLE

The gold covered box, called 'The Ark of the Covenant', had been placed in the tabernacle by Moses. It was the place where God had promised to meet with His people. When it was moved it had to be covered and carried on poles.

EXTRA INFO

Once the people had settled in their own land, the ark no longer needed to be carried from place to place.

One day there was a battle between the Philistines and the Israelites. The Philistines won and many Israelites were killed. The Israelite leaders sent for the ark. They thought that if the ark was with them, they would win.

GOD'S WORD

1 Samuel chapter 4 verses 4-9.

The Philistines thought that the ark was an idol like the ones they worshipped. They fought hard and won the battle again. They captured the ark and killed Eli's sons. Israel had made a big mistake. They thought that God would help them if they brought the ark. But God had promised to help them if they obeyed Him. Eli's sons had not obeyed God so God did not protect them in the battle.

Eli was ninety-eight years old now, and unable to see. He knew that the ark should not have been taken. A messenger came to tell him that Israel had lost the battle and that both his sons had died. The worst news of all was that the ark of God had been captured.

BY MYSELF

When he heard this, he fell from his chair and died.

ASK ABOUT

What were the names of Eli's two sons? How long had Eli been one of Israel's judges? (1 Samuel chapter 4 verse 18).

Day 123: THE RETURN OF THE ARK

After the Philistines had captured the ark they took it to Ashdod and carried it into the temple of their idol.

This idol was called Dagon. The Philistines placed the ark of God in Dagon's temple.

1 Samuel chapter 5 verses 1-5.

God would not allow the Philistines to treat the ark as another idol. He brought illness to them: wherever they moved the ark, the illness followed. After seven months, they decided to send it back to the Israelites. They placed it on a cart that was pulled along by two cows. The cows went straight to the Israelite town of Beth-shemesh. The people there were glad to see the ark return. But some of them died, because they looked into it. Sinful men and women can only come to God in the way that God chooses.

The people remembered that God is Holy.

The people of Beth-shemesh asked the people of Kirjath Jearim to take the ark. The ark stayed there for twenty years. During that time, the Israelites began to feel sorry for disobeying God. Samuel told them that they could not love God and idols. If they would obey God, then God would save them from the Philistines. Samuel gathered the people together at Mizpah. The people were sorry for their sin and Samuel prayed to God for them. This time God helped His people to defeat the Philistines. God always keeps His promises. If we love and obey Him, He will be with us and will help us.

What happened to the idol when the ark of God was beside it? How long was Samuel a judge? (1 Samuel chapter 7 verse 15).

Day 124: ASKING FOR A KING

We have read about Israel's judges in the time of Moses. We have also read about the judges who were Israel's leaders after Joshua died.

It was important that the leaders of the people should be honest men.

If two people had a quarrel and went to see the judge about it, the judge had to decide what to do. He must not take sides with a rich person who might give him money. Samuel was an honest judge because he loved and obeyed God. He travelled about helping the people with their problems. But his two sons were not honest. They took the side of those who paid them.

1 Samuel chapter 8 verses 1-9.

Samuel was sad because the people of Israel wanted to have a king like the other nations. God was their king, and He chose the men who would be their leaders.

God told Samuel to warn the people what it would be like to have a king.

Samuel spoke to the men who had come to see him at Ramah. He explained that a king would take many of the people to work for him. He would want some to be soldiers, some to look after his crops, some to be servants in his house. A king would also take some of their animals and their crops. The men still wanted a king. Other nations had a king to lead them into battle. The Israelites wanted to be the same.

What were the names of Samuel's sons?
Whose side did Samuel's sons take?

Day 125: ISRAEL'S FIRST KING

Have you ever searched for something that was lost? A man named Kish had some donkeys that were lost. He sent his son Saul with a servant, to find them.

They travelled a long way, but did not find the donkeys.

Saul said that they ought to go back in case his father was worried. But the servant thought that Samuel might be able to help them.

1 Samuel chapter 9 verses 14-21.

'Seer' is an old word meaning 'prophet'.

Samuel invited Saul and his servant to a meal. They stayed the night and then in the morning, Samuel had a message for Saul from God. The servant was sent on ahead so that only Samuel and Saul remained together. Samuel poured oil on Saul's head. He told him that God had anointed him to lead His people.

After Saul had gone, Samuel called the people together to Mizpah. As the people came before Samuel in their tribes, the tribe of Benjamin was chosen. From that tribe, Saul was chosen, but he was nowhere to be seen. Saul had hidden himself. At last he was brought to the people as the one God had chosen to be king. The people shouted, 'Long live the king'.

Samuel explained how things should be done now that Israel had a king. Some of the people were pleased to follow their new king, but others wondered whether Saul was the right person.

Who told Samuel that Saul should be Israel's king? What happened to the lost donkeys?

Day 126: A BATTLE WON

Not everyone was pleased that Saul had been chosen as king. Then something happened that made a difference.

Sometime after Saul was anointed the city of Jabesh Gilead was surrounded by people called Ammonites. Saul sent messengers all over the land of Israel. Soon a large army was ready to follow him. They fought against the Ammonites and set the people of Jabesh Gilead free. The Israelites were glad Saul was king.

EXTRA INFO

When a king or queen is crowned we have a ceremony called the coronation.

Samuel called the people together at the city of Gilgal. This time no one said anything against Saul. A great celebration was held. Samuel, now an old man, spoke to the people. He asked them if he had ever treated them unfairly. They knew that Samuel had always been honest. They knew that he had done all that he could to help them. Then Samuel reminded the Israelites of what God had done for them. He talked about the days of Moses and of the Judges, Gideon, Barak and Jephthah. Samuel was not afraid to tell the people that it had been wrong to ask for a king.

GOD'S WORD

1 Samuel chapter 12 verses 19-25.

BY MYSELF

Samuel told the people that God would still be with them.

Samuel promised that he would keep praying for them. He promised that he would still be there to teach them to do right.

ASK ABOUT

What did the people ask Samuel to do?
What did he tell the people to do?

Day 127: SAUL DISOBEYS GOD

It is good to start a job well but it is even better to finish well. When Saul was made king he began well, but as time went on, he did not always obey God.

Many thousands of Philistines came to fight against Israel. The men of Israel were so afraid that they hid from them. Saul waited at Gilgal where Samuel had promised to meet him. But Saul did something wrong.

1 Samuel chapter 13 verses 8-14.

Saul should not have done this: God had chosen the tribe of Levi to look after the tabernacle and offerings.

Samuel belonged to the tribe of Levi, and after Eli died, he took Eli's place offering sacrifices to God.

There were many battles against the Philistines. Saul's son Jonathan fought bravely against them.

One day Samuel had a message from God.

Saul was told to fight the Amalekites because of the wrong things that they had done. Saul fought the battle, but did not do all that God had told him to. Samuel was very sad when he heard this. He spent the night praying to God. Early the next day he went to see Saul. Saul told Samuel that he had done as God had said. Then he began to make excuses for the things he had done wrong. At last, he admitted that he had disobeyed God. God would now choose someone else to be king. Because of Saul's disobedience the next king would not be Jonathan, his son.

What should we do when we do wrong? (1 John chapter 1 verse 9).

Day 128: JESSE'S SONS

Have you ever felt disappointed about someone? Maybe a friend has been unkind to you or someone has broken a promise. Samuel was disappointed that Saul had not obeyed God as he should have done. But God had chosen the person who would be king after Saul. He told Samuel to go to Bethlehem. He was to take some oil to the house of a man named Jesse. One of Jesse's sons was to be Israel's next king.

1 Samuel chapter 16 verses 6-13.

Samuel thought at first that Jesse's oldest son would be God's choice. He was probably tall and strong.

We see what people look like, but God knows us as we really are.

It was Jesse's youngest son, David, who was to be anointed as king.

David did not become king straight away: Saul remained king for some years. But Saul was no longer the brave leader that he had been at first. He had disobeyed God and knew that God was no longer helping him. Saul's servants thought that if someone played the harp to Saul, he would feel better. One of them knew that David could play the harp. So Jesse was asked to send his son David to king Saul. Of course Saul did not know that God had chosen David to be king after him. When David played on his harp, Saul felt happier. He was pleased to have David with him. David was made an armour-bearer to the king.

Who were Jesse's grandfather and grandmother? (Matthew chapter 1 verse 5).

If you knew someone who was nearly two metres tall, you would think that they were very big. But long ago there was a man who was almost three metres tall. He was Goliath the Philistine, and with his helmet and suit of armour, he must have looked very frightening.

The Israelite and Philistine armies were at war again. This time they faced each other across a valley. Every day the soldiers prepared for battle. But instead of the armies fighting, Goliath called for someone to come and fight him.

Saul's soldiers were afraid. For forty days Goliath waited for someone to come and fight.

Jesse sent David to find out whether his brothers were safe and well. They were soldiers in Saul's army. David brought food for them and their commander.

1 Samuel chapter 17 verses 20-25.

David heard the giant shouting but David loved and trusted God.

David believed that Goliath was not just shouting against Israel, but against Israel's God. Some of the soldiers told David that the king had promised a reward to the man who fought Goliath. King Saul would make the man rich and would let him marry his daughter. David's oldest brother, Eliab, was angry with David for talking with the soldiers. But David continued asking questions.

How many loaves and cheeses did David bring? (Verses 17 and 18). What did the Israelites do when they saw Goliath?

Day 130: DAVID AND GOLIATH

King Saul heard that David had been talking to the soldiers about Goliath. He sent for him. David told the king that he would fight the giant. Saul thought that he was too young. But David told Saul of how God had helped him look after his father's sheep.

1 Samuel chapter 17 verses 34-40.

While he was young, David learned to trust God. He knew that God was with him. He was not afraid of Goliath because God was still with him.

A soldier carrying a shield went in front of Goliath.

Goliath came towards David. The giant had armour on and carried a sword. He was very angry when he saw how young David was. He was sure that he would soon kill him. David wore no armour. He had his shepherd's sling and five smooth stones. Unafraid, he ran towards Goliath and placed one stone in his sling. He whirled the sling round and the stone hit Goliath on his forehead.

The giant fell to the ground.

David had trusted God to help him, and the giant that the Israelites had been so afraid of, was dead. The Philistine army began to run away. The Israelites went after them and won the battle. We need to trust God in our everyday lives at school or work. Then when there are difficult things to face, like David we will know that God is with us.

What two animals had attacked the sheep that David looked after? What did David take with him to fight Goliath?

Day 131: SAUL'S JEALOUSY

We are pleased when we win a game or do well at school. It is not quite so easy to be pleased when other people do well. After Goliath had been killed, the women sang as they celebrated Israel's victory. But king Saul realised that their song praised David more than him. He felt jealous. As he saw how David continued to win battles against the Philistines, Saul felt afraid. He knew that he had displeased God by his disobedience. He could see that God was with David, helping him in everything he did.

David married king Saul's daughter, Michal. Jonathan, the king's son, became a very good friend to David. He was sorry that his father had become so jealous.

1 Samuel chapter 19 verses 1-7.

Saul knew that Jonathan was right and that he should not harm David. But is was not long before he was once again planning to have him put to death. He sent men to watch David's house during the night. David's wife, Michal, realised what was going to happen. She was sure that there was a plan to kill David when the morning came.

David's wife helped him to escape through a window without Saul's men seeing him.

Then she dressed up an idol and placed it in David's bed. She pretended that David was ill. It was some time before the men realised that he was not there. This gave David time to get away. He went to see Samuel and told him all that king Saul had done.

Why did Saul want to kill David? Who told him that this was wrong?

153

Day 132: DAVID AND JONATHAN

It is good to have a friend you can rely on, even when things go wrong. David needed to know whether Saul still planned to kill him. If so, then he would have to go away. David trusted Jonathan to talk to the king and then tell him whether he should stay or go. They chose a festival meal, when David would be expected to eat with the king. David would not be there: Jonathan would find out whether the king was still angry with him. David and Jonathan made a promise that they would always be friends.

David promised to be kind to Jonathan's family.

1 Samuel chapter 20 verses 18-23.

On the first day when king Saul saw that David's place was empty, he thought that there must be a good reason why David was not there. But on the second day, he spoke to Jonathan about it and became very angry. Jonathan now knew that his father would kill David if he could capture him. He went out into the field with his arrows. David who was hiding nearby heard Jonathan call to the boy who was with him. He heard him say that the arrow was beyond him. This was the sign that Jonathan was going to use if David must go away. After Jonathan had sent the boy away, David came out of hiding. The two friends were very sad. Their friendship meant a lot to them, but they would have to be separated from one another.

David and Jonathan never forgot the promises they had made.

What sign would Jonathan give if it was safe for David to stay? What sign would he give if David must go away?

Day 133: IN HIDING

David knew that God had chosen him to be the next king of Israel. And yet, for a time, he had to go from place to place, hiding from king Saul.

David stayed in the Cave of Adullam with about 400 followers. His parents came there, until he found a safe place for them.

David heard that the city of Keilah was being attacked by Philistines who were stealing the food. David asked God whether he should fight the Philistines. When he was sure that God would help him, he led his men to Keilah. They won the battle and saved Keilah. But king Saul heard about this and he led his soldiers there.

Saul thought that David would be trapped in the city and that he would be able to capture him.

When David heard that Saul was coming, he prayed for God's help. He left the city and moved from place to place. Saul was so jealous of David that he kept on searching for him. But God kept David safe. Saul could not find him. One day Jonathan went to meet David. He helped David to trust God. Jonathan knew that God would protect David. One day David would be king.

Saul entered a cave one day. He did not know that David and his men were there. David's men wanted to kill Saul, but David would not. He cut a piece from Saul's robe to show it to the king later. Then Saul would know that David had spared his life.

1 Samuel chapter 24 verses 16-22.

Did king Saul know that he was wrong to keep trying to kill David? Do you think David could trust Saul?

Day 134: NABAL AND ABIGAIL

A man named Nabal owned three thousand sheep and a thousand goats. He was wealthy, but mean and unpleasant. He had a beautiful wife, named Abigail.

In Old Testament times, one way of knowing that someone was rich was if they owned lots of animals.

David and his men were living for a time near to where Nabal kept his flocks. They treated Nabal's shepherds well and protected them from thieves. When the time came to shear the sheep, David sent a message to Nabal. He asked Nabal to send some food for him and his men. Was Nabal grateful for David's kindness to the shepherds? No! Nabal refused David's request. When David heard he set off with four hundred men armed with their swords.

1 Samuel chapter 25 verses 14-19.

Abigail quickly prepared food and went to meet them. When she saw David, she bowed and asked him to forgive Nabal. Abigail told David that he would be king one day. It would be better for him if he didn't kill them. If he did his conscience would be troubled in the future. David thanked God for sending Abigail. He accepted her food and did not pay Nabal back for his unkindness. When Abigail told Nabal what had happened, he fell ill. A few days later he died. David asked Abigail to be his wife. She agreed.

David knew that Abigail was wise as well as beautiful.

Who told Abigail that Nabal had refused to help David? What did Abigail do to put things right?

Day 135: SAUL'S LAST BATTLE

Life was hard for David during the years that Saul tried to capture him, and yet David tried to show Saul that he would never harm Israel's king. One day, Saul heard where David was hiding. He took three thousand men to search for him. But David saw where their camp was. He asked someone to go there with him. A man named Abishai said that he would go.

1 Samuel chapter 26 verses 7-12.

David stood on a hill facing Saul's army. He called out to Abner who was in charge of the soldiers. He told Abner that he had not guarded the king properly. Saul heard David's voice and called to him. David showed Saul his spear. king Saul could see that David had spared his life a second time. David knew that he could not trust Saul, even though at times Saul admitted that he had been wrong.

Saul's heart was not changed. He was still jealous.

David decided it would be safer to live outside Israel.

A Philistine named Achish gave him the city of Ziklag. David lived there with his men and their families.

The Philistines again fought against Israel. king Saul and his three sons Jonathan, Abinadab and Malchishua died in the battle. David was very sad. king Saul had done many wrong things, but David was still sorry that he had died in the battle. Most of all, he was sad to have lost his true friend, Jonathan.

What did Abishai want to do to king Saul? What did David take to prove to Saul that he could have harmed him?

Day 136: KING DAVID

Three of Saul's sons were killed by the Philistines, but he did have another son whose name was Ishbosheth. A man named Abner had been in charge of king Saul's army. He made Ishbosheth king over all the tribes who lived in the northern part of the land of Israel.

When a king dies, his eldest son usually becomes king. If he has no son, but does have a daughter, she will become queen.

David knew that God had chosen him to be king. He prayed that God would show him what to do. God told him to go to Hebron. This was in the land belonging to the tribe of Judah in southern Israel. The men of Judah came to Hebron and made David their king. David was king there for seven and a half years. His army was led by Joab. Ishbosheth's army was led by Abner.

There was war between the two armies for a long time. But Abner became angry with Ishbosheth. He told David he would make him king over all Israel. Abner took twenty men and went to meet David at Hebron.

David made a feast for Abner and his men.

Abner promised to bring the people together to make David their king. Joab was not pleased that David had let Abner go. Without telling David, he sent for Abner and killed him. David made sure the people knew that he had not wanted Abner to be killed. The people believed him: they wanted him to be king of all Israel.

2 Samuel chapter 5 verses 1-5.

How old was David when he became king? How long was he king in Hebron? How long was he king in Jerusalem?

158

Day 137: THE ARK AT JERUSALEM

Which tribe looked after the tabernacle? It was the tribe of Levi. The Book of Numbers explains which parts of the tabernacle the different Levite families were to take care of. Before the ark was moved, priests had to cover it with the curtain that hung between the two rooms of the tabernacle. They were not allowed to look at the ark. They had to carry it on poles.

EXTRA
INFO

After David became king in Jerusalem, he prepared a tent so that the ark could be placed there.

GOD'S
WORD

2 Samuel chapter 6 verses 1-7.

The people had not followed God's instructions. They had put the ark on to a cart, when it should have been carried by the Levites. They had to learn once again that sinful people can only come to God in God's way. David was afraid to bring the ark to Jerusalem that day. He left it at the house of a Levite named Obed-Edom, and it remained there for three months. Then David called the Levites together so that the ark could be brought to Jerusalem in the right way. David confessed that they had not done this before. This time the Levites carried the ark with the poles on their shoulders. It was a very happy day. Some of the Levites played musical instruments, such as harps and cymbals, and some of them sang. Then king David wrote a Psalm of thanks to God. (We can find this in 1 Chronicles chapter 16).

BY
MYSELF

David called on the people to remember all God's goodness and to thank Him.

ASK
ABOUT

What did David try to use to bring the ark to Jerusalem? Who should have carried it and what should they have used?

Day 138: WHEN GOD SAID 'NO'

Have you ever wanted to do something, only to find that someone else has been asked to do it instead? This happened to king David, but he was not angry or upset about it. As he looked at his palace in Jerusalem, he thought about the tent where the ark of God was. No building had been made for the ark. He spoke to the prophet Nathan about it, and Nathan thought that the king should go ahead and build. But that night, God spoke to Nathan.

GOD'S WORD

2 Samuel chapter 7 verses 8-13.

Nathan told David that God had not asked anyone to build a house for Him. However, God promised that He would build a house for David. He did not mean a building, but that David's family would continue forever. David's son would build God's house.

EXTRA INFO

When the Lord Jesus came, He was born into the family of king David.

Later, David said that he knew why he had not been chosen to build the temple. While he was king, he had many battles to fight. The temple would be built by his son in a time of peace. After Nathan had spoken to him, David thanked God for all that He had done for him. He also thanked God for all that He had done for the people of Israel. He praised God for His greatness.

BY MYSELF

David asked God to keep His promise so that people would see how great God is.

ASK ABOUT

What work did David do before he became king? What was the name of the prophet who brought God's message to David? (2 Samuel chapter 7 verse 17).

Day 139: DAVID'S PROMISE

Do you remember the name of David's special friend? David had promised to be kind to his friend's family.

2 Samuel chapter 9 verses 1-7.

king Saul had made David's life very hard. Saul had wanted to kill him. Some people would have taken revenge on Saul's family. But David remembered his promise. David set out to help Mephibosheth, Jonathan's son, and not to harm him.

Life was not easy for Mephibosheth. When he was five years old, his father was killed in battle. The nurse who was looking after him tried to run away with him when she heard the bad news. Mephibosheth fell, and both his feet were hurt and never got better. Years later, when king David gave him king Saul's land he gave Mephibosheth help to farm the land.

David ordered Ziba, with his fifteen sons and twenty servants, to work for Mephibosheth.

After this, Mephibosheth lived in Jerusalem. He was invited to have his meals with the king's family. In 2 Samuel chapter 9 verse 3 king David said that he wanted to show 'the kindness of God' to Saul's family.

God's kindness is kindness that we do not deserve.

Mephibosheth did not deserve David's kindness. We do not deserve God's kindness to us, and yet He sent Jesus into the world to die for us.

Why did king David want to show kindness to Saul's family? Who was going to look after the land given to Mephibosheth?

Day 140: DAVID DOES WRONG

God chose David to be king and he became a great king. He trusted in God and won many battles. In the Book of Psalms there are wonderful words that he wrote. But David was not perfect: he did some things that were wrong. One day he saw a beautiful woman named Bathsheba. She was married to Uriah who was away fighting for the Israelite army. David sent for her, even though he knew she was Uriah's wife.

In Exodus chapter 20, it says we must not commit adultery. A man must not take someone else's wife, and a woman must not take someone else's husband.

David disobeyed this commandment. He made plans so that Uriah would be killed. He wrote a letter to Joab who was in charge of the army.

2 Samuel chapter 11 verses 14-27.

Joab's messenger told David that the Israelite soldiers had fought against a city. Men on the city walls had shot arrows at the Israelites and Uriah had been killed.

David knew that Joab had done as he was told.

Uriah had been brave, but Joab had made sure he would be killed. Bathsheba was sad when she heard the news. But after a while, king David sent for her. She became his wife and soon had a baby boy. It is hard to understand why David did such a wrong thing. When we are tempted to do wrong, we need to ask God to help us to say 'no'. king David did not do this.

Who had seen all that king David had done?

Day 141: FORGIVENESS

God had seen what David had done. He sent the prophet Nathan to speak to the king. Nathan began by telling David a parable.

EXTRA INFO

A parable is a story that teaches us something.

GOD'S WORD

2 Samuel chapter 12 verses 1-6.

Nathan told David that the story was about him. God had made him king and given him many things. But David had killed Uriah so that he could take his wife. Even though Uriah was killed in battle, God knew that it was David who had planned it. There would always now be fighting in David's family.

BY MYSELF

Because he truly loved God David wasn't angry with Nathan for speaking in this way.

David realised what a terrible thing he had done. He owned up to his sin. Nathan told David that God forgave him, but that Bathsheba's baby boy would die.

After Nathan went back to his house, the baby became very ill. David prayed that God would make the child well, but after a week the baby died.

This part of king David's life makes us feel very sad. But because of the wrong that he had done, David wrote some words that have helped many people. We will read of some of David's words in Psalm 51 when we look at the Book of Psalms. Christians who have done wrong and wondered if God could ever forgive them, have read this Psalm and remembered how God forgave king David.

ASK ABOUT

Who was sent by God to speak to king David? How did he begin his talk with the king?

Day 142: ABSALOM LEAVES HOME

Have you ever broken someone's toy and been afraid to tell them what had happened? If, instead of being angry your friend forgives you, what a difference this makes.

It is wonderful to know you are forgiven.

David knew that he deserved to be punished for the wrong things that he had done, but God had forgiven him. However difficult life might be, David knew that God would be with him.

Bathsheba had another little boy and he was given the name Solomon.

Good news came to king David from Joab. The battle against the Ammonites was almost won. Joab asked the king to lead the army to victory. He agreed to do this, and soon the crown from the Ammonite king was placed on king David's head.

Now David had more than one wife, as other men did in Old Testament times. This caused difficulties in David's large family. At times his family brought him great sorrow, as Nathan had told him it would. There was such trouble between two of David's sons, that one, named Absalom, ran away from home. He went to Geshur, where his mother's family lived. He was away for three years and as time went by, his father longed to see him again. Joab knew this and sent a wise woman to speak to David about it.

2 Samuel chapter 14 verses 21-27.

Did king David agree to let Absalom come back? Did he say that Absalom could come and see him?

Day 143: CONSPIRACY

Today we read about a conspiracy against king David. The one who planned to harm David was his own son, Absalom.

A conspiracy is a secret plan to do wrong.

Two years went by after Absalom returned to Jerusalem. He was not allowed to see his father. He asked Joab to speak to the king about it. The king listened to Joab and sent for Absalom and kissed him.

2 Samuel chapter 15 verses 1-6.

Without the king knowing, Absalom was making sure that the people thought that he cared about them more than his father did. After four years, Absalom told his father that he wanted to go to Hebron. The king let him go, and he took two hundred men with him. These men did not know about Absalom's plans. Absalom wanted to be king instead of David. Secretly he sent messengers throughout Israel, calling on the people to make him king. A lot followed Absalom, including David's friend and adviser, Ahithophel. When David was told about the conspiracy, he left Jerusalem. Many went with him as he climbed the Mount of Olives just outside the city.

David was sad when his son plotted against him.

When he heard that Ahithophel was helping Absalom, David prayed that Absalom would get wrong advice.

How many men went ahead of Absalom's chariot? Why did Absalom get up early and stand at the roadside?

Day 144: A GOOD FRIEND

It is good to have friends. But when life gets difficult, it is very good to have friends that we can trust.

David had some brave friends who helped him.

One was named Hushai. The king knew that Absalom would ask Ahithophel's advice. David asked Hushai to go to Absalom and pretend to give him better advice.

2 Samuel chapter 16 verses 15-20.

Hushai pretended to help Absalom. Ahithophel thought that David and his men should be attacked quickly, because they would be tired after their journey. Hushai gave Absalom different advice. He wanted to give the king time to get ready for battle. Absalom did not attack his father quickly as Ahithophel had suggested. Hushai sent secret messengers to the king, and David escaped with all his soldiers across the River Jordan. By the time Absalom led his followers into battle, David was ready for the fight. He wanted to lead his soldiers, but they asked him not to. They loved their king, and did not want his life to be put in danger.

Three men were in charge of Davids army: Joab, Abishai and Ittai.

David told his men not to harm Absalom. Even though Absalom wanted to make himself king, the king still loved his son. Nathan had told David that he would always have trouble in his family!

Who was a true friend to king David, even though he pretended to help Absalom?

Day 145: A REBELLION ENDS

Although David was in trouble because of his son Absalom, he had many people who were loyal to him.

EXTRA INFO

What does it mean to be loyal to someone? It means to be a real friend, even when things go wrong.

A great battle was fought between those who were loyal to David, and those who had followed Absalom. Those who fought for king David won the battle.

GOD'S WORD

2 Samuel chapter 18 verses 9-13.

The man who saw Absalom hanging in a tree did not harm him because of king David's orders. But Joab, and some soldiers, quickly put Absalom to death. Joab disobeyed the king, but he knew that if Absalom was killed, the rebellion would be over. Absalom's followers would soon want David to be king again. But how did David hear the news about his son? Two men hurried to tell him. The first messenger gave good news, but did not tell him about Absalom. The second messenger told David that Absalom was dead.

BY MYSELF

David was very, very sad and cried for his son.

Joab went to see the king. He told David he should meet the soldiers who had fought for him. If he didn't the men would think that he cared more for Absalom than he did for them. David knew that what Joab said was right. He went out to meet the men who had been loyal to him. After this, king David crossed the River Jordan and returned to his palace in Jerusalem.

ASK ABOUT

Where did one of Joab's soldiers see Absalom? Why did the soldier do nothing to harm Absalom?

1 AND 2 KINGS: FROM BLESSING TO CAPTIVITY

Here we read of the nation of Israel from the death of David to the Babylonian captivity. Solomon succeeded his father David as king and built the temple at Jerusalem. God granted his request for wisdom to rule, but sadly he joined his wives in idol worship.

He ruled for forty years over a united kingdom, but after his death the nation was divided into the southern kingdom of Judah (including the tribe of Benjamin) and the northern kingdom, known as Israel, consisting of the remaining ten tribes. Whilst Judah had some godly rulers such as Jehoshaphat, Hezekiah and Josiah, none of the kings of Israel were faithful to God. We read about Elijah and Elisha, prophets to the northern kingdom and also of Isaiah and Jeremiah's prophecy to Judah. In spite of the repeated warnings given by the prophets, both kingdoms became idolatrous. Israel was taken captive by the Assyrians, and over a century later (586 BC) came the Babylonian captivity of Judah.

DAYS 146-182: Kings and Chronicles

1 AND 2 CHRONICLES: KINGDOM OF JUDAH

The first nine chapters of 1 Chronicles consist of genealogies, including some interesting detail, such as the responsibilities of the Levites. Chapter ten records the death of Saul, the remainder of the Book being concerned with the reign of king David. The closing chapters tell us of David's preparations for the building of the temple and the importance he placed on this.

2 Chronicles begins with Solomon's reign and the construction and dedication of the temple. After the division of the kingdom, we read of Judah and it's kings: details of the northern kingdom are only included when they affect Judah.

The Books of Chronicles differ from the Books of Kings in the events they include or exclude. This is because the Chronicles were written from the Priestly point of view.

Day 146: PREPARING TO BUILD

What was it that king David wanted to build, but God told him that it would be built by his son Solomon?

1 Chronicles chapter 22 verses 6-13.

king David had wanted to build thetemple but this would be a job for his son to do. David did however collect the building materials: gold, silver, bronze, iron, wood and stone.

The king asked the leaders of the people to help Solomon with the building. He made sure that the priests and Levites were ready to do their duties in the temple, as they had in the tabernacle. David encouraged Solomon to begin to build the temple.

He knew that God would help him.

Before building can start, there has to be a plan.

When the Israelites made the tabernacle, God gave Moses the plan. king David had plans ready for the building of the temple. God had helped him to write down all that must be done. Then the king called the people together. He asked them who would be willing to give towards the building of the temple. The leaders of the people were glad to give to the work. They gave gold, silver, precious stones, bronze and iron. There was great joy that day when the people saw their leaders giving so willingly. king David thanked God for all His goodness in giving them so much. He knew that all that they had given for the temple had first of all been given to them by God.

Who does everything belong to? (1 Chronicles chapter 29 verses 11 and 14-16).

Day 147: A NEW KING

king David had grown old and was no longer able to lead the people as he had done. One of his sons, Adonijah, made himself king. Joab and Abiathar the priest, were on Adonijah's side. Adonijah invited his brothers and the leaders of the people to a great feast. But he did not invite Solomon or Nathan the prophet or those who were loyal to king David.

Nathan told Bathsheba, Solomon's mother, what had happened. He said that she should go to king David and remind him that Solomon was to be the next king. Bathsheba did as Nathan had said, and told the king what Adonijah had done. Then Nathan the prophet also went in to speak to the king.

GOD'S WORD

1 Kings chapter 1 verses 32-40.

When Adonijah and the people with him heard the celebrations, they wondered what was happening. Abiathar's son Jonathan told them the news that David had made Solomon king. Adonijah was afraid that Solomon would have him put to death. But the king sent him home without punishing him.

BY MYSELF

David knew that he was near the end of his life.

He gave some last words of advice to Solomon. He reminded him that he must keep all the laws that God had given to Moses. If he did this, things would go well for him and his son would be king after him.

EXTRA INFO

When David died, he had been king for forty years.

ASK ABOUT

Which of king David's sons tried to make himself king? (1 Kings chapter 1 verse 5). Who anointed Solomon as king?

Day 148: THE SHEPHERD PSALM

We learn a lot about David's life from the two books of Samuel and the first book of Chronicles. But we learn about his love for God in the Psalms he wrote.

The Psalms are poems which were sung in the temple, and quite a lot of them were written by David.

Many psalms praise God for His greatness. Others thank Him for His goodness and help. Some are prayers, asking for God's help or forgiveness. Those who wrote the palms were helped by God the Holy Spirit, just as the writers of the rest of the Bible were. David was able to write Psalms about the Lord Jesus many years before His birth at Bethlehem.

Psalm 23, written by king David.

When he was young, David looked after sheep. He knew that God cares for His people, as a shepherd cares for his sheep. A shepherd in Israel led his sheep. He gave them all they needed. Passing through a dark valley, the sheep would not be frightened, because the shepherd was with them. David knew that throughout his life, God had led him and provided for him.

He had difficult times, but God had been with him.

When the time came for him to die, God would take him to be with Him for ever. David trusted in God's promised Saviour, even though he lived a thousand years before the Saviour came.

David said: The Lord is my Shepherd. For how long did David say that he would dwell in the house of the Lord? (Verse 6).

Day 149: THE TEMPLE

What is it like to be a king or a queen? Kings and queens may seem to do whatever they like, but they have many duties too. When Solomon became king, he wanted to please God and rule the people well.

2 Chronicles chapter 1 verses 7-12.

Wisdom means knowing what is the right thing to do, even when it is very difficult to decide.

Solomon asked for wisdom so that he could be a good king.

God was pleased that he had not asked to be rich or famous.

God promised to give Solomon wisdom as well as the riches he had not asked for. Soon Solomon began building the temple. king David had given him the plan as well as the gold, silver, bronze, iron, wood and stone that he had collected. Solomon set thousands of men to work quarrying stone for the building. He also sent for wood from the land of Lebanon.

In the temple there were two rooms: the smaller room was called the Most Holy Place. The rooms were lined with gold and had a curtain between them called 'the veil'. Solomon made furniture for the temple. The bronze altar was larger than the one in the tabernacle. There was a large bronze basin for the priests to wash their hands and their feet. There were also ten smaller basins. Solomon made ten golden lampstands and ten tables. All this work took seven years to complete.

What did Solomon ask God to give him? What else did God promise to give to Solomon?

Day 150: SOLOMON'S PRAYER

The people of Israel gathered at the temple when all the work was finished. They brought sacrifices and offerings and the Levites brought the ark containing the Ten Commandments. The priests placed the ark in the Most Holy Place. Some Levites played instruments and others sang to thank God for His goodness.

A cloud filled the temple and the people knew that God was with them.

Solomon stood in front of the people and thanked God for keeping His promise to David. He knelt on a raised platform so all could see him and he prayed to God.

2 Chronicles chapter 6 verses 18-21.

Solomon knew that God is so great He cannot be contained in a building. But he also knew that God had chosen the temple as the place to meet His people. He asked God to hear the prayers made in that place, and to forgive the people when they did wrong. After his prayer, fire came down from heaven onto the sacrifices. The people saw it and worshipped God.

A great feast was held for seven days and then the people returned home with thankful hearts.

God told Solomon that He had heard his prayer. He promised to hear His people's prayers. He reminded Solomon to obey God as his father had done. God warned him that if the people did not obey God, they would be taken away from their land.

What two things did Solomon ask God to do? (2 Chronicles chapter 6 verse 40).

Day 151: A ROYAL VISITOR

We have many ways of hearing news from all over the world, such as television, radio, or telephone. These did not exist in Solomon's day, but news still travelled.

Letters were sent, and traders carried news from one land to another.

People in the lands around Israel heard of the wisdom of Solomon. The Queen of Sheba, who lived a long way from Israel, decided to find out if he was as wise as she had been told. Her servants loaded camels with precious things as presents for king Solomon.

2 Chronicles chapter 9 verses 1-6.

The queen found that the wisdom of Solomon was even greater than she had been told. She realised that God had made him a great king. She gave gifts of gold, precious stones and spices. Kings from many other lands also came to see Solomon. Each brought presents of gold, silver and other precious things. king Solomon became very rich. He had ships that sailed to different lands and brought back many valuable things. He also had thousands of horses and chariots.

God had kept His promise to king Solomon, giving him the wisdom he had asked for. He also gave him the riches He had promised, and so Solomon became a very great king.

During Solomon's forty year reign, the land of Israel was at peace.

What was the name of the queen who came to visit king Solomon? Who had made him such a great king?

Day 152: IDOLS

Do you remember the ten commandments that God gave? We read about them in Exodus chapter 20.

The second commandment teaches us that we should not worship idols.

People who lived in the lands around Israel did bow down to the idols they had made. God said that the people of Israel should not marry people from these lands. God knew that if they did so, they would become like the other nations.

1 Kings chapter 11 verses 1-4.

Solomon was a great and wise king. It is sad to read that he disobeyed God by marrying women who worshipped idols. He also built special places for the idols of his wives. God had warned Solomon not to have anything to do with these false gods. Now God spoke again to Solomon. He told him that because of his disobedience, his son would not be king over the whole land of Israel. Ten of the tribes of Israel would have another king who did not come from the family of king David. Solomon's son would be king over the large tribe of Judah (which included the small tribe of Benjamin).

Solomon gave an important job to a man named Jeroboam. Ahijah the prophet told Jeroboam that he would rule the ten tribes of Israel. Solomon must have heard about this, because he wanted to kill Jeroboam.

Jeroboam went to live in Egypt until Solomon died.

In 1 Kings chapter 11 verse 6 who was not as true to God as his father had been?

Day 153: REHOBOAM'S ADVISERS

Solomon was king of all the people of Israel for forty years. After he died, his son Rehoboam became king. At this time, Jeroboam was still living in Egypt. The people sent for him and he went with them to speak to the new king.

GOD'S WORD

1 Kings chapter 12 verses 4-7.

The people felt that they had to work very hard in the time of Solomon. They asked Rehoboam to make life easier. The old men who had helped Solomon said that Rehoboam should speak kindly to the people and help them. Rehoboam sent for some of his young friends. Their advice was quite different. They said that the king should tell the people that he would make their lives much harder. Rehoboam took the advice of his young friends and told the people that life would be much harder now.

BY MYSELF

The people went away very disappointed.

EXTRA INFO

The family of King David belonged to the tribe of Judah whose land was in the southern part of Israel. The tribe of Benjamin shared this part of the land with them.

The other ten tribes decided that they wanted Jeroboam to be their king. At first Rehoboam thought that he should try to become king over all the tribes as his father had been. He began to get his soldiers ready to fight. But God told him not to do this and he obeyed God.

ASK ABOUT

Did king Rehoboam take the advice of the older men or his young friends? (1 Kings chapter 12 verses 13 and 14).

Day 154: GOLDEN CALVES

In the United Kingdom, kings and queens have a palace in London, the capital city. king David had a house in Jerusalem. Solomon built a palace there. The temple was also at Jerusalem. Jeroboam did not want his people to visit the temple. He did not want them to remember when Israel had one king.

They might be sorry that they had made him king.

1 Kings chapter 12 verses 26-29.

The two gold calves became idols. The people worshiped idols just like the other nations did. It is hard for us to understand why people bow down to idols. Idols are statues made out of gold, silver, wood or stone. They cannot see, hear, or do anything. Even today some people bow down to false gods. Because of his wickedness God spoke to Jeroboam by his prophets. God told Jeroboam that he had done wrong and had also taught the people to do wrong.

A prophet is someone who tells people the things that God wants them to know.

Jeroboam was king over the ten tribes of Israel for twenty-two years. His part of the land became known as 'Israel'. The other part where the kings still came from the family of king David, was called 'Judah'.

Jeroboam's son Nadab was king for two years. He worshipped the idols that his father had made. He was killed by a man named Baasha who became the next king. No one else from Jeroboam's family became king because he had disobeyed God.

What did Jeroboam say the golden calves were?

Day 155: KING ASA

The Bible always tells us the truth about people, so that we will learn the truth about ourselves. One thing we learn is that it is easier to start well than to continue well. Both King Saul and King Solomon began well, but neither of them continued to do right. King Rehoboam also obeyed God during the first years of his reign. Then, when he had become a strong king, he stopped following God's law. He did nothing to stop the people making idols for themselves.

Rehoboam was king for seventeen years and then his son Abijah was king for three years.

When Abijah's son Asa became king there was a real change. Asa took away the idols and destroyed the places where the people worshipped them. He also taught the people to obey God's commandments.

Asa loved God and obeyed Him.

2 Chronicles chapter 14 verses 2-6.

Asa made sure that the cities of Judah were strong and that the soldiers were able to keep the land safe. A great army from Ethiopia came against the land of Judah. Asa knew that the Ethiopian army was larger than his. He prayed for God's help. God heard his prayer. Because God helped King Asa, the Ethiopians began to run away from the battle. God gave the people of Judah a great victory. A man named Azariah came with a message from God to King Asa. He told the king that while he obeyed God, God would be with him. He warned him not to stop doing what was right.

Who did Asa command the people to serve?

Day 156: PAYING FOR HELP

Sometimes it seemed that Israel had forgotten all the good things that God had done for them. They bowed down to idols and did many wrong things. But there were always some people who loved and obeyed God. They still went to the temple, even though idols had been set up for them to worship instead. The people who did not belong to Judah heard how God was helping Asa. Many left their homes to live in Judah.

When he had been king for nearly fifteen years, Asa called the people together. People from Judah and Benjamin came to Jerusalem as well as those from the other tribes who had joined them. They sacrificed many sheep and bulls.

They promised to seek God with all their hearts.

There was great joy at this time and there was no war until the thirty-fifth year of King Asa's reign.

Then the King of Israel began to make life difficult for the people of Judah. King Asa sent gold and silver to the King of Syria. The King of Syria then helped King Asa by fighting against Israel.

God sent a man named Hanani to King Asa. He reminded the king of how God had helped him when the Ethiopian army came. At that time Asa had trusted in God and prayed to Him. Now he had asked the King of Syria for help instead of God. Instead of telling God that he was sorry for what he had done, King Asa was angry with Hanani and put him in prison.

2 Chronicles chapter 16 verses 7-10.

Who did King Asa ask to help him? Who should he have asked?

Day 157: BY THE BROOK

Asa was King of Judah for forty years. About three years before he died, a man named Ahab became King of Israel. King Ahab married a woman from a country near to the land of Israel. Her name was Jezebel and she did not love God. She worshipped a false god called Baal.

Ahab also bowed down to idols and he built a temple for people to worship Baal.

God sent Elijah the prophet to speak to Ahab. The message he gave was very frightening.

1 Kings chapter 17 verses 1-7.

If there was no rain, the crops would not grow and the people would not have enough food.

The people needed to learn that it is God who sends rain, not idols. It was not easy for Elijah to bring this message. Ahab became very angry with him. However, God told Elijah exactly what to do and Elijah obeyed.

The brook would provide him with water to drink. Even the ravens did as God told them to: they provided Elijah with food to eat. While Elijah was at the brook there was no rain, and so the brook dried up. Elijah could not live without water and so God spoke to him again. This time God told him to set out on a journey to a city called Zarephath. This was in the land where Queen Jezebel came from. Once again Elijah obeyed God and set out on the journey.

What did the ravens bring Elijah in the morning and in the evening?

As we read the Bible we find that God does not always choose great, rich, or famous people to do His work. When He told Elijah to go to Zarephath, God said that the food he needed would be provided by a widow who lived there.

EXTRA INFO

A widow is a woman whose husband has died. In Bible times they often became very poor.

GOD'S WORD

1 Kings chapter 17 verses 8-12.

The widow that Elijah met was very poor. She and her son were about to eat the only food they had left. After that she thought that they would starve. But Elijah gave her a message from God.

BY MYSELF

Her flour and oil would last until God sent rain.

The woman believed Elijah. She brought him some food as he had asked her to. Elijah stayed there. Every day there was enough flour and oil to bake bread.

While Elijah was living in Zarephath, the widow's son became so ill that he died. She told Elijah that she was afraid she was being punished for doing something wrong. Elijah took the boy to his room and prayed that God would give him life again. God answered Elijah's prayer and he brought the boy back to his mother. Every day this widow had seen the miracle of the flour and oil. Now she saw the miracle of her own child being brought back to life. She was certain that Elijah was a man who spoke the words God gave him. At last the time came when God told Elijah to go to King Ahab: God promised that he would send rain.

ASK ABOUT

What was the widow doing when Elijah first saw her? (1 Kings chapter 17 verse 10).

Day 159: A TIME TO CHOOSE

Ahab was a wicked king and yet Obadiah, who looked after his palace, loved and trusted God.

Queen Jezebel had tried to kill all the true prophets of God, but Obadiah rescued one hundred. He hid them in caves and provided food for them.

When Elijah returned to Israel he met Obadiah. It was so long since there had been any rain that there was hardly any grass left. Obadiah was searching for grass to keep the animals alive. Elijah told Obadiah to tell the king that he had come. Obadiah was afraid to do this. He told Elijah that Ahab had been trying to find him, even sending men to other countries to search for him. Obadiah was afraid that Elijah would go away again, but Elijah said that he must see Ahab that day. Obadiah told the king that Elijah had come, and the king came to meet him.

1 Kings chapter 18 verses 16-20.

Elijah was not afraid to tell the king that he had brought trouble on Israel by worshipping false gods. King Ahab did as Elijah asked and sent for the false prophets. He called the people together to Mount Carmel and Elijah spoke to them there.

He told them that it was time to choose between the true God and their false gods.

He asked the prophets of Baal to prepare a sacrifice and ask their gods to send fire on it. Elijah would do the same but he would ask the true God to send fire.

Where did Obadiah hide the prophets and what did he provide for them?

Day 160: GOD'S ANSWER

Elijah watched the prophets of Baal. From morning until midday they called on Baal to send fire on their sacrifice, but nothing happened. Elijah told them to shout louder in case Baal was busy, or on a journey, or even asleep.

Elijah knew that no one would answer. But he allowed them to continue shouting for Baal until evening. Then he told the people to come near to him. He built an altar with twelve stones and prepared an animal to sacrifice. A trench was dug around the altar and water was poured over the sacrifice.

1 Kings chapter 18 verses 36-39.

Elijah did not have to spend hours shouting for God to hear him. All the people could see that God had answered Elijah's prayer by sending fire.

The prophets of Baal were put to death as God had said they should be. Then Elijah told Ahab to go and have something to eat as there would soon be rain. Ahab did so, but Elijah climbed to the top of Mount Carmel to pray. While he was there he sent his servant to look toward the sea to see if there was any sign of rain. The servant could see nothing, so Elijah kept sending him to look again. The seventh time he looked the servant saw a very small cloud. Then the sky became dark with clouds and it began to rain heavily.

This was the first rain in the land of Israel for more than three years.

How many times was water poured over the sacrifice before Elijah prayed? (1 Kings chapter 18 verse 34).

Day 161: NABOTH'S VINEYARD

Next door to King Ahab's palace in the town of Jezreel there was a vineyard that belonged to a man called Naboth. Ahab wanted this vineyard for himself.

A vineyard is a piece of land used for growing grapes. Grapes grow on a plant called a vine.

1 Kings chapter 21 verses 1-4.

Naboth was quite right not to sell his land because God had said that the land should stay in the family. It seems that because the king could not have what he wanted he did something that I hope you never do: he sulked. When Queen Jezebel heard all about it, she told Ahab that she would get the vineyard for him.

Jezebel did something that was very wrong.

Jezebel wrote letters to the important men of the city and signed the letters with the king's name. She told them to send for Naboth and two wicked men who would be prepared to tell lies. With people looking on, the two men were to say that Naboth had said bad things about God and the king. This was a lie but the letters said that Naboth must be put to death. When all this had taken place Jezebel told Ahab that he could have the vineyard. However, there was one thing that Ahab and Jezebel had forgotten: God knew what they had done. God sent Elijah to tell the king that He would punish him and his wife for their sin. This time Ahab was sorry for what he had done.

What did King Ahab wear instead of his royal robes to show that he was sorry? (1 Kings chapter 21 verse 27).

Day 162: A WRONG FRIENDSHIP

While Ahab was King of Israel, Asa's son Jehoshaphat became King of Judah. Jehoshaphat loved and obeyed God. He continued to take away any idols that were in the land of Judah, as his father had done. He also sent priests, Levites and other leaders to teach the people God's law. These men travelled through all the cities of Judah, so that the people understood the way God wanted them to live.

Even the people of the countries around Judah realised that God was with His people. They did not fight against Jehoshaphat at that time.

Even though Jehoshaphat was a good king, he did bring trouble upon himself and his family. This was because he made a friend of King Ahab and arranged for his son Jehoram to marry Ahab's daughter. As both Ahab and his wife Jezebel worshipped idols, it was not likely that their daughter would be a good wife for Jehoram.

One day Jehoshaphat visited Ahab. King Ahab wanted to free one of the cities of Israel from the King of Syria. He asked King Jehoshaphat to help him.

2 Chronicles chapter 18 verses 3-8.

King Ahab's false prophets pretended they knew what God said.

However, there was just one true prophet who Ahab did not like, because he spoke the truth. Micaiah warned the king that he would lose his life in the battle.

How many false prophets did King Ahab have?

Day 163: JEHOSHAPHAT'S DANGER

It is good to help others. But, as King Jehoshaphat discovered, it is not right to help someone who has made up his mind to disobey God.

Ahab decided that he would go in disguise to fight the King of Syria. He would not wear his royal robes. He would wear ordinary clothes so that no one would know who he was.

Jehoshaphat was asked to wear his royal robes as usual and come with him to the battle.

The King of Syria told his soldiers not to fight anyone except King Ahab. When they saw Jehoshaphat in his robes they thought that he was Ahab. Jehoshaphat cried out and the men realised that he was not the king they were looking for. Although they could not see Ahab, someone shot an arrow which wounded him.

Ahab stayed in his chariot until the evening and as the sun was setting he died.

Jehoshaphat was able to return safely to Jerusalem.

2 Chronicles chapter 19 verses 1-4.

King Asa had been angry with Jehu's father when he brought God's message. But Jehu was not afraid to tell Jehoshaphat that God was not pleased with him.

It seems that Jehoshaphat knew that Jehu spoke the truth. He made sure that the people understood God's commandments and set judges over them so that problems were answered fairly.

Which king did Ahab fight against? (2 Chronicles chapter 18 verse 30).

Day 164: ELISHA

There are only two people who we read about in the Bible who did not die. One was Enoch (Genesis chapter 5) and the other was Elijah the prophet. Elijah had been true to God during Ahab's wicked reign. Then a day came when God took Elijah up to heaven.

God had already chosen Elisha to be a prophet after Elijah. He would continue to speak God's words to the people.

2 Kings chapter 4 verses 1-7.

God showed Elisha how to help the poor woman. She did what Elisha said and was able to pay her debts. One day Elisha travelled to a place called Shunem, where another woman invited him to a meal. After that, he ate at her house whenever he passed that way. Because the woman saw that Elisha served God, she asked her husband to make a room for him to use.

Elisha must have been glad to have somewhere to rest from his journeys.

He was grateful for the woman's kindness and asked her if there was anything he could do for her. She would not ask for anything, but Elisha's servant, Gehazi told his master that she had no son. Elisha told the woman that she would have a son. At first she found it difficult to believe what Elisha had said. Her husband was old and she did not expect to have any children. But when the year had gone by, she had a baby boy, just as Elisha had told her.

Can you name the four items of furniture that were in Elisha's room at Shunem? (2 Kings chapter 4 verse 10).

Day 165: THE SHUNAMMITE

The Bible does not tell us the name of the woman who was so kind to Elisha.

She is often called 'the Shunammite woman' because the place where she lived was called Shunem.

Life must have changed a lot after the little boy was born. They watched over him as he learned to walk and talk. As he grew bigger he was able to go out into the fields with his father. One day, when he was watching the reapers, the boy became ill. He told his father that his head hurt. His father told a servant to carry him to his mother. The Shunammite woman nursed her little boy until midday but he did not get better. He became so ill that he died. His mother laid him on Elisha's bed.

2 Kings chapter 4 verses 22-26.

The woman knew that the best person to speak to was Elisha, the man of God. He saw that she was very sad and soon realised why. He gave Gehazi his staff and told him to hurry and lay it on the boy's face. Then Elisha followed the woman to her home. Gehazi came to meet them, to tell them that the child had not recovered. Elisha went to his room and closed the door. He prayed for the child and God answered his prayer. The boy opened his eyes: God gave him back his life.

The woman knew that only God could have brought her son back to life.

Who else prayed that life would come back to a child and God answered his prayer? (1 Kings chapter 17 verse 22).

Day 166: NAAMAN

At some time in our lives most of us will fall ill. It may be a very slight illness that only lasts a few days or it may take a long time to get well again, or you may not recover.

Leprosy is a serious illness, nowadays medicines can help to cure people with leprosy.

In 2 Kings we read about an important man who had leprosy long ago. There was no medicine to help him.

2 Kings chapter 5 verses 1-5.

The prophet that the little girl wanted Naaman to see was Elisha. The King of Syria sent Naaman to the King of Israel. The king was upset because he could not make Naaman better. He was afraid that the King of Syria would be angry. When Elisha heard what had happened, he asked for Naaman to come to see him. But when Naaman arrived at the prophet's house, Elisha sent a messanger to tell Naaman that he would be cured if he washed seven times in the River Jordan. Naaman was very angry.

He thought that Elisha should have come himself and called on God to heal him.

He also thought that the rivers in his own country were better than the rivers in Israel. He was ready to go back to Syria, but his servants persuaded him to do as Elisha had said. He dipped seven times in the River Jordan, and the leprosy was gone.

Why was the little girl from Israel living in Naaman's house? How did she help Naaman to get well?

Day 167: ELISHA'S SERVANT

Leprosy made the person's skin look different from normal. So when Naaman came out of the water, everyone could see that he was better. He went to see Elisha, to tell him that he knew now that Israel's God was the only true God. He also wanted to give Elisha a present: he had brought silver and gold and clothing with him. Elisha would not take anything. It was God who had made Naaman well and Elisha did not want to be paid. But Gehazi, Elisha's servant, did want something for himself.

GOD'S WORD

2 Kings chapter 5 verses 20-24.

EXTRA INFO

Did you notice that Gehazi told lies? Sadly, when we begin to do wrong, one sin often leads to others.

When Elisha next saw his servant, he asked him where he had been. Gehazi said that he had not been anywhere. He should have remembered that his master was a prophet. Elisha knew exactly where Gehazi had been and what he had taken from Naaman. It was a very serious thing to have told lies about Elisha to Naaman. Now Naaman would think that he had paid for his healing. Elisha had wanted him to know that it was God who had healed him.

BY MYSELF

He could not pay for something that was God's gift to him.

Elisha said that Gehazi would now have Naaman's leprosy. As he went out, his skin showed that he now had the illness from which Naaman had been cured.

ASK ABOUT

What two things did Gehazi say that were not true? (2 Kings chapter 5 verses 22 and 25).

Day 168: FINDING FOOD

A capital city is the most important city in the country. In the United Kingdom the capital city is London. The Royal family have a palace there. The capital city of the United States is Washington. King Ahab's capital was Samaria. When Ahab's son Jehoram was king, the King of Syria brought his army to besiege Samaria.

To besiege a city means that soldiers are all round the city so that no one can go in or out.

The Syrian army besieged Samaria for so long that there was no food left there. Jehoram was very sad when he saw that the people did not have enough to eat. He went to see Elisha.

Elisha told the king that God said there would be plenty of food on sale tomorrow.

An officer who had come with the king did not believe this. Elisha told him that he would see it happen but would not eat any food himself. Now four men who had leprosy lived just outside the gates of Samaria. They decided to give themselves up. It would be no worse than starving in Samaria. But when they came to the Syrian camp, all the soldiers had gone. The army had run away and left all their goods behind.

2 Kings chapter 7 verses 8-11.

News that there was food in the Syrian camp soon reached the people. The officer who had not believed Elisha, was put in charge of the city gate. As the people rushed out he was trampled to death.

How many lepers went to the Syrian camp? What was their good news?

Day 169: A WICKED QUEEN

Jehoshaphat King of Judah loved and obeyed God. Yet he arranged for his son Jehoram to marry Athaliah, King Ahab's daughter. Jehoram was king for just eight years. He worshipped idols like his father-in-law King Ahab had done. He died when he was about forty years old and his son Ahaziah became king.

Ahaziah only reigned as king for one year.

When Ahaziah died, his mother did a terrible thing. She decided that she would be Queen of Judah. In order to achieve this she killed Ahaziah's children — her own grandchildren. However, the children's aunty, Jehosheba, rescued one little boy. His name was Joash. and he was one year old.

Jehosheba was married to Jehoiada the priest. They kept Joash hidden in a room in the temple for six years. This must have been a sad time for people in Judah who still trusted in God. God had promised that there would always be someone from the family of King David to be their king. For six years it seemed as though God had forgotten His promise.

When Joash was seven years old, his uncle, Jehoiada, decided that the time had come to show the people their king. He planned everything carefully. He sent men to bring all the Levites and leaders of the people to Jerusalem.

He knew that he must keep Joash safe from his wicked grandmother.

2 Chronicles chapter 23 verses 2-7.

How long was Joash hidden in the temple? (2 Chronicles chapter 22 verse 12).

Day 170: JOASH IS CROWNED

Coronation day is when a king or queen is crowned. Joash had a coronation when he was just seven years old. It was a special day. His uncle, Jehoiada, had planned it carefully. The Levites and officers did as Jehoiada asked.

Joash was protected from danger.

When he was crowned he was given a copy of God's commandments. Jehoiada and his sons anointed him and said - 'Long live the king'. Athaliah heard a noise and wondered what was happening in the temple.

2 Chronicles chapter 23 verses 11-13.

After the coronation all the people rejoiced because they had a king from the family of David as God had promised. Athaliah was so angry when she discovered what was happening she shouted out 'Treason'.

Treason is the word that is used for trying to kill or overthrow the king or queen.

Athaliah was actually the one guilty of treason. She was put to death. Jehoiada made a promise with the people and the king that they would be true to God. The people destroyed the idols and the altars. Jehoiada then made sure that the work of the temple was properly carried out. He appointed priests to offer sacrifices. He made sure that the singers and gatekeepers were ready. The people were glad Athaliah was no longer queen.

How old was Joash when he became king? (2 Chronicles chapter 24 verse 1). Who heard a noise and came to the temple?

Day 171: JOASH BEGINS WELL

Joash was able to be a good king at only seven years old because Jehoiada the priest helped him.

Jehoiada lived to be a very old man, and while he lived Joash did what was right.

Joash grew up, got married and had children of his own. The temple had been neglected and precious things had been taken from it. Now Joash decided that the temple should be repaired.

2 Chronicles chapter 24 verses 8-13.

This was a good work for Joash to do, but once Jehoiada died, some of the leaders of the people began to talk to him. Joash joined them in worshipping idols.

God sent prophets to remind them that they were doing wrong, but they would not listen.

Jehoiada's son Zechariah spoke to the people. He told them that God would not help them if they disobeyed Him. Instead of being sorry for the wrong things he had done, Joash said that Zechariah should be killed. Jehoiada and his wife had saved Joash's life and cared for him when he was young. Jehoiada had helped him to rule as he was growing up. How terrible that Joash should forget all this and have Jehoiada's son put to death. Because of this God did not help the people of Judah when the Syrian army came against them. The battle was lost and Joash was wounded.

How was the money collected to repair the temple? How old was Jehoiada when he died? (2 Chronicles chapter 24 verse 15).

Day 172: THE LEPER KING

One king of Judah who reigned for a long time was Uzziah, the grandson of Joash. He became king when he was sixteen years old and his reign lasted fifty-two years.

2 Chronicles chapter 26 verses 3-8.

Uzziah had a large army which was well prepared to fight against the enemies of Israel. He also built towers in the walls of Jerusalem.

God helped Uzziah and he became a strong king. But instead of thanking God for making him strong, Uzziah became proud. He went into the temple to do some of the work that only the priests were allowed to do. God had chosen the family of Aaron for this special work. It was wrong for Uzziah to do this. The priests went into the temple to tell the king that he should not be there. Instead of admitting that he had done wrong, he became very angry.

As the priests looked at the king, they saw that something had happened to him. The skin of his forehead had changed: he had leprosy. Uzziah knew that God had done this to him because he had done wrong. He hurried out of the temple.

Because of his illness he had to live in a house away from other people.

Uzziah's son, Jotham, helped with some of the king's work. Uzziah had been a good king until he became proud. If he had remembered that it was God who had made him strong, this would never had happened.

**How old was Uzziah when he became king?
How long did he reign?**

Day 173: KING AHAZ

After Uzziah's long reign, there were two kings who each reigned for sixteen years. Jotham was a good king who obeyed God and did what was right.

Because he wanted to please God in all that he did, God helped him to become a strong king.

After Jotham's death, his son Ahaz became king. He was different from his father. Instead of trusting God, he worshipped idols. This brought trouble on Judah because God did not help them to fight against their enemies. The King of Syria took many people captive. Then the King of Israel brought his army against Judah. Many men were killed and many of the people were taken from their own land.

King Ahaz even paid the King of Assyria to come and help him, but he would not help.

2 Chronicles chapter 28 verses 22-25.

These verses tell us two things about King Ahaz. He made places for the people to worship idols throughout the land of Judah. He closed the temple so that the work of the priests stopped. It seems very strange to us that people should bow down to idols that are made of wood or stone, gold or silver. The nations around the land of Israel and Judah had their idols. But God had taught His people that He was their Creator. They should love and obey Him. When they did this, He helped them, and other nations could see that there is one true God.

Ahaz worshipped false gods. Where did these false gods come from? King Ahaz closed the doors to what place?

Day 174: A TIME OF REJOICING

Sometimes people say 'Isn't she like her mother' when they look at a little girl, or, 'Isn't he like his father' when they see a young boy. Quite often children do take after their parents. Whether Hezekiah looked like his father King Ahaz we do not know. We do know that he was very different from him in his ways.

Hezekiah was twenty-five years old when he became king. In the first month of his reign he opened the doors of the temple and called the priests and Levites together. After he spoke to them, the priests and Levites cleaned the temple. By the sixteenth day of the month the work was finished. Then the king and the leaders went to the temple. The priests offered sacrifices and the Levites sang praises to God. It was a time of great rejoicing for the king and the people.

2 Chronicles chapter 29 verses 26-30.

Hezekiah then sent letters to everyone in Israel and Judah. He asked them to come to Jerusalem to keep the feast of the Passover.

The people of Judah were glad to obey the king and gather at Jerusalem.

Those who carried the letters to Israel were laughed at. But some people there did come to the feast.

There had not been such a wonderful time in Jerusalem since the days of Solomon. The people were so glad to be together in this way that the feast continued for two weeks instead of one.

When the Levites praised God whose words did they use?

Day 175: ASSYRIAN SOLDIERS

When Jeroboam became king, he set up golden calves for the people to worship. Not one of the kings of Israel who came after him took those idols away.

Some of the kings obeyed some of God's commands, but none fully obeyed God.

The last King of Israel was called Hoshea. In the ninth year of his reign, the King of Assyria took the people away from their own land into the land of Assyria. This was what God had warned them would happen, if they did not obey Him. The people of Israel were taken captive while Hezekiah was King of Judah.

King Hezekiah continued doing all he could to make sure that the priests and Levites carried out their work in the temple at Jerusalem.

2 Chronicles chapter 31 verses 4-10.

At this time, when everything seemed to be going well in the land of Judah, Sennacherib, the King of Assyria, sent a great army against Jerusalem.

One of the officers in charge of the Assyrian soldiers tried to frighten the people of Jerusalem. He called out to them that their God would not be able to save them from the King of Assyria. He told them not to listen to King Hezekiah who would tell them to trust in God.

Three of Hezekiah's officials came to tell him what was happening. When he had heard their news, he went into the temple. He then sent a message to the prophet Isaiah.

What was the name of the King of Assyria? (2 Chronicles chapter 32 verse 1).

Day 176: JERUSALEM KEPT SAFE

We all have times when we are happy and times when we feel sad. There are times when we feel safe and also times when we face danger.

God wants us to learn to trust Him whatever is happening.

Hezekiah knew what to do when trouble came. He knew that God would speak to him through Isaiah the prophet. Isaiah sent a reply to Hezekiah, telling him not to be afraid of what the Assyrians had said. Then Hezekiah received a letter from the King of Assyria. In the letter Sennacherib said that no one had been saved from the Assyrians by their gods. He also said that the God of Judah would not save Hezekiah and his people.

When Hezekiah read the letter, he went to the temple.

2 Kings chapter 19 verses 14-19.

Hezekiah wanted God to keep the people of Judah safe. Hezekiah wanted the people in the lands around Judah to know that there is only one true God. He knew that people could not be helped by idols. He trusted in the God who could save His people. He wanted others to worship the living God, not useless idols.

God heard Hezekiah's prayer and gave His answer through the prophet Isaiah. God promised that He would keep Jerusalem safe and that the King of Assyria would go back to his own land. Sennacherib did return to Assyria without fighting the people of Jerusalem.

What did Hezekiah do with the letter Sennacherib sent to him?

Day 177: KING MANASSEH

King Hezekiah became very ill and Isaiah told him that he must prepare himself to die. When Hezekiah prayed, God heard him and promised that he would get well and live for fifteen more years.

About three years after this, Hezekiah's son Manasseh was born.

Manasseh became King of Judah when he was only twelve years old. He was king for fifty-five years. Instead of continuing the good things that his father had done, Manasseh encouraged the people to worship idols. He placed altars for the idols around the temple. He even placed an idol inside the temple, where God had chosen to meet with His people.

God sent prophets to warn Manasseh that the people would suffer because they had disobeyed God. Manasseh would not listen to the prophets. Soldiers came from the King of Assyria and took Manasseh away to Babylon.

While he was there the king prayed that God would help him.

2 Chronicles chapter 33 verses 12-16.

Manasseh would not give up his idols or the other wicked things he did, until God brought great trouble on him. After he was brought back to Jerusalem he did show that he was truly sorry for his sin. We know this because he took the idols away and told the people that they must worship God.

How old was Manasseh when he became king? For how long did he reign? (2 Chronicles chapter 33 verse 1).

Day 178: GOD'S LAW IS FOUND

For two years Manasseh's son Amon was king. He was a very wicked king and he was killed by his own servants. Amon's son Josiah was only eight years old when his father died. The people of Judah made him their king. Josiah was very different from his father and his grandfather.

When he was about sixteen years old Josiah began to want to know God.

Four years later he started to destroy the idols and images that were all over the land. After a few more years had passed, Josiah realised that a lot of work needed to be done at the temple. Workmen were brought in and the Levites made sure that the repairs were done properly.

While the work was being done, Hilkiah the priest found something in the temple.

2 Chronicles chapter 34 verses 14-18.

Many people think that the part of the Bible that Hilkiah found was Deuteronomy. In that book, Moses told the people that God would be with them to help them, if they obeyed Him. But He also warned them that if they disobeyed God, they would be taken away from their own land. Josiah heard what was in the book, and was very sad. He knew the people had disobeyed God. For many years they had worshipped idols. Josiah sent men to see a lady named Huldah who was a prophetess. He did this because he wanted to hear what God would say about His people.

What did Josiah destroy and what did he repair?

Day 179: A PROMISE TO OBEY

It is good to be warned when there is danger. You may have seen notices on the beach telling you where it is safe to bathe and where it would be unsafe. When warnings like that are given, it is wise to obey.

God had given many warnings to His people, but they had disobeyed Him. Huldah told Josiah that God said that terrible things would happen to the people of Judah because of their disobedience. But this would not be while Josiah was king. God knew that Josiah was truly sad because of the sins of the people. When the king heard the words of the prophetess, he gathered the people together at the temple.

GOD'S WORD

2 Chronicles chapter 34 verses 29-33.

Josiah stood before the people just as King Solomon had done many years before.

BY MYSELF

Josiah promised to obey God and he made sure that the people promised too.

After this, Josiah called the people together to keep the Passover. The king and the leaders of the people gave many lambs and goats from their own flocks. These were given to the people, so that all could take part in the feast.

EXTRA INFO

At Passover time the people remembered how God had brought them out of Egypt. It was a time of giving thanks to God for all that He had done for them.

ASK ABOUT

In what year of his reign did Josiah keep the Passover feast? (2 Chronicles chapter 35 verse 19). Can you name another king who kept the Passover feast? (2 Chronicles chapter 30 verse 1).

Sometimes we think a lot about what other people think of us. We would like people to think that we are very good, or clever, or good-looking. But it is much more important to know what God says about us.

We find what God says about King Josiah in 2 Kings chapter 23 verse 25.

Josiah loved God with all his heart. Sadly, when he had been King of Judah for thirty-one years, he was killed in a battle with the King of Egypt.

After Josiah's good reign, there were four kings of Judah who did not love or obey God. The first one, Jehoahaz, was king for just three months. After this he was taken away to the land of Egypt. The second one, Jehoiakim was king for eleven years. He was taken to Babylon by the King of Babylon whose name was Nebuchadnezzar. The next king was Jehoiachin. He was also taken to Babylon when he had been king for three months and three days. Many of the important people of Judah were taken captive at this time.

During the time of these three kings, God sent Jeremiah the prophet to tell them that they must change their ways.

Jeremiah chapter 36 verses 1-4.

God was ready to forgive His people if they would obey Him and do what was right.

When Jeremiah's words were read to Jehoiakim, he burned the writing in the fire. He would not ask God to forgive him. He was not willing to change.

Who wrote down the words of Jeremiah?

Day 181: JEREMIAH IS RESCUED

God had given Jeremiah a job to do that was not easy. He had to warn the kings and people of Judah that they would be taken away from their own land, if they did not obey God. But the people did not want to listen. They wanted to go their own way, worshipping idols and doing many things that were wrong.

The fourth king after Josiah was Zedekiah. Sometimes he listened to Jeremiah sometimes he didn't.

He would even listen to those who wanted Jeremiah to be kept in prison or put to death. One day some of the important men of Judah put Jeremiah down into a muddy dungeon. The king's servant, Ebed-Melech, saw this. He knew that Jeremiah was being left in the dungeon to starve to death. He decided that he would speak to the king about it.

Jeremiah chapter 38 verses 9-13.

After Jeremiah had been rescued from the dungeon, Zedekiah sent for him.

The king wanted Jeremiah to tell him what God said would happen to him.

Jeremiah told him to give himself up to the Babylonian princes. If he did not, the city of Jerusalem would be burned. Although the king knew that Jeremiah told him the truth, he did not do as he said. Zedekiah was afraid of what other people would say. He listened to the men who advised him instead of obeying God.

What was the name of the servant who rescued Jeremiah? (Jeremiah chapter 38 verse 7).

Day 182: CAPTIVITY

Do you remember what a siege is? It is when soldiers camp all round a city so that no one can go in or out. During Zedekiah's ninth year as King of Judah, the King of Babylon brought his army to besiege Jerusalem. The soldiers were there for more than a year, until there was no food left in the city. One night, King Zedekiah and his soldiers managed to escape from the city. They were not free for long: the Babylonian army went after them and Zedekiah was captured. He was chained and taken away to Babylon.

EXTRA INFO

Nebuzaradan came from Babylon to Jerusalem. He was an important man in King Nebuchadnezzar's army.

GOD'S WORD

2 Kings chapter 25 verses 8-12.

All the important people from Judah were captured. Only the poor were allowed to stay. The King of Babylon sent a message to Nebuzaradan. He said that Jeremiah should be allowed to stay in Judah.

God had sent the prophets Isaiah and Jeremiah to warn the people of Judah that they would be taken away from their land if they disobeyed God. Some of the kings, such as Hezekiah and Josiah, did love and obey God. But the people's hearts were not changed: they wanted to go their own way. How sad to see the temple and all the important buildings burnt down.

BY MYSELF

The walls of Jerusalem were broken down and in ruins. But God had not forgotten His people.

ASK ABOUT

Find God's promise to the people of Judah. (Jeremiah chapter 29 verses 10).

DAYS 183-185: JONAH

THE RELUCTANT PROPHET

Jonah was a prophet in the northern kingdom of Israel in the days of Jeroboam the 2nd. He was commissioned by God to warn the people of Nineveh of impending judgement. Nineveh was the capital city of Assyria and its people were both idolatrous and cruel. The account of Jonah's voyage away from Nineveh and his rescue by a large fish is well known. His subsequent obedience resulted in repentance by both king and people. Jonah learns a lesson about God's love and pity for the inhabitants of Nineveh. We see God's mercy towards Nineveh, but also His patience with Jonah, who received God's calling a second time.

There can be no doubt about the historical facts of this Book: the Lord Jesus Christ referred to both Jonah's experience inside the fish and also the repentance of the people of Nineveh.

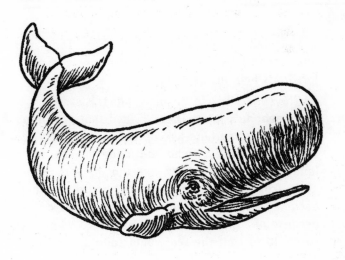

Day 183: JONAH DISOBEYS

Long ago, a man named Jonah lived in the northern part of the land of Israel.

He probably lived about eight hundred years before the birth of the Lord Jesus.

Jonah was a prophet: a man who God spoke to, so that he would give God's message to others.

Jonah chapter 1 verses 1-5.

Jonah knew that Nineveh was a great city in Assyria. The people there worshipped idols and were cruel to their enemies. Jonah did not want to go. He paid his fare and went on board a boat going the opposite way.

The storm that God sent caused even the sailors to be afraid.

They called on their idols to help them. They could not understand why Jonah was sleeping instead of praying for God's help in the storm.

The sailors began to think that this storm must be somebody's fault. They decided that Jonah must have done something wrong. Jonah told them that he worshipped the God who had made the sea and the land. Jonah also told the men that he was running away from God. When the sailors heard this they became even more afraid. If the storm had come because of Jonah, the sailors wondered what they could do so that the sea would calm down again.

Where did God tell Jonah to go? Where did he go instead?

Day 184: JONAH OBEYS GOD

Jonah thought that he could run away from God, but that is something that no one can do. With a terrible storm raging around them, the sailors asked Jonah what they should do.

Jonah chapter 1 verses 12-17.

Jonah told the men to throw him in the sea. The men did not want to. The sailors saw God's power when imediately the storm ended.

They realised that the God Jonah had spoken about was the true God.

God did not leave Jonah to drown. A big fish swallowed Jonah. For three days and nights he was inside an enormous fish. We cannot imagine what that was like. God heard Jonah's prayer, and caused the fish to vomit Jonah onto dry land. Then God spoke to Jonah for the second time and told him to go to Nineveh. This time Jonah obeyed.

As he walked into the great city, Jonah called out to the people. The message that he brought from God was a serious one. He simply told the people that in forty days a terrible disaster would strike the city. The people of Nineveh believed what Jonah said. They took off their usual clothes and put on sackcloth instead.

This was their way of showing that they were sorry for the wrong things they had done.

Even the king did this. He also said that no one should eat or drink, but that they should all cry out to God.

How long was Jonah inside the fish?

Day 185: A LESSON FOR JONAH

There were two things that Jonah knew. One was that the people of Nineveh were very wicked and deserved to be punished. The other was that if they were truly sorry for their sin, God would forgive them.

This was why Jonah did not want to go to Nineveh. He did not want those people to be forgiven.

God saw that they believed the message Jonah brought. They were willing to stop their wrong-doing. As Jonah had expected, God did not bring disaster on them.

God forgave their sin.

Jonah chapter 3 verse 10 and chapter 4 verses 1-3.

Jonah was God's messenger to Nineveh, and yet he had a lot to learn. He made a shelter to get away from the hot sun and sat outside the city. God prepared a plant that grew up and provided shade for Jonah. Jonah was glad to be protected from the strong sunlight. The next morning, God prepared a worm, that damaged the plant so much that it withered. Without the shade from the plant, Jonah began to feel ill. For the second time he said he wanted to die. Then God spoke to Jonah. God asked him whether it was right to be so angry about a plant. If Jonah felt so sorry about a plant, surely God should feel sorry for the people of Nineveh.

We should not want God to punish those who we think are very bad. We should remember that we too are sinful and need God to forgive us.

How many people lived in Nineveh? (Jonah chapter 4 verse 11).

DAYS 186-192: DANIEL

GOD'S PURPOSE AND GOD'S SERVANT

Chapters 1-6 of Daniel are mainly historical, 7-12 are mainly prophetic. As a teenager removed from Judah to exile in Babylon, Daniel's desire to obey God caused him to shun compromise. This loyalty to God characterised his life of high office in Babylon, Media and Persia.

The prophetic visions form an overview of the rise and fall of world empires, so accurate that at times the Book has had rough handling by critics. There can be no doubt, however, that the author was Daniel under the inspiration of the Holy Spirit.

Daniel was faithful in prayer, even when a political plot against him made prayer, for a time, illegal. His prayer in chapter 9 shows us the heart of this man of God as he intercedes for his people.

Day 186: DANIEL SAYS NO

In the days of the last Kings of Judah, some of the people were taken captive to the land of Babylon. Nebuchadnezzar, King of Babylon, decided to take the cleverest and best-looking young men from Judah.

He wanted young men who could learn the language of Babylon and serve him in his palace.

They would be given good food and wine, and would have teachers to prepare them for work.

Among these young men were Daniel, Hananiah, Mishael, and Azariah. Daniel decided not to eat the food or drink the wine that the king provided. The Bible does not tell us why he did this. It could be that the food had been offered to idols before it was brought to the table. Or it may have been that Daniel wanted to be sure that he did not eat anything that the people of Israel had been taught not to eat. Very politely, Daniel asked the king's servant if he and his three friends might have plainer food: vegetables to eat and water to drink. The servant was afraid that the king would be angry if these four young men did not look as strong as the others.

Daniel chapter 1 verses 11-16.

Daniel was a young man, probably a teenager. Even though he had been taken away from home and family, he was determined to obey God. At the end of three years training, Nebuchadnezzar found Daniel, and his friends better than the wise men of Babylon.

How long did Daniel and his friends ask to try the plain food, to make sure they did not become ill?

Day 187: THE KING'S DREAM

Sometimes we have good dreams. Sometimes we have bad dreams. Sometimes we have dreams that we cannot remember. One day Nebuchadnezzar called for all his wise men. He asked them to tell him what he had been dreaming about. The king was sure that his dream had an important meaning. His wise men said that they would tell him the meaning of his dream, if he would tell them what he had dreamed about. The king became angry and said that they would all be killed if they did not do as he asked. Of course no one could possibly know someone else's dream and the wise men told the king so.

Daniel chapter 2 verses 13-19.

Daniel believed that God could tell him what the king wanted to know. He asked his three friends to pray. God heard them. Daniel thanked God and was brought before the king. Nebuchadnezzar asked him to tell him about his dream. Daniel told the king that it was God who had shown him the dream and its' meaning. Daniel told Nebuchadnezzar about the great image he had seen in his dream. Like a great statue, it was made of gold, silver, bronze, iron and clay. The image was to teach Nebuchadnezzar about the great kingdoms that would arise in the world. The golden head meant Babylon.

The silver, bronze, iron and clay meant other kingdoms that would come afterwards.

Daniel also told the king about God's Kingdom that will last for ever.

What did Nebuchadnezzar say after Daniel had spoken? (Daniel chapter 2 verse 47).

Nebuchadnezzar made a golden statue that was nearly twenty-eight metres high and nearly three metres wide. All the important men in the land gathered around the statue. When they heard music being played, they had to bow down to the image. There was a terrible punishment for any who would not bow down: they would be thrown into a fiery furnace. So the people bowed down as they had been told.

EXTRA INFO

It seems that Daniel was not present while all this was going on, but his three friends were.

They had been given Babylonian names: Shadrach, Meshach and Abed-Nego. Some people saw that they did not bow down to the statue. When the king heard this, he became angry and sent for the three men. He gave them another chance to obey him.

GOD'S WORD

Daniel chapter 3 verses 16-18 and 23-25.

BY MYSELF

Daniel's friends knew that God did not want them to bow down to idols.

They believed that God could save them, but whether God saved them or not, they were determined to obey Him. They were put into the fiery furnace. When the king looked into the fire, he saw someone with them. The Bible does not tell us who this was, but either the Lord Jesus came Himself or He sent an angel. God protected Shadrach, Meshach and Abed-Nego. They were not hurt at all. The king realised that the God they worshipped is a great and powerful God.

ASK ABOUT

What Babylonian names were given to Hananiah, Mishael and Azariah? (Daniel chapter 1 verse 7).

Day 189: WRITING ON A WALL

Daniel stayed in Babylon for many years. One of the Kings who came after Nebuchadnezzar was called Belshazzar.

GOD'S WORD

Daniel chapter 5 verses 1-6.

The king was frightened when he saw fingers writing on the wall. He offered a great reward to anyone who could tell him what the writing meant. None of the wise men of Babylon could tell the king what it meant. The Queen Mother told the king about Daniel and very soon he was sent for. The king offered gifts to Daniel if he would tell him the meaning of the writing.

BY MYSELF

Daniel did not want the king's gifts.

He spoke truthfully to Belshazzar about how proud he was. He also made it very clear to the king how wrong it was to praise the idols of Babylon while drinking wine from golden cups taken from the temple at Jerusalem. Daniel told the king about the true God, who sent the fingers to write on the wall. Daniel then went on to explain the writing.

God helped Daniel to understand three things from the writing on the wall. Firstly, Belshazzar's kingdom had come to an end. Secondly, God was not satisfied with Belshazzar's life. Thirdly, Babylon was about to be taken over by other nations, the Medes and the Persians. That night Belshazzar was killed.

EXTRA INFO

A man named Darius the Mede became king. The great kingdom of Babylon had been conquered.

ASK ABOUT

What were the Babylonian idols made out of?

215

Day 190: A PLOT AGAINST DANIEL

Kings and Queens need people to help them rule over their lands. King Darius chose one hundred and twenty men to take charge of his empire.

These men were called satraps and over them were three governors.

Daniel was a governor. The king was so pleased with Daniel, and thought about making him the most important of all his people. The other governors and satraps did not like this. They decided to complain to the king about Daniel. But he did his work so well that they could not find anything wrong. However, these men knew that Daniel loved and obeyed God.

Daniel chapter 6 verses 4-10.

Even though Daniel had many things to do, he made sure that he prayed to God three times every day. The men who were planning against him knew that Daniel prayed. The new law that they had persuaded the king to sign, meant that anyone praying would be punished by being put into the lion's den. When Daniel heard about the law that the king had signed, he continued to pray just as he had done before.

He did not try to hide, but kept his window open towards Jerusalem.

He had been away for many years, but Daniel never forgot the temple at Jerusalem where God had promised to meet with His people.

How many times each day did Daniel pray?

Day 191: IN THE LION'S DEN

Who do you think was watching Daniel when he went to his room to pray? Of course, the governors and the satraps were all there, ready to hurry away to tell the king. When these men told the king that Daniel had broken the new law, Darius was very sorry. He probably realised that it had all been a plot to trap Daniel. All day long he tried to think of a way to save Daniel from the terrible punishment. Nothing could be done.

In that land, once the king had signed his name, the law could not be changed.

When evening came, Daniel's enemies made sure that the king did as the law said. Darius gave the order for Daniel to be taken to the den of lions. As he did so, he told Daniel that his God would save him. That night, the king could not eat or sleep. He got up very early in the morning and hurried to the den of lions.

Daniel chapter 6 verses 19-23.

The king was so glad to know that Daniel was safe. He sent for the governors and satraps who had wanted Daniel to be killed by the lions. They were punished by being put into the den themselves. They did not escape. Darius wrote to all the people of his empire to tell everyone about Daniel's God.

The king knew that the God Who saved Daniel from the lions is the true and living God.

Which king saw Daniel's friends saved from the fiery furnace? (Daniel chapter 3 verse 28).

When we read about the Kings of Israel, we find that some of them began well, but did not continue well. Even the wise King Solomon did not always obey God. In the Book of Daniel we read about a man who loved and obeyed God from when he was young to when he was very old. Living in a land where the people worshipped idols, Daniel worshipped the true God. If we, like Daniel, want to live lives that please God, then God Himself will help us.

God has not changed. The same God who was with Daniel, can be with us.

Do you remember the promise that God gave to the people of Judah in the time of Jeremiah the prophet? God promised that after seventy years of captivity, the people would return to their own land. Daniel read God's promise. He also knew the words that Moses had spoken many years before. Moses had warned the people that if they did not obey God, they would be taken away from their land. But Moses also said that if they began to obey God once again, then God would bring them back from captivity. Daniel prayed that God would forgive the sin of His people.

Daniel chapter 9 verses 3-6, and 18-19.

We do not read that Daniel was able to return to the land of Judah. But as God had promised, many others were able to do so.

Can you find some of the words Daniel used when he prayed? (1 Kings chapter 8 verse 47). Who had said these words? (1 Kings chapter 8 verse 22).

DAYS 193-198: EZRA

RETURN FROM EXILE

Ezra was a priest and scribe, with knowledge and understanding of God's Law. Chapters 1-6 of Ezra concern the first group of Jews who returned to Judah after seventy years captivity. At this time about fifty thousand made the journey led by Zerubbabel, who was a descendant of King David, born in exile. They met with opposition as they rebuilt the temple, but were encouraged by the prophets Haggai and Zechariah. It was at least sixty years after Zerubbabel's return that Ezra travelled to Jerusalem. Almost fifteen hundred men are listed who went with him. Ezra's great desire was to teach the Law to God's people. He was greatly distressed to learn of marriages with idol-worshippers, and wept as he confessed the sin of the people to God. Painful as it was, he had to deal with the situation. Idolatry led to many sinful practices: the people of God had to separate themselves from such things.

Day 193: THE JOURNEY BACK

It had been such a sad time for the people of Judah when King Nebuchadnezzar's soldiers took them from their own land to the land of Babylon. Years went by, and the Kingdom of Babylon was replaced by the Kingom of Persia. God had told Isaiah the prophet that there would be a king called Cyrus. God had said that this king would allow the people to go back to Jerusalem and build their temple again.

Ezra chapter 1 verses 1-5.

Not everyone was going to return to Judah. Some who stayed at Babylon gave gifts to help those who were setting out on the journey back.

About fifty thousand people travelled back to Judah, led by a man named Zerubbabel. Zerubbabel came from the family of King David. There was something very special that these people had to carry with them. King Cyrus gave them all the gold and silver that had been taken from the temple at Jerusalem. Altogether they had five hundred items of gold and silver to take back.

The people owned many horses, mules, camels and donkeys. They loaded their belongings on to their animals.

It was a long journey back to Jerusalem, but a much happier journey than the one the captives had made seventy years before. Ahead of them was a lot of work rebuilding their houses, the temple and the walls of the city.

Who told King Cyrus that the temple at Jerusalem should be rebuilt?

Day 194: A TIME TO GIVE THANKS

I wonder what were the most important things for the people to do when they arrived back in their own land? The first thing we read is that the heads of the families gave gifts so that the temple could be rebuilt. The second thing was for people to begin living in the cities that their families came from.

GOD'S WORD

Ezra chapter 3 verses 1-6.

You may remember that there were three special occasions in the seventh month of the year. The people came to Jerusalem even though the temple had not yet been rebuilt.

EXTRA INFO

Jeshua was the High Priest.

BY MYSELF

It was important that the altar was set up so that the people could bring their offerings.

After seventy long years of captivity, the Feast of Tabernacles could again be celebrated in Jerusalem. Soon money was collected to pay stonemasons and carpenters to work at the temple. Wood was brought by sea from Lebanon, as it had been in Solomon's time. The priests and Levites took charge of the work, to make sure everything was done properly. When the foundation of the temple was laid there was a special time of giving thanks to God. The priests sounded the trumpets and the Levites sang praise to God. The people joined in praising and thanking God: they shouted for joy. Some very old men who remembered Solomon's temple felt sad. They remembered the temple as it used to be.

ASK ABOUT

Who was Zerubbabel? What was the name of the High Priest?

Day 195: THE TEMPLE REBUILT

Have you ever started to make something and then found it to be more difficult than you expected? After the foundation of the temple had been laid, difficulties began to arise for the builders. Some people living in the land of Judah had been moved there from their own lands by the King of Assyria. They wanted to help build the temple. The people of Judah knew that this would hinder the work. They said that King Cyrus had told them to build the temple, and no one else. These people didn't like this and tried in every way they could to stop the building. For some years the work did stop. Then God sent two prophets to encourage the people to complete the work.

EXTRA INFO

One prophet was called Haggai and the other was named Zechariah.

Zerubbabel and Jeshua began to build again. Just at that time a letter was sent to King Darius. The Governor of the land wanted to know if King Cyrus had really said that the temple should be rebuilt. Cyrus was no longer king, but Darius said that a search must be made for Cyrus's words. A scroll was found with the words of Cyrus written on it. Darius sent a reply to the Governor, saying that the people of Judah must be given help to build the temple.

GOD'S WORD

Ezra chapter 6 verses 6-10.

The priests, the Levites and all the people gathered to celebrate and to give thanks to God.

BY MYSELF

At last the temple was finished.

ASK ABOUT

What did King Darius want the priests to do for him?

Day 196: EZRA'S JOURNEY

The people who had come to the land of Judah with Zerubbabel settled down in their own homes. Sixty or more years went by and the Persian Empire had a new king named Artaxerxes. At this time Ezra the priest was living in Babylon. He studied the laws that God had given in the time of Moses. He wanted to make the journey to Judah so that he could teach the people God's law. Ezra knew that it was important that the people should obey God. They had been taken away from their land because of their disobedience. Now they needed to know the way God said they should live their lives.

King Artaxerxes wrote a letter giving Ezra permission to go to Jerusalem. He was to take with him any of the people, especially the priests and Levites, who wanted to go. The king also gave gold and silver for the temple to Ezra. In his letter the king gave Ezra a job to do in the land of Judah.

GOD'S WORD

Ezra chapter 7 verses 25-28.

The Kings of Persia ruled many lands. They wanted people to live peacefully in their own countries. King Artaxerxes saw that Ezra was the right man to help the people of Judah. Ezra believed that it was God who had caused the king to think in this way.

BY MYSELF

He thanked God for the king's help.

EXTRA INFO

He began gathering around him those who were willing to go to Jerusalem with him. Ahead of them was a journey of about nine hundred miles.

ASK ABOUT

What was the name of the very first High Priest? (Ezra chapter 7 verse 5; Exodus chapter 28 verse 1).

Day 197: A SAFE ARRIVAL

Travelling was not easy in Old Testament times. It was not only that there were no aeroplanes, trains or cars but it was also very dangerous. Men sometimes lay in wait to rob travellers of the goods they carried with them.

Ezra knew all about the dangers on the long journey to Jerusalem. He could have asked the king to send some soldiers with them to protect them. He had not done this because he told the king that God would look after His people. So at the beginning of the journey, Ezra called the people to pray.

They asked God to take care of them and their children, and to keep all their belongings safe.

God answered their prayers. Four months after leaving Babylon, they arrived safely at Jerusalem.

On the fourth day after arriving in Jerusalem, Ezra made sure that the gold and silver from the King of Babylon was taken to the temple. After that was done, Ezra received some very sad news. The leaders of the people came to tell him that some of the men had married women from other nations. This meant that once again there would be idol-worshippers among the families of Judah. Ezra was very, very sad. He knew that it was because they had worshipped idols that the people had been taken away from their land years before. God had been so good to them, allowing them to return home and yet His people were disobeying Him again.

Ezra chapter 9 verses 4-10.

What did Ezra tell the people to do at the beginning of their journey?

Day 198: THE PEOPLE ARE SORRY

The things that we do wrong often hurt others. The Bible calls the wrong things that we do 'sin'. The worst thing about sin is that when we sin, we disobey God.

God is very great and very wise. He is our Creator – He made us – and He knows what is best for us.

The men of Judah should not have married idol worshippers. God had warned them about this. Those who worshipped idols did many wicked things.

God's people should have shown other nations the right way to live, not copied them.

Ezra knew that what the people had done was very serious. As he prayed, he wept. Many of the people gathered around him weeping.

Ezra chapter 10 verses 1-4.

Ezra announced that all the men were to come to Jerusalem on a certain day. On that day, it rained heavily. It would take too long to speak to each person in turn so the men were told to go home. They would be sent for at set times to speak to their leaders.

We do not know what the leaders said to them. If the women were willing to give up their idols and obey God, they probably would have been allowed to stay. But those who would not obey God were sent back to their own people. This must have caused a lot of sadness. The people were learning to be truly sorry for their sin.

Who was it that said there was still hope?

DAYS 199-204: NEHEMIAH

PRAYER AND ACTION

Nehemiah was cupbearer to the Persian King Artaxerxes and a contemporary of Ezra's. Chapters 1-6 show how Nehemiah made the journey to Jerusalem, where he oversaw the rebuilding of the city walls in spite of opposition. Chapter 7 gives a list of those who returned to Judah with Zerubbabel. The remaining chapters show how the preaching and teaching of God's Word by Ezra and the Levites resulted in the people entering into a covenant to keep the Law of God. But they failed to keep it and Nehemiah, after a further period at the court of Artaxerxes, returned and dealt with the situation. Nehemiah a man of action and a man of prayer, ever conscious of the greatness of the God he served.

Day 199: NEWS FROM JERUSALEM

In Persia, which we now call Iran, there was a city called Susa. In this city the Kings of Persia had their palaces. One day some men from Judah came to Susa. There they met Nehemiah who was cupbearer to King Artaxerxes.

The cupbearer was in charge of the king's wine. He tasted the wine first to make sure it wasn't poisoned.

Nehemiah was able to ask his visitors about Jerusalem and the people who had returned to Judah.

The news that they gave him was not good.

Nehemiah chapter 1 verses 1-6.

Nehemiah was troubled about the state of Jerusalem. For several months he thought and prayed about it. Then one day, when Nehemiah took wine to King Artaxerxes, the king noticed that Nehemiah was sad. Nehemiah was able to tell the king how sorry he was about Jerusalem, the city his family had once lived in. The king asked Nehemiah what he wanted. Without speaking aloud Nehemiah prayed to God. He asked the king for permission to go to Jerusalem to rebuild the city walls. King Artaxerxes agreed to allow Nehemiah time to do this. He also gave letters to Nehemiah, saying that he could travel to Judah and also have wood from the king's forest for the city gates. The king sent soldiers to protect Nehemiah on his journey. God had answered Nehemiah's prayers. He had all he needed to make the journey to Jerusalem.

What was the name of the keeper of the king's forest? (Nehemiah chapter 2 verse 8).

Day 200: THE WORK BEGINS

When people work for God, they often find that there are difficulties to overcome. Two men were unhappy to hear that Nehemiah had come to help the people of Judah. Their names were Sanballat and Tobiah.

Nehemiah stayed for three days in Jerusalem without telling anyone what he hoped to do.

One night he went round the walls of the city to see exactly what needed to be done. Then he called together the leaders of the people.

Nehemiah chapter 2 verses 16-20.

Nehemiah encouraged the people to work.

They were laughed at by Sanballat and Tobiah as well as by a third man named Geshem. In the Book of Nehemiah chapter 3 we have a list of people who helped to build the walls of Jerusalem. The priests and the Levites, the people and their leaders all joined in. But one group of people did not work as hard as they should have done. This chapter reminds us that God knows each of us by name. He knows when we try to please Him and help others to know about Jesus. He also knows when we are lazy.

Sanballat was angry when he saw that the walls were being rebuilt. Tobiah made fun of the work. He said that even a fox climbing on to the wall would break it down. Nehemiah knew what they were saying. He prayed to God about it and the building went on.

Who laughed at the builders?

Day 201: THE ENEMIES' PLANS

Sanballat, Tobiah and others, planned a secret attack on the men who were building the walls of Jerusalem. But Nehemiah heard about it.

Nehemiah chapter 4 verses 11-16.

Nehemiah reminded the people that they had a great God. He set men to guard those who were working on the wall. Even the builders carried swords. They were ready to help others whenever the trumpet sounded as a signal that there had been an attack. The plan to attack the builders failed because they were so well protected. Sanballat, Tobiah and Geshem tried to think of other ways to stop the work.

Four times they sent a message to Nehemiah, asking him to meet them, but he would not go.

Then a letter was brought to Nehemiah by Sanballat's servant. The letter said that the people of Judah were planning to rebel against King Artaxerxes, and make Nehemiah king. Nehemiah knew this was not true. They were trying to make him afraid so he would stop working. When this did not succeed, Nehemiah was invited to a secret meeting in the temple. He knew that Sanballat and Tobiah were still plotting against him. He did not go to the temple. Instead, he prayed and kept on with the work.

In spite of their enemies, the Jews finished the wall of Jerusalem in just fifty-two days.

How many times did Sanballat send the same message to Nehemiah? (Nehemiah chapter 6 verses 4 and 5).

Day 202: HEARING GOD'S LAW

The builders had faced so many difficulties that when the wall was finished even their enemies knew that God had helped them. When the gates were put in place, Nehemiah gave instructions about when they should be opened and how they should be guarded.

The gates had names such as Sheep Gate, Water Gate, Fish Gate and Horse Gate.

In front of the Water Gate was an open square. The people gathered there on the first day of the seventh month. They asked Ezra to bring the Book of the Law of Moses. Ezra stood on a platform that the people had made. All through the morning the people listened as he read God's law. The Levites helped them to understand it. God's law tells us how we should live: the things that we should do and the things that we must not do. When we read what God has said, we see what is wrong in our lives. This is what happened to the people of Judah as they listened to Ezra. They began to weep. Nehemiah, Ezra and the Levites comforted them. They told them that this was a day to rejoice and to share their food with one another.

The next day, all the people met together again.

Nehemiah chapter 8 verses 13-18.

The feast of tabernacles was a very happy time of giving thanks to God. The people brought branches from the trees to make shelters for themselves. This had been forgotten, until Ezra came to teach them the words that Moses had written long before.

What did the people make for Ezra? (Nehemiah chapter 8 verses 4 and 5).

Day 203: REMEMBERING

Sometimes it is good to remember things that have happened to us. We can remember kind people that we've met and places that we have visited. We can even remember the mistakes we have made so that we will be careful not to make the same mistakes again.

One day some Levites reminded the people of Judah of all that God had done for them. They spoke about how God had chosen Abram and promised the land of Canaan to his family. They spoke about the time when God brought His people out of Egypt and how Moses became their leader. They remembered how God had led them through the desert for forty years until they were able to live in their own land. The Levites spoke of how patient God had been when His people disobeyed Him. and how he forgave them and saved them from their enemies. But then they had been taken captive by other nations, because of their sin.

GOD'S WORD

Nehemiah chapter 9 verses 32-35.

EXTRA INFO

The Levites spoke to God, but with all the people listening.

Then Nehemiah and the people made a promise that they would obey God. They promised not to marry those who worshipped idols. They promised to keep the Sabbath day as a special day. They also promised that they would look after the temple and bring their offerings to the priests and Levites.

BY MYSELF

The people of Judah knew that while they obeyed God, He would be with them and protect them.

ASK ABOUT

What words did the Lord Jesus say about obeying God's commands? (John chapter 14 verse 15).

Day 204: BROKEN PROMISES

When we make a promise we should do what we have said. Sometime after the people of Judah had made promises to God, Nehemiah went back to King Artaxerxes. On his return to Jerusalem, he found that the people had already broken their promises.

In the temple there was a large storeroom where food for the Levites was kept. The priest, whose name was Eliashib, had given this room to Tobiah. It seems strange that this man who had caused so much trouble when the walls were being built, was now living in the temple. The Levites who were not being provided with food, had gone back to their homes. Nehemiah was very sad to see this. He removed Tobiah from the temple and made sure that the offerings for the Levites were stored as they should have been.

Nehemiah remembered his promise to care for the temple, even though others had quickly forgotten.

Nehemiah chapter 13 verses 15-18.

The people had broken their promise to keep the Sabbath day special. Nehemiah made sure that the gates of Jerusalem were shut on the Sabbath day. The third promise they made was not to marry people who worshipped idols. Some had even broken this promise. Nehemiah reminded them that even King Solomon had sinned in this way.

Nehemiah loved and obeyed God. With Ezra, he taught the people to do this too.

What were the three promises that the people of Judah made?

SAVED FROM DESTRUCTION

The events recorded in this Book took place between the return to Jerusalem under Zerubbabel and that under Ezra. The Book shows the providential overruling of circumstances by God, although the name of God does not appear in it. Whilst in exile, during the reign of King Ahasuerus, the Jews became the subject of a plan to annihilate them. It is no coincidence that the elimination of the Jewish nation would have meant the elimination of the Messianic line. The book of Esther reminds us that no circumstance can thwart the purposes of God. Mordecai's insight in this matter is seen in his question to Esther in chapter 4 verse 14. God's solution was in place before the evil plan was drawn up.

Day 205: THE KING'S FEAST

We have read about three separate journeys from
Babylon to Judah. The first was when Zerubbabel led
the people back to their own land. The second was
Ezra's journey bringing more people back to Judah.
Then Nehemiah travelled to Jerusalem. Not all of the
Jewish people returned. Some remained in the places
where their families had been taken captive.

In the Book of Esther we read about events in the land
of Persia after Zerubbabel had gone to Judah. The King
of Persia after King Darius, was called Ahasuerus.

He is sometimes called King Xerxes.

The king decided to hold a great feast to show
everyone how wonderful his kingdom was.

Esther chapter 1 verses 1-7.

Queen Vashti made a feast for the women who lived
in the palace. She was very beautiful. On the last day
of his feast, the king sent for her. King Ahasuerus
had been drinking wine and wanted to show off his
beautiful queen. Vashti would not come. The king
was very angry. He sent for his wise men to ask their
advice. One of them, whose name was Memucan, said
that women all over the kingdom would hear about
what the queen had done. They would then begin to
disobey their husbands. Memucan suggested that the
king should send out letters to all the countries of the
empire. The people should be told that Vashti was no
longer queen because she had not obeyed the king.
Every husband was to be the master of his own house.

**For how many days did King Ahasuerus
display his wealth and splendour?**

Day 206: THE NEW QUEEN

Sometimes, when we are angry, we do things that we feel sorry about afterwards. It may be that King Ahasuerus was sorry that he had sent Vashti away. As time went by he thought about her and about why she was no longer queen.

The king's servants suggested to the king that beautiful young women should be brought from all over the kingdom. Ahasuerus would be able choose a new queen. The plan was agreed to and many young women were brought to the palace at Susa.

At the time this was happening, a man named Mordecai lived in Susa. Mordecai's family had been taken away from Jerusalem in the days of King Nebuchadnezzar. Mordecai had a young cousin named Esther who had no mother or father. He had looked after her as though she was his own daughter. She grew into a beautiful young woman and was one of those who were taken to the palace.

Out of all the women the king loved Esther the best and chose her to be the queen.

He placed the royal crown on her head. The king did not know that Esther belonged to the Jewish nation. Mordecai had told her not to mention this and she obeyed him. One day Mordecai heard two of the king's servants plotting against the king.

Esther chapter 2 verses 20-23.

No reward was given to Mordecai for saving the king's life, but what he had done was written down.

Can you find three things that the king did to celebrate Esther becoming queen? (Esther chapter 2 verse 18).

King Ahasuerus chose Haman to be the most important man in the land after himself. The king ordered all his servants to bow to Haman, but Mordecai would not.

GOD'S WORD

Esther chapter 3 verses 1-6.

Mordecai must have believed it was wrong to bow to Haman. He would not have known how angry Haman would get or that he would plot to destroy the Jews.

Haman told the king that some people in his kingdom did not obey his laws. He asked the king to destroy them. The king did not try to find out whether it was true. He gave Haman permission to do as he thought right. Haman sent letters to every part of the empire, in the name of the king. On the thirteenth day of the twelfth month, every Jew, young or old, was to be killed. The Jews heard this and were very distressed.

EXTRA INFO

People wore sackcloth instead of their usual clothes in order to show their sorrow.

Mordecai went about the city dressed in sackcloth. Esther's servants told her about this and she sent clothes to him. Mordecai would not take the clothes.

BY MYSELF

Esther sent one of the king's servants to find out what was wrong.

Mordecai told the servant all about the letter and gave him a copy to show to Esther. He thought that when Esther understood her people's danger, she could go and speak to the king about it.

ASK ABOUT

What was the name of the servant that Esther sent to Mordecai? (Esther chapter 4 verse 5).

Day 208: THE GOLDEN SCEPTRE

When a king or queen is crowned, they are given a sceptre. This is a golden staff, or stick, which is a sign of royal power. King Ahasuerus had a golden sceptre and he used it to show his power over his people.

When Esther knew that Mordecai expected her to go to the king, she explained that no one was allowed to go to the king unless they had been sent for. Anyone trying to reach the king would be put to death, unless the king held out the golden sceptre.

Mordecai sent a reply to Esther. He told her that she would not be safe just because she was in the palace. He asked her whether she may have become queen just for this time, so she could help her people. Esther knew that she must do as Mordecai had asked her.

It was dangerous for Esther to approach the king uninvited, even though she was the queen.

She asked Mordecai to gather all the Jews in Susa for three days of fasting. Fasting means going without food so as to give time to pray for God's help. Esther also kept the days of fasting before going to the king.

Esther chapter 5 verses 1-5.

In the Book of Esther we do not read God's name, but we find that God is looking after His people.

Esther was allowed to speak to the king, but she did not hurry to explain why she had come. She invited the king and Haman to a special meal the next day.

What happened to anyone who came to see the king if he did not hold out the golden sceptre?

Day 209: MORDECAI'S GREAT DAY

After he had been to the first of Esther's banquets, Haman was very happy. He told his wife and friends that he was the only person invited to go with the king. But one thing made Haman angry: Mordecai still would not bow down to him. His wife and friends told him to make a gallows about twenty-three metres high and ask the king's permission to hang Mordecai on it. After that, Haman would be able to enjoy the queen's second banquet. Haman agreed that he would do this.

Esther chapter 6 verses 1-10.

At last the king knew that Mordecai had once saved his life but had not been rewarded. The great honour that Haman wanted for himself was now for Mordecai.

Proud Haman, who had been planning to kill Mordecai, had to lead him through the city square.

While Haman was telling his wife what had happened, the king's servants came to remind him that Queen Esther's banquet was ready. This time, when the king asked Esther what it was that she wanted, she asked him to spare her life and the lives of her people.

Esther explained that she and her people were going to be destroyed.

Ahasuerus asked who would do such a thing. Esther told him that it was Haman. Haman had been proud to be the king's favourite. He had made wicked plans to destroy the Jews. Now he waited in great fear to know what would happen to him.

What happened to Mordecai that Haman had really planned for himself?

Day 210: HAMAN'S PUNISHMENT

King Ahasuerus was very angry when he heard what Haman had planned to do. He left the banquet and went into the palace gardens. The person he had trusted, was really very wicked.

Haman knew his life was in danger. He pleaded with Esther to save him. When the king came in from the garden, a servant told him about the gallows that Haman had made. The king gave the command for Haman to be hanged on them.

Everything that had belonged to Haman was given to Esther. She had told the king that Mordecai was related to her. The king then gave Mordecai the position that had been Haman's. He became the most important person in the land apart from the king.

In the days of the Kings of Persia, once a king had issued a command, it could not be altered.

Letters had been sent all over the empire ordering the destruction of the Jews on the thirteenth day of the twelfth month.

Esther spoke to the king about this.

Esther chapter 8 verses 3-8.

What Haman had written in the name of the king could not be altered. But Esther and Mordecai were given permission to send out another letter. This letter told the Jews that they could gather together to defend themselves against anyone who attacked them.

What happened to Esther when she went to see the king for the second time?

Day 211: THE JEWS ARE SAVED

God is not actually mentioned by name in the Book of Esther, but we can see how He was looking after the Jewish people. When King Ahasuerus chose Esther to be his queen, God was in control. Can you remember one very important reason why God would not allow anyone to destroy the Jews?

We read in the Book of Genesis of how, long ago, God called a man named Abraham to leave his home and travel to the land of Canaan.

God said that the promised Saviour would come into the world through the family of Abraham.

Abraham's family grew into the nation of Israel.

The people of Israel became known as the Jews. Haman's plot to destroy the Jews could not succeed because no-one can change what God has planned.

When the thirteenth day of the twelfth month came, the Jewish people fought against those who attacked them. Some of the people were killed, but the Jews did not take any of their possessions for themselves. They did not hurt anyone who did not attack them. The Jews were not destroyed as Haman had planned: they were saved from their enemies.

Queen Esther and Mordecai sent letters to all the Jewish people in every land. They said that every year there should be a special day of celebration to remember how they had been kept safe. This was to be known as the feast of Purim.

Esther chapter 9 verses 29-32.

Who became the next most important person to the king? (Esther chapter 10 verse 3).

WHEN THE RIGHTEOUS SUFFER

The book of Job is probably the oldest book in the Bible, written during or before the Patriarchs. It deals with the suffering of a godly man, who is condemned by friends who should have comforted him. Chapters 1 and 2 give us a behind-the-scenes view which Job did not have. In fact he was never given a specific answer to his problem. Chapters 3-37 record the lengthy discussion between Job and his four friends. Job defends his integrity against his friends' accusations. In the closing chapters of the book, Job received such a view of the wisdom and power of God that he ceased to question God's dealings with him. The book ends with blessings not only restored but increased.

Day 212: A TERRIBLE DAY

In the book of Genesis we read about God's enemy the devil who tempted Eve to disobey God.

He is sometimes called by another name, Satan.

The Bible tells us that he was once like one of the angels but he became proud and wanted to be like God. He has continued to tempt people to do wrong.

The devil tries to stop people understanding and loving God.

Long ago there lived a man whose name was Job. Job was a very rich man and he loved and obeyed God.

Job chapter 1 verses 1-5.

God said that Job did what was right more than anyone on earth. Satan said that Job only loved God because God was good to him. If God took away Job's riches, Satan said that Job would hate God instead of loving Him. God let Satan do as he wished with Job's possessions, but he was not to hurt Job himself.

Then there came a terrible day for Job. All his oxen, donkeys and camels were stolen. His sheep were burned and most of his servants were dead. Then the worst news of all: his sons and daughters had all been killed when the house they were in fell on them. In one day Job had lost so much and yet he still worshipped God. He believed that the God who had given him his riches and his family had now taken them from him. He was not angry with God as Satan had expected.

How many children did Job have? How many sheep? How many camels?

Day 213: JOB'S FRIENDS

God knew everything that had happened to Job. He knew that Job still loved Him. He saw that Job still did what was right. Satan said that this was only because Job was fit and healthy. If Job had a dreadful illness Satan was sure that he would no longer love God. God allowed Satan to bring illness upon Job, but not an illness that would cause him to die. So after losing his family and his possessions, Job became very ill.

His whole body from his feet to the top of his head was covered with painful sores.

Job's wife saw his pain and distress. She told him that it was time he gave up his love for God.

Job said we must accept whatever God sends - good or bad.

News of all that had happened to Job reached his friends and they came to visit him.

Job chapter 2 verses 11-13.

At first his friends were so sorry that they could not speak. Because of his great sorrow and pain Job said that it would have been better if he had never lived at all. Job's friends began to talk. Each tried to persuade Job that he must be a wicked man. They were sure that God gave good things to those who obeyed Him, but punished those who did wrong. They were sure that Job was being punished. They wanted him to own up. A fourth friend joined in. None of them comforted Job in all his trouble.

What were the names of Job's friends? (Job chapter 2 verse 11 and chapter 32 verse 6).

Job had been a very rich man but he had not been selfish. He had given food and clothes to the poor. He had opened his house to travellers who needed somewhere to rest. Now that he was in trouble, it was hard to have friends who argued with him, instead of comforting him. Job did not understand why such terrible things had happened. But he still trusted in God and waited for God to speak to him.

God spoke to Job, but did not tell him why he had suffered so much. God asked Job questions instead.

GOD'S WORD

Job chapter 38 verses 4-11.

God spoke to Job about His creation: the earth and the sea; the sky and the stars; the birds and animals that He had made. As God spoke to him, Job realised how wise and how powerful God is. He no longer needed to ask God any questions. He knew that he could trust this great God.

God said that Job's friends must bring an offering and that Job would pray for them, because they had said things about God that were not right.

God made Job even more wealthy than he had been before. Once again he had seven sons and three daughters. He lived to be a very old man.

BY MYSELF

The book of Job shows us that life is not always easy, even when we love and obey God.

EXTRA INFO

When sad things happen, we can learn to trust in God. The God who made the world will not make any mistakes in our lives.

ASK ABOUT

What were the names of Job's three daughters? (Job chapter 42 verse 14).

HYMNS AND PRAYERS

The book of Psalms is a hymnbook for private use and public worship. It is also a book of prayer, where we see the people of God in every situation of life: times of sorrow, suffering and conflict; times of thanksgiving, praise and blessing. In introducing children to this book, we show them that God's people will want to give Him praise and thanksgiving. We show them also that they can bring their sorrow over sin, their questions, doubts and fears to the God who is the same today as He was when the Psalmist called upon Him.

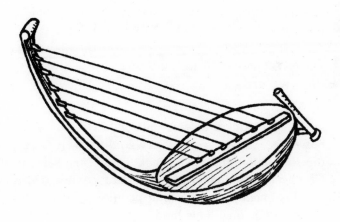

Day 215: THE BOOK OF PSALMS

When Christians meet together, they often sing hymns or songs to thank God for His goodness and praise Him for his greatness.

The Book of Psalms was the hymnbook of the people of Israel. They are still sung by Christians today.

Many Psalms were written by David, and some by a man named Asaph. At least one Psalm was written by Moses and there are some whose writers are not known. All those who wrote the Psalms were helped by God, just as other writers of the Bible were. Today we will look at two Psalms that tell us about God's Power. In Psalm 8 verses 3 and 4 David was thinking about the sky at night.

Psalm 8 verses 3-4;
Psalm 19 verses 1-4.

These verses teach us that God is much greater than we are.

In Psalm 19 David tells us that by looking at what God has made we can see how powerful He is. It is as if the sun, moon and stars speak to us. They seem to say 'The God who made us is very great'. As we read the Old Testament, we learn that people often bow down to idols that they have made. Idols of gold, silver, wood or stone cannot see or hear. They cannot help those who pray to them. In Psalm19 David tells us that all over the world people can see what God has made. As we look at the sun, the moon and the stars, we know that the one who made them is a great God.

What is it that we are to look after? (Psalm 8 verses 6-8)

Day 216: PSALMS OF PRAISE

Do you know what it means to praise somebody? We praise those who do a job well or make something useful or beautiful. We also praise people because we admire them and want them to know that we do.

There are many Psalms that praise God for who He is and for what He has done. We should certainly want to praise God for the wonderful world that He has made. The words of the Psalms help us to do this.

We should thank God for giving us life and so many good things.

Psalm 100.

We do not know the name of the person who wrote these words, but he tells us that we should praise God joyfully and gladly. The reasons why he says this are in the last verse of the Psalm. God is good: we can be sure that what God does will always be right. We can also be sure that God always does what is best for His people. God's mercy and His love last for ever.

God's mercy means that we do not receive the punishment we deserve for the wrong things we do.

God shows mercy to all those who trust in the Lord Jesus, because He has taken their punishment.

The third reason we find in this verse for praising God, is that God's truth lasts forever. People may change their minds and even forget their promises. God is not like that. He does not change. He always does what He says He will do. Think about things that you can say thank you to God for.

In what way should we praise God? (Psalm 100 verse 2).

Day 217: PSALMS FOR A JOURNEY

You will remember that the people of Israel had special days such as the Passover and the Feast of Tabernacles. They used to travel to Jerusalem for these feast days each year. There were certain Psalms that they would sing together on their journey.

These Psalms are Psalms 120 –134, which in many Bibles are each called 'A Song of Ascents'. Today's Bible reading, Psalm 122 was written by King David.

Psalm 122.

David loved the place where the people met to worship God.

In David's lifetime the Jewish people still worshipped God in a tent. The temple was built by Solomon. In the temple there was the gold-covered box called the 'Ark of the Covenant'. We read about this in Exodus. The temple was where God had promised to meet with His people. Each time they made the journey there they must have been reminded that God was with them.

Sometimes people go on a pilgrimage: a journey to a place they think is special. The journey to Jerusalem was God's choice: He told His people to gather there.

The visits to Jerusalem each year must have been very happy, but we do not have to go to a special place to meet with God. The Lord Jesus promised to be with His people always. Wherever we are, we can know that God hears us when we pray to Him.

What made King David glad?

Day 218: PSALMS THAT SAY SORRY

Have you ever felt sad because you have done something wrong? Perhaps you have said something that was not true, or maybe you have been unkind to a friend or to someone in your family. When we have done wrong, we know that we need to be forgiven. We need to tell the person we have hurt that we are truly sorry for what we have done. In the Bible we read that God says we should love others as much as our selves.

The Lord Jesus said that we should do the things for others that we would like them to do for us. When we do wrong to someone, we disobey God.

Some of the Psalms were written by men who felt very sad because of their sins.

In Psalm 38, King David says that his sins are like a heavy load, making him very sorrowful. You will remember that he also wrote Psalm 51, after he had taken another man's wife for himself.

Psalm 51 verses 1-4, and verse 10.

David knew that his sin was against God and so he asked God to have mercy on him: not to treat him as he deserved to be treated. He depended on God's mercy and love for forgiveness.

These Psalms help us when we are sad because of our sin. King David could only look forward to the time when God would send a Saviour into the world. We know that the Saviour has come and that because of His death we can be forgiven.

What sort of heart did David ask for?

Day 219: PSALMS OF PROMISE

When Adam and Eve sinned, God promised that He would send someone to overcome the evil that had entered the world. We learn more about this promised person as we read through the Old Testament. You will not be surprised then, to find that some of the Psalms are about the coming Saviour.

One of these, Psalm 22, was written by King David about a thousand years before the Lord Jesus was born in Bethlehem.

Psalm 22 describes what would happen when the Lord Jesus was crucified. David could only have written these words because God's Holy Spirit helped him.

We have seen that there are Psalms about God's power and about praising God. There are also Psalms for the journey to Jerusalem and Psalms about being sorry for our sin. Today we have seen that some Psalms tell us about God's promise to send a Saviour.

The longest Psalm in the Bible is about God's Word. We call the Bible God's Word because those who wrote the Bible were helped by God the Holy Spirit. The words that they wrote were from God Himself.

Psalm 119 verses 97-105.

The man who wrote this Psalm says that he loves God's law. This is because God's commandments teach us how to live.

We must remember that God made us and God knows what is best for us.

Which verse of Psalm 119 tells us that the Bible is like a light to show us where to go?

HOW TO LIVE WISELY

This book deals with many subjects which can be followed through its chapters. There are many contrasts, such as wisdom and folly, purity and impurity, diligence and laziness, soberness and drunkenness. As far as the notes are concerned, headings have been given which are easy to remember. The short readings have been chosen to show something of the wise teaching the book of Proverbs gives.

Day 220: WISE ADVICE

Have you ever heard anyone say 'Fine feathers do not make a fine bird', or, 'A stitch in time saves nine'? These are called proverbs, or wise sayings. There are lots of them and your Mums or Dads might be able to tell you some more.

In the Bible there is a book that is called The Book of Proverbs. Many of these wise sayings were written by King Solomon. God had given King Solomon great wisdom, so we could call this book 'How to live wisely'.

The Book of Proverbs contains wise advice. King Solomon tells us that only foolish people will not listen to advice.

A foolish person thinks that he knows everything. A wise person wants to find out what God says.

Proverbs chapter 3 verses 1-6.

People do all kinds of things to make themselves happy. Some people spend all their time trying to become rich and have lots of money. Others want to enjoy themselves all the time and never think of being helpful to other people. The verses we have read today remind us that we need God to show us the right way to live. If we will trust in God and always ask Him to help us, He promises that He will do so.

When we are travelling we use a map to help us find the way. God has given us this book full of wise advice so that we can find the right way through life.

What two things come to those who take the advice found in the Book of Proverbs?

Sometimes we see signs that warn us of danger. At the zoo we might see a sign that tells us not to put our hands into a cage.

If we take no notice of the warning, we are likely to have our fingers bitten.

Our parents warn us about things that would hurt us such as playing with fire or sharp knives. Our parents warn us about these things because they love us and do not want us to get hurt. In the Book of Proverbs God gives us many wise warnings. If we want to live wisely, we will take notice of these.

One thing this Book warns us about is the way we choose our friends. Proverbs chapter 12 verse 26 and chapter 13 verse 20 tell us to choose friends carefully. Wrong friendships harm us.

There are many verses in this Book that warn us about being lazy. The following verses remind us that we should work hard or expect to be poor.

Proverbs chapter 24 verses 30-34.

The Book of Proverbs warns those who tell lies or do other wrong things that one day they will be punished.

God wants us to be truthful and kind to others.

If we think that we do not need wise warnings we are foolish. If we listen to God in the Bible and ask Him to help us understand, we will be wise.

What happens at harvest time to a farmer who has not ploughed? (Proverbs chapter 20 verse 4)

Day 222: WISE THINGS

Sometimes we can learn lessons from the creatures that God has made.

When a man named Agur wanted to write about four wise creatures, he chose four that are very small.

Proverbs chapter 30 verses 24-28.

Have you ever watched ants scurrying about? They may not appear to be doing very much and yet they collect food for themselves. Even while you are quite small, you can store up words from the Bible that will help you as you grow up.

There are small animals called conies or rock badgers that are not very strong. These little creatures make their home in the rocks so that they can be safe.

God is like a Rock to everyone who trusts in Him. We may be weak, but He is strong.

We read about locusts in the Book of Exodus. They are like large grasshoppers. Each locust is quite small, but many go about together. This teaches us there are things that we cannot do on our own.

Some people do not like spiders very much, and would like to clear them out of their houses. But spiders even spin their webs in kings' palaces. They work at their webs and if one is swept away they begin again on another one. The Lord Jesus has work for even the youngest boy or girl who trusts in Him.

What were the four wise creatures from the Book of Proverbs chapter 30?

Day 223: WISE STEPS

However many miles you may walk, the distance you travel is made up of many steps. Every day we are on a journey through life, and that journey is made up of many steps. In Proverbs, God gives us directions so that we will take the right steps.

Proverbs chapter 1 verse 7.

The word fear in this verse does not mean that we are afraid of God as if He wanted to harm us. It means that we always remember that God made us.

God is very great and we are very small and weak compared with Him.

The first step in knowing how to live is to see God as much greater than we are. When we think of God in this way, we learn to love God and hate evil.

Proverbs chapter 3 verse 5.

This verse teaches us that an important step is to trust God. Every word He speaks is true. God is so powerful. He can always do what He says He will do.

Proverbs chapter 8 verse 33.

When we are born we do not have a map to help us through life. We need to listen to God. When we read our Bibles we listen to God. As we grow up we have many things to decide. If we listen to God, He will help us to find the right answers to these questions.

What is more precious than silver or gold? (Proverbs chapter 3 verses 13 and 14)

Day 224: WISE CHOICE

After the Lord Jesus rose from the dead, He was able to show His disciples that the Books of the Old Testament looked forward to His coming into the world. If you read all the wise sayings in the Book of Proverbs, you might wonder whether there is anything about the Lord Jesus in this Book.

There is one particular chapter where King Solomon begins by writing about wisdom, but as we read on, we realise that he is writing about the Son of God.

Proverbs chapter 8 verses 22-31.

In these verses we can see that God's Holy Spirit helped Solomon to write about the Lord Jesus. Before the earth was created, Jesus was with God his Father. When the sky and the sea and the dry land were made, Jesus was there. He was especially interested in the people He had made to live in His world.

The Lord Jesus has all the wisdom of God.

To know Jesus is to live wisely. To trust Him is to find life which lasts forever.

King Solomon was a wise man. He saw many people who were foolish, who would not listen to wise warnings. He saw people who chose to live for things that do not last.

In the Book of Proverbs God asks us to choose wisely. It is wise to ask the Lord Jesus to forgive us for the wrong things we have done. He will then be the One who teaches us to live in a right way.

Which verse tells us that the Lord Jesus was especially interested in people?

DAY 225: ECCLESIASTES

LIFE UNDER THE SUN

Here we have man's search for satisfaction and happiness in life. Knowledge, pleasure, wealth — in fact, everything the writer experiences fails to give what he seeks. Only at the close of the book are we directed to God and His commandments. How different from the futility of life seen in Ecclesiastes, is the abundant life which the Lord Jesus Christ gives to those who are His.

Day 225: THE PREACHER

Solomon wrote many of the wise words in Proverbs. He also wrote the next book in our Bible, 'Ecclesiastes', which means 'The Preacher'. We are to listen to these words just as we listen to a preacher in church.

This book tells us all about the things that people do to try to make themselves happy.

Being very wise, although it was good, did not make him happy. Even enjoying himself was not satisfying. Solomon had great houses and beautiful gardens made for himself. He had many servants and became rich.

Ecclesiastes chapter 2 verses 4-9.

Solomon enjoyed planning and working. But having everything he wanted, did not bring lasting happiness. Solomon thought about peoples' lives. Some people had very sad lives. Others were always working but never enjoyed their money. He saw people who were wicked and others who were kind and helpful. He saw the difference between wise people and foolish people.

This Book is all about life 'under the sun' which means life in this world.

Ecclesiastes teaches us that having lots of things only makes us happy for a time. In the last chapter Solomon tells us to remember the God who made us.

Knowing the Lord Jesus as our Saviour and Friend brings real happiness.

When does Solomon tell us to remember God? (Ecclesiastes chapter 12 verse 1)

PROCLAIMER OF GOD'S HOLINESS

It has not been possible to include readings from all the prophetic books. The last nine days of Old Testament readings give a simple introduction to the message of three of the prophets.

Isaiah prophesied about seven hundred years before Christ, through the reigns of Uzziah, Jotham, Ahaz and Hezekiah. After being given a vision of the Holiness of God, he was commissioned by God to speak to a people who would not want to hear the message he brought. Although chiefly addressed to Judah, Isaiah's prophecies also involved other nations. He exposed the shallowness of a religion which did not include care for the needy. He knew that the Babylonian captivity would come, because of the disobedience of the people. Isaiah spoke of the majesty and greatness of God, and of the birth, ministry and suffering of the Messiah. The idea of there being more than one author of this Book is not upheld by the New Testament writers, who consistently name Isaiah as the author of the words they quote.

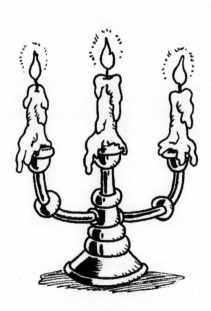

Day 226: GOD SENDS ISAIAH

A lady was pleased with her freshly washed, white sheets. Outside there was snow on the ground. She held up a sheet near the window, but it looked quite grey when she saw it against the pure white snow! Today we read about Isaiah, the prophet, who saw someone who is even purer and whiter than snow. When he saw the Lord Jesus on the throne he felt sinful and unclean, because Jesus is pure and Holy.

Isaiah the prophet also saw some angels called, seraphim.

Isaiah chapter 6 verses 1-5.

Isaiah lived in Jerusalem about seven hundred years before Jesus was born in Bethlehem. He saw the Lord Jesus as He was before He came to earth.

Jesus was always with God the Father in Heaven.

Even the seraphim, who are not sinful like us, cover their faces as they stand near God. When Isaiah was given this vision of Jesus, it is not surprising that he realised how sinful he was.

One of the seraphim touched Isaiah's mouth with a live coal from the altar. He told Isaiah that his sin had been taken away. Isaiah heard the Lord asking him who could He send. Now he knew that his sin was forgiven, Isaiah answered, 'Here am I! Send me'.

Isaiah was willing to take God's message to His people. He knew that this would not be easy and that the people would not want to listen to God.

Isaiah had a vision in the same year as somebody died. Who was the king who had died?

Day 227: THE NEED TO CHANGE

Sometimes we think we are good. We are like the lady with her white sheets. She thought they were as white as could be, until she saw how white the snow was.

When we begin to understand what God is like, we know that we are not good enough to please Him.

Isaiah had to remind the people that God is Holy and that God knew all about them.

They brought their offerings to the temple and kept the Sabbath days and feasts. But they did not look after the poor people. They did not help the widows, or children who had no one to care for them. When they brought offerings to the temple they were not truly sorry for their sin. They were pretending to be sorry, and then doing the same wrong things again.

Isaiah chapter 1 verses 16-20.

It was no use the people making offerings, while all the time they were greedy and would not share with the poor. When God shows us that we are sinful, He wants us to ask for his forgiveness and His help to do what is right. God promised that if the people would change their ways, He would forgive them.

Isaiah warned them that if they did not obey God, they would be taken away from their own land to the land of Babylon. God wanted His people to care for one another and to treat each other fairly. God's laws are good, but the people did not want to listen. They did not want to change their ways.

Who does God want his people to care for and look after?

Day 228: LOOKING FORWARD

In the Book of Isaiah we read messages that God gave to the prophet. There are warnings to Judah and some chapters about other nations. But there are also promises about the coming of the Lord Jesus. Isaiah looked forward to the time when the Son of God would come to the world. Lets look at a few of these verses.

Isaiah chapter 9 verses 6 and 7.

These verses tell us that a Child will be born, who is God. He will be a king from the family of King David. These things are difficult to understand because God is much greater than we are. We can never explain how the Son of God came from Heaven to be born as a baby. But it happened exactly as God said it would.

Isaiah chapter 53 verses 5 and 6.

Many years before Jesus was born, God told Isaiah what would happen when Jesus died on the cross.

These verses tell us about Someone who will be hurt because of the wrong things we have done.

We have all gone our own way instead of living as God says we should.

But God has laid the wrong things we have done on His own Son, so that He can take our punishment.

What Isaiah wrote in this chapter happened to Jesus. Only God could have given these words to Isaiah hundreds of years before Jesus came.

Can you find two words for the wrong things we do? (Isaiah chapter 53 verse 5)

COSTLY OBEDIENCE: THE MESSAGE REJECTED

Jeremiah prophesied from the time of King Josiah until Judah went into captivity. Appointed by God while he was still young, he called the people to return from their backsliding but his message was rejected. He suffered greatly at the hands of the people, at one time being put in the stocks and on another occasion lowered into a dungeon where he was left to sink into the mud. He also suffered because of his true concern for a people who refused to believe that they would not escape the consequences of their disobedience. He was greatly distressed by the presence of false pastors, prophets and priests who misled the people. There is, however, a message of hope in the Book of Jeremiah. He foresaw that the captivity would be for a limited period: after seventy years the exiles would return.

Day 229: GOD SPEAKS TO JEREMIAH

Jeremiah was the prophet rescued from a muddy dungeon. God sent him to speak to the people of Judah. Isaiah had brought God's messages to the people from the time of King Uzziah to the time of King Hezekiah. After this there were two Kings who taught the people to worship idols. Then the young King Josiah began to destroy the idols and called the people to love and obey God. In the thirteenth year of King Josiah's reign, God spoke to Jeremiah.

Jeremiah chapter 1 verses 6-9.

Jeremiah was still a young man when God told him that he was to be a prophet.

He felt that he could not speak to the people. God promised to be with him and give him the words to say.

Jeremiah continued speaking to the people of Judah until they were taken to Babylon in the days of King Zedekiah. Jeremiah was very sad when he saw the people bowing down to idols. He saw that they were turning away from the God who could help them, to pray to idols made of wood and stone. Jeremiah longed for them to listen to God.

God reminded Jeremiah of what had happened to the people living in the northern part of the land. They had broken God's commandments, until they were taken captive to the land of Assyria. The people of Judah knew about this and yet they did the same wrong things. God sent Jeremiah to tell them to leave their idols and call on the one true God.

Who was king when God first spoke to Jeremiah? (Jeremiah chapter 1 verse 2)

Day 230: AT THE POTTER'S HOUSE

Have you ever watched someone using a potter's wheel? A skilful potter, will be able to make something beautiful from a piece of clay.

While the wheel moves quickly round, the potter shapes the clay.

One day God told Jeremiah to go to the potter's house.

Jeremiah chapter 18 verses 1-6.

Jeremiah watched the potter at work. The bowl or pot that he was making got spoiled. Jeremiah might have expected the potter to throw away the broken pieces of clay. But the potter did not do this. Patiently he re-shaped the same clay until he was satisfied with what he had made.

God's people had not become the nation He wanted them to be, because they had disobeyed Him. But, like the potter, God is patient. God was willing to forgive His people and to teach them how they should live.

Jeremiah spoke to the people of Judah. He told them that God would bring a great disaster unless they stopped living such wicked lives. Their answer was that they would not change, but would live as they wanted to. Then Jeremiah had to tell the people that because they had prayed to idols that could not hear them, when they needed help, no help would be given. The people of Judah should have thanked God for sending Jeremiah to them. Instead they decided that they would not take any notice of what he said.

What is the word that God uses to describe the idols of the people of Judah? (Jeremiah chapter 18 verse 15)

Day 231: FALSE PROPHETS

Ill people need a doctor to tell them what is wrong and how to get better. A doctor who says nothing is wrong and lets an illness get worse, is no use.

Jeremiah told the people that if they changed their ways, God would help them. Other people said something quite different. There were men who were false prophets. God had not spoken to them, but they pretended that He had. They told the people not to listen to Jeremiah; everything would be all right. They did not warn the people that their enemies would overcome them because of the wrong things they did. The people of Judah liked listening to the false prophets. They treated Jeremiah cruelly even though everything he said was for their own good.

The message that Jeremiah gave the people was that they would be taken away from their own land to the land of Babylon. They would be kept there for seventy years. After that they would be allowed to return.

GOD'S WORD

Jeremiah chapter 29 verses 10-14.

Even though the people did not listen to Jeremiah, we can still learn from what he said. We learn how patient God is with His people. He is the One who truly cares for them.

BY MYSELF

God wants His people's lives to show that they belong to Him.

EXTRA INFO

Jeremiah had a hard life, but he knew that God was with him. Jeremiah's life shows us that God never leaves those who live for Him.

ASK ABOUT

When would God's people eventually turn to him and pray to him?

DAYS 232-234: Malachi

THE MESSENGER

Malachi was the last Old Testament prophet and he exercised his ministry about four hundred and fifty years before the birth of Christ. He had to oppose the people's wrong attitude to the worship of God and the priests' failure to instruct them. He reminded the people that God would bless them when they gave to Him what was rightfully His. Even after the hard lesson of captivity, the people of God were once again guilty of backsliding. But chapter three contains a message for those who remained faithful: God spoke of them as His special treasure. Genesis chapter three contains the first promise of the Old Testament and Malachi chapter four contains the last. Both speak of the coming of the Saviour.

Day 232: GOD'S MESSENGER

The Book of Malachi was written about 450 years before Jesus was born. God sent Malachi to speak to His people when they returned to Judah after the captivity. The temple had been rebuilt and the priests were there when the people brought their offerings.

EXTRA INFO

Malachi means messenger. He was the last Old Testament prophet to bring God's message to Judah.

The first message that Malachi brought the people was that God loved them. Life was not easy for them. They wondered whether God really did love them. Malachi had to tell them that the problem was in themselves.

BY MYSELF

God loved His people, but His people were not showing real love and obedience to Him.

When they brought offerings they should have brought the best that they had. Instead, they brought worthless animals. The priests should have taught the people to live as God had commanded. But they did not. They helped rich people before they helped the poor.

GOD'S WORD

Malachi chapter 2 verses 7-9.

These words are hard to understand. They teach us that God gave the priests a special task, but they did not care about it. The people knew this and so they did not respect the priests as they should have done.

There had been such joy when the temple was rebuilt. It is sad to find the people forgetting their great God. But God loved them so much that He sent Malachi to tell them what was going wrong.

ASK ABOUT

Who else should have been God's messenger as well as Malachi?

Day 233: GOD'S SPECIAL TREASURE

Moses spoke to the Israelites in the very last year of his life. He told them that if they obeyed God, God would keep them safe and they would have all they needed. If they disobeyed God then they would go through great trouble.

These words of Moses should have been read to the people, including the children, every seven years.

The words that Moses spoke were God's words and they came true. Yet they did not seem to learn their lesson.

In the time of Malachi, the people of Judah blamed God for their troubles. But they were doing things that were wrong. Some men married women who worshipped idols. Some left their wives because they wanted to be married to someone else. They still brought offerings to the temple, but they were not really sorry for the things they had done wrong.

Malachi told the people to obey God and to bring their offerings to the temple. God said that if they did this, He would give them so many good things that they would not know where to put them all.

There were still people in the land of Judah who loved God. God said that He would remember them and they would be His special treasure.

Malachi chapter 3 verses 16-18.

It is not easy to do right when all around you people do not love God or obey Him. These verses remind us that pleasing God is what really matters.

What did the people who loved God do? Who heard what they said?

Day 234: WAITING

All through the Old Testament we find God's promise to send a Saviour. It was first given after Adam and Eve sinned. It was repeated to Abraham and to King David. It is in the Psalms and in the Book of Isaiah. God reminds His people of the One who is coming. In Malachi we read the promise again.

Malachi chapter 3 verse 1.

The promised One is called 'The Lord': the One who has power over everything. He is also called 'The messenger of the covenant': the One who comes so that we can know God as our friend. The verse also speaks of one who will tell the people to prepare for the Saviour's coming. After Malachi brought God's message to the people, there were four hundred years when God did not send any prophets. During these years battles were fought and Israel was not free to manage its own affairs.

Israel came under the power of the Roman Empire.

In many parts of the Old Testament, the people of Israel were often in trouble because they did not obey God. Instead of teaching other nations about the One true God, they began to worship idols themselves.

But some people still loved and obeyed God.

They remembered God's promises and looked forward to when the Saviour would come.

Who will the people be told to prepare for? (Isaiah chapter 40 verses 3-5)

THE FOURFOLD WITNESS

In order to deal with events as far as possible in chronological order, readings have been taken from all four Gospels. After four hundred years of prophetic silence, the good news of the coming of the promised Saviour was announced. The life of the Lord Jesus Christ was recorded by four men: four accounts, distinct and yet confirming and complementing each other.

MATTHEW

Matthew was a tax collector called by the Lord Jesus Christ to be one of the twelve disciples. This Gospel contains many references to the fulfilment of Old Testament prophecy. Christ is particularly presented as the King of the Jews, being referred to in the very first verse as the Son of David, although the genealogy which follows begins with Abraham.

MARK

Mark knew Peter and others who were disciples even though he himself was not one of the twelve. This Gospel does not include either a genealogy or account of the birth of Christ. It begins with the ministry of John the Baptist and moves rapidly through events. Many people believe that much of the material in Mark's Gospel came to him directly from the Apostle Peter.

DAYS 235-312: The Gospels

LUKE

Luke was not one of the twelve disciples. He was a doctor, who accompanied Paul on some of his journeys. He begins his Gospel with an account of the birth of John the Baptist not found in the other three. He includes a genealogy which goes back to Adam, and is placed at the beginning of Christ's public ministry. As a Gentile, he wrote particularly for Gentiles.

JOHN

John was a fisherman who was called to become one of the twelve disciples of the Lord Jesus Christ. His stated purpose in writing was to witness to the deity of Christ, so that the reader would believe and find life (see John chapter 20 verse 31). Like Mark, he does not include a genealogy or account of the birth of Christ. He begins his Gospel with a statement of the Eternal nature of the Son of God. He includes a full account of the teaching the Lord gave to the disciples immediately before His trial and crucifixion.

Day 235: THE ANGEL'S MESSAGE

When a king or queen plans to visit a town, someone is sent on beforehand to make sure that everything is ready.

When the time came for God to send His Son into the world, He chose one man to tell the people to get ready.

Zacharias the priest and his wife Elizabeth loved God. They obeyed God's commandments and prayed to Him. As the years went by and they grew older, they still did not have a child of their own. Then one day, Zacharias went into the temple to burn incense. In the temple, beside the altar of incense, he saw an angel.

At first he was frightened, but the angel told him not to be afraid.

Luke chapter 1 verses 11-17.

Zacharias found it hard to believe what the angel had said because he and his wife Elizabeth were older than people usually are when they have children. The angel, whose name was Gabriel, told him that because he did not believe what he had said, he would not be able to speak until the baby was born.

The people who had been praying outside the temple, wondered why Zacharias had been such a long time. When he did come out, he could only make signs to them, because he could not speak. They realised that he had seen something special in the temple that day.

What name was Zacharias to give his son? Which verse tells us that he was to make people ready for the Lord?

Day 236: THE ANGEL VISITS MARY

While Zacharias and Elizabeth waited for their baby to be born, the angel Gabriel was again sent by God to speak to someone. This time he visited a lady whose name was Mary.

Mary lived in the town of Nazareth, and she belonged to the same family as Elizabeth.

Luke chapter 1 verses 26-33.

Mary was engaged to be married to a man named Joseph. An angel also appeared to Joseph in a dream. The angel explained to Joseph about the special baby who was to be born. He was told, just as Mary had been, that the baby was to be given the name Jesus.

'Jesus' means 'Saviour' for He would save His people from their sins.

Mary and Joseph were married, and Joseph looked after Mary until the baby was born.

In the first chapter of Matthew's Gospel there is a long list of names. The list begins with Abraham and ends with the Lord Jesus. Abraham lived about two thousand years before Jesus was born. The list of names shows us that the Lord Jesus was born into the family of Abraham. Does this remind you of God's promise to Abraham? Look at Genesis chapter 22 verse 18. God promised that through Abraham's family, good would come to people all over the world. As we read the New Testament, we will see how God did as He had promised.

What was the name of the mother of the Lord Jesus? Which verse tells us that Jesus is the Son of God?

Day 237: ZACHARIAS SPEAKS

Do you know what is one of the very first things that happen after a baby is born? The baby is given a name. The name is usually chosen by the baby's mother and father.

When Elizabeth's baby was born her friends and her family were very pleased. They knew that Zacharias and Elizabeth had waited a long time for their baby. They expected that the baby would be called Zacharias like his father, but Elizabeth told them that he was going to be called John.

This was a surprise. No one in the family was called John.

The people who had come to see the new baby looked to see what Zacharias would do. Zacharias had been unable to speak since the angel had spoken to him. He wrote the words, 'His name is John'. As soon as he had done this, Zacharias was able to speak again. The news of all that had happened to Zacharias and Elizabeth spread to the people who lived nearby.

Everyone who heard about it wondered what sort of person John would be when he grew up.

They thought that God must have some special job for him to do. Now that Zacharias was able to speak, he praised and thanked God for remembering His promise to Abraham. God's Holy Spirit helped him to understand the work that John would do one day.

Luke chapter 1 verses 76-80.

Why had Zacharias been unable to speak? Why were the people surprised that the baby was to be called John?

Day 238: BETHLEHEM

Long ago, there was a great empire called the Roman Empire. The Roman Empire ruled over many countries, including the land of Israel.

The ruler was not called a king: his title was 'Caesar'.

While Mary and Joseph waited for the promised baby to be born, Caesar Augustus gave an order. Everyone in the Empire must go to their own town to have their names registered.

If you look at Matthew chapter 1, you will find the name of King David in verse 6. King David's home town was Bethlehem, and so it was to Bethlehem that Mary and Joseph had to go. They had to travel about eighty-five miles - this was a long journey in those days when there were no cars or aeroplanes. When they reached Bethlehem, there was no room for them at the inn. Mary knew that her baby would soon be born. But they found found shelter in a stable.

There was no cot or soft blankets. When Jesus was born, Mary laid Him in a manger. This was full of straw for the animals to eat.

Luke chapter 2 verses 8-18.

The shepherds soon told other people about the message of the angels, and the Baby who had been born. But Mary thought quietly about everything that had taken place, so that she would always remember the time when the promised Baby was born.

Why did Mary and Joseph have to go to Bethlehem? Can you find three names for the Lord Jesus used by the angel?

In the city of Jerusalem in the land of Israel, there lived a man named Simeon. Simeon loved God and obeyed His commandments. God had told him that before he died, he would see the Christ.

'Christ' means 'anointed one' and is a name given to the Lord Jesus.

Simeon believed God, and waited for the day when he would know that the Saviour had come. When the Lord Jesus was almost six weeks old, Mary and Joseph brought Him to the temple. They had come to offer a sacrifice as God's law said they should after a baby had been born. Simeon went to the courtyard of the temple, and there he saw Mary and Joseph with the baby Jesus. Simeon took the baby in his arms.

Luke chapter 2 verses 29-32.

Simeon knew that this child was the One who God had promised to send. Just then, a very old lady called Anna also came in. When she saw the Lord Jesus with Mary and Joseph, she said thank-you to God. Like Simeon, she knew that God had done as He had promised and sent the Saviour into the world. Anna knew that there were other people who were looking forward to the Saviour's coming.

Anna told them about the Baby she had seen at the temple, and how God had kept His promise.

What names are given to the Lord Jesus in Isaiah chapter 9 verse 6? Anna said thank-you to God for sending the Lord Jesus. Have you done this?

Matthew chapter 2 verses 1-12.

GOD'S WORD

We do not know who the wise men were, or how many there were. When they arrived at Jerusalem, King Herod was not pleased that a new king would be born. He pretended to want to worship the special child. God knew that Herod would try to destroy Jesus. God warned the wise men not to return to the king, and so they went home a different way.

BY MYSELF

An angel told Joseph to take Jesus to Egypt.

The angel explained in a dream that Herod wanted to kill Jesus. Joseph obeyed God's message. He got up while it was still night. With Mary, he set off to the land of Egypt. They took the Lord Jesus out of the land of Israel before the king began his search.

King Herod was angry because the wise men did not return to tell him where the new King had been born.

EXTRA INFO

He gave a very cruel command. All the little boys in or near Bethlehem who were two years old or under, must be killed.

Herod did not know that the One he really wanted to destroy was no longer in Bethlehem. Mary and Joseph stayed in the land of Egypt until King Herod died. Then an angel spoke to Joseph in a dream again, telling him that it was now safe to return to Israel.

ASK ABOUT

Was the Lord Jesus still in the stable when the wise men came? What presents did the wise men bring?

Day 241: AMONG THE TEACHERS

Have you ever been on an outing when someone got lost? It is very frightening for the one who is lost and for those who are looking for him. But how happy everyone is when the missing person is found!

When they left Egypt, Mary and Joseph returned to their home in Nazareth. Once a year, they made the journey to Jerusalem for the Feast of the Passover.

This was when the people of Israel remembered the night when God had brought His people out of Egypt.

Many people from the same town or village would travel together to the Feast. It must have been a very happy time, and a time of giving thanks to God.

When the Lord Jesus was twelve years old, He went with Mary and Joseph to Jerusalem. At twelve years old he would have been thought of as a 'grown up'. A boy of twelve in the land of Israel was considered old enough to understand God's law.

Luke chapter 2 verses 41-50.

Mary and Joseph were very worried when they realised that Jesus was not with them.

They thought that He was lost. But the Lord Jesus was not really lost. He was in the courts of the temple, and He called the temple 'My Father's House'. This shows us that He knew that God was His Father. It was right that Mary and Joseph should know this too.

What did the teachers at the temple think about the Lord Jesus? The Lord Jesus was the Son of God. How did He behave with Mary and Joseph? (Luke chapter 2 verse 51)

Day 242: AT THE RIVER JORDAN

When Zacharias' and Elizabeth's son grew up, he knew that God had chosen him to tell the people to prepare for the Saviour. He told the people to repent, so that their sins - the wrong things they had done - could be forgiven.

'Repentance' is a long word, but it is not too hard to understand. Imagine you see a road sign which shows that you are going the wrong way. If you are sensible, you will turn round and go the right way! Repentance is like that. It means realising that we have not been living as God wants us to, and being willing to change. It is more than being sorry for the wrong things we have done. It is asking God to change us, so that we will want to do the things that please Him.

People came to John to be baptised in the River Jordan. The water could not wash their sins away, but being baptised meant that they wanted to change.

They wanted to leave their sins behind and live a life that pleased God.

Because so many people came to John to be baptised, he became known as John the Baptist.

John told the people that Someone greater than he was coming. One day Jesus came to the River Jordan.

Matthew chapter 3 verses 13-17.

The Lord Jesus was baptised by John even though He had no sins to repent of. John uunderstood that Jesus was the promised Saviour.

**What did God say about the Lord Jesus?
What did John say about the Lord Jesus?
(John chapter 1 verse 34)**

Day 243: IN THE DESERT

When Adam and Eve were in the Garden of Eden, Eve was tempted to disobey God. Satan used the serpent to speak to Eve. Another name for Satan is 'the devil'. The Bible teaches that he was perfect when God created him. But he became proud and wanted to be like God Himself. Now he is against God and against everything that is good. He tempted Eve to do wrong, and he has been tempting people to do wrong things ever since. When the Son of God came into the world, the devil tempted Him to disobey God His Father.

GOD'S WORD

Matthew chapter 4 verses 3-11.

We do not know everything that happened during the forty days that the Lord Jesus was in the desert. But we do read of three temptations which the devil used. Each time, the Lord Jesus answered with words from the Bible.

BY MYSELF

We should read our Bibles. Then when we are tempted to do wrong, God's Holy Spirit will help us to remember what God says we should do.

The writer of the Book of Hebrews tells us that the Lord Jesus was tempted just as we are. Because of this, He understands our difficulties and is able to help us. But He never gave in to temptation.

EXTRA INFO

Jesus lived a perfect life. In everything He did, He pleased God His Father.

ASK ABOUT

How many days was the Lord Jesus in the desert? (Matthew chapter 4 verse 2) Who helped Him after this time of temptation?

Day 244: THE LAMB OF GOD

When John the Baptist began to tell people to prepare for the Saviour, he did not know who this was. When Jesus was baptised John understood who He was.

John had some disciples: men who wanted to learn from him. One day two of John's disciples were with him. John saw the Lord Jesus. He told his disciples that Jesus was the Lamb of God. They knew that John meant that Jesus was the promised Saviour.

GOD'S WORD

John chapter 1 verses 35-42.

The word Messiah means 'anointed one'. The word Christ means the same thing. Old Testament priests and Kings were anointed. Oil was poured on them as a sign that God had chosen them to do a particular job.

EXTRA INFO

Jesus was God's anointed One, with work that only He could do.

Andrew told his brother that he had found the Messiah. The following day, Andrew, Peter and another of John's disciples met Jesus.

BY MYSELF

Jesus called a man named Philip to follow Him.

Philip came from the town of Bethsaida. He found a man named Nathanael and told him that they had found the One that Moses had written about. But when Nathanael heard that Jesus came from Nazareth, he did not think that He could be anyone very special. Philip took him to Jesus. Nathanael found that Jesus knew all about him. He told Jesus that he knew that He was the Son of God.

ASK ABOUT

What was the name of Andrew's brother? Who brought Nathanael to Jesus?

Day 245: A MIRACLE AT A WEDDING

Have you ever been to a wedding? At a wedding the bride and bridegroom usually invite their families and friends to have a lovely meal together. The Lord Jesus and His disciples were invited to a wedding at a place called Cana in Galilee. Mary the mother of Jesus was also invited. Someone would have been asked to look after the meal, to make sure that there was plenty of food and drink for the guests. But at this wedding there was not enough to drink.

GOD'S WORD

John chapter 2 verses 1-11.

People living at that time could not turn on a tap to get water. Water had to be brought from a well, and so every home would have some water pots. How did the water become wine? We call this a 'miracle'.

EXTRA INFO

Usually wine is made from the juice of grapes and it would take a long time to make. When the Lord Jesus changed the water into wine, it happened straight away.

This was the first miracle that the Lord Jesus did.

BY MYSELF

Jesus changed the water into wine so that people would know that He is the Son of God.

When we read the first chapter of Genesis, we learned that only God can create by His own power. When the Lord Jesus made the wine, He was showing God's power to create.

ASK ABOUT

What did the master of the feast say about the wine? Which verse tells us that this miracle helped the disciples to believe in the Lord Jesus?

Day 246: IN THE TEMPLE

Do you remember why God wanted the people of Israel to make the tabernacle? God wanted to be with His people and He chose the tabernacle to be the place where He would speak to them. Later, when the people had settled down in the Land of Canaan, the temple was built and it replaced the tabernacle. People brought their offerings to the temple, just as they had brought them to the tabernacle when it was at the center of their camp in the desert.

Many people travelled to Jerusalem at the time of the Passover Feast. They could not always bring an animal with them to offer at the temple: they would need to buy one. Men brought sheep and cattle and doves to the courtyard of the temple. They sold them there, and probably charged too much.

GOD'S WORD

John chapter 2 verses 13-17.

If you look at Isaiah chapter 56 verse 7, you will see that God calls the temple 'a House of Prayer'. Sadly, people were so busy buying and selling that they had forgotten what the temple was for. Those who really loved God must have been sad to see the poor people being cheated and charged too much. They must have been sad to hear so much noise and confusion in God's House of Prayer.

EXTRA INFO

The Lord Jesus called the temple 'His Father's House' so that people would see He was the Son of God.

BY MYSELF

Jesus cared very much about what the temple was meant to be.

ASK ABOUT

What do we read in the Book of Isaiah about the temple? What did the Lord Jesus call the temple?

Day 247: NICODEMUS

When the Lord Jesus lived on earth, there were some people called 'Pharisees'. They were very strict about keeping God's law.

A strict person always wants things done in a certain way: everything must be 'just right'.

Being strict about God's Law should be a good thing, but the Pharisees added lots of their own rules to God's commands. As time went by, they thought more about their own ideas than about what God had said. A Pharisee named Nicodemus wanted to meet Jesus.

John chapter 3 verses 1-8.

Why do you think Nicodemus talked to Jesus at night? Perhaps he didn't want people around. Nicodemus did not understand what Jesus meant when He told him that he needed to be born again. He knew that no one can start life again as a baby. But Jesus was talking about being born into God's family. To find out what 'repent' means look back at Day 242.

When someone repents and asks God to forgive their sins, then God gives that person new life: a real new beginning.

Jesus knew that Nicodemus did not understand His words. Jesus talked to him about how the Son of God had come into the world so that people could be saved from sin.

What happened when Moses lifted up the snake in the desert? (John chapter 3 verse 14 and Numbers chapter 21 verse 9). Learn John chapter 3 verse 16 off by heart.

Day 248: AT THE WELL

Long ago, many people were taken away from their homes in the northern part of the land of Israel. This part of the land was called Samaria. People from other lands were brought to live there instead. They were called 'Samaritans'. Those who lived in other parts of Israel were called 'Jews'.

The Jews and the Samaritans did not like each other. They had as little to do with each other as possible.

One day the Lord Jesus was travelling back to Galilee. On the way, He stopped to rest at a well in Samaria.

John chapter 4 verses 7-15.

The Samaritan woman was surprised when Jesus spoke to her. He spoke in a way that showed that He knew all about her.

Jesus told her that He was the One who God had promised to send into the world.

When the disciples arrived at the well, they were surprised to find The Lord Jesus talking to a Samaritan woman. The woman left her water pot by the well and went into the city. She told people about Jesus and what He had said. The people asked Jesus to stay with them. He stayed for two days. As they listened to Him, many believed that He was the promised Saviour. At first they had believed, because of what the woman had told them. Now they believed in the Lord Jesus because they had heard Him for themselves.

What did Jesus tell the Samaritan woman about herself? (Verse 18). What did she tell other people? (Verse 29).

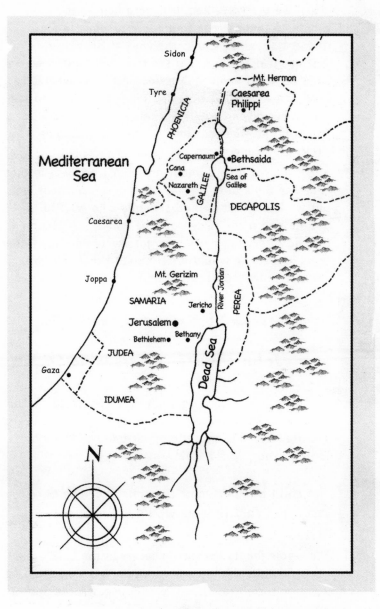

A map of Israel in New Testament times

Day 249: A FATHER BELIEVES

When we are travelling, it is very helpful to have a map so that we can find our way. Have a look at the map which shows the land of Israel in New Testament days. Can you see the River Jordan where John baptised people? Can you find Cana where the Lord Jesus changed water to wine? You will also see the names given to different parts of the land: Judea, Samaria and Galilee. Close to the Sea of Galilee was the city of Capernaum.

There was a very important man who lived in that city. The Bible does not tell us very much about him, but we know that he had servants who worked for him and he had a son. One day, the man's son became ill. Instead of getting better, he got worse until his father thought that he would die. He heard that the Lord Jesus had arrived back in Cana.

Cana was about fifteen miles from Capernaum.

John chapter 4 verses 46-54.

You may find verse 48 quite hard to understand. The Lord Jesus knows whether we truly believe in Him or not. He gave this man the opportunity to show his faith in what He could do.

The child got better at the time that the Lord Jesus had said that he would live.

The whole family became believers in the Lord Jesus. Verse 54 calls this miracle 'a sign'. This means that it was a miracle that shows us that Jesus is the Son of God with power to heal.

Who came to meet the man on his way home? What news did they bring?

Day 250: AT NAZARETH

Before books were made as they are now, writing was done on a long roll of paper, leather, or parchment. (Parchment is thicker than ordinary paper.) Usually each end of the roll was joined to a piece of wood or metal, which it could be wound on to. It was called a scroll.

As a scroll was read, one end was unrolled while the other end was rolled up again. The books of the Old Testament were written on scrolls.

The Jewish people used to meet on the Sabbath day to hear the reading from the Old Testament. The building where they met was a synagogue. One Sabbath day, the Lord Jesus went to the synagogue at Nazareth.

Luke chapter 4 verses 16-22.

The words that Jesus read from the scroll are found in Isaiah chapter 61. When He told the people that the scripture was fulfilled, He meant that He was the One that Isaiah had written about. God's Holy Spirit had helped Isaiah to write things about Jesus more than seven hundred years before He was born in Bethlehem.

Jesus talked to the people about Elijah and Elisha who had lived many years before.

The people did not like the things that the Lord Jesus said. They became very angry and would have hurt Him. But the Lord Jesus walked quietly away.

Which book of the Old Testament did the Lord Jesus read from in the synagogue? Read Luke chapter 4 verse 29 to find out what the people wanted to do.

Day 251: FISHERS OF MEN

Have you ever seen fishing boats returning with a catch? We have already read about Simon Peter and Andrew. They were fishermen. Jesus spoke to them by the Sea of Galilee. He also spoke to James and John.

GOD'S WORD

Mark chapter 1 verses 16-20.

What do you think the Lord Jesus meant when He told Andrew and his brother that He would make them fishers of men? In future instead of catching fish, they would be helping people to come to know God.

Near the Sea of Galilee was a town called Capernaum. Jesus and his disciples went into the synagogue there and Jesus taught the people. He spoke so differently from their usual teachers that they were surprised at what He said and how He said it.

When they came out of the synagogue they went to Andrew and Simon Peter's house. They found that Simon Peter's mother in law had been taken ill. She was lying down, too ill to prepare for visitors.

BY MYSELF

When Jesus was told about it, He took her hand and helped her up.

The fever went away so quickly that she was able to get up and prepare a meal for them. That evening, many people gathered at the door of the house where Jesus was. They brought those they knew who were ill.

EXTRA INFO

The Lord Jesus healed the sick because He is the Son of God. Seeing these miracles of healing should have helped people to understand who He was.

ASK ABOUT

What was the first miracle that Jesus performed? (John chapter 2 verse 9).

Day 252: AN UNUSUAL WAY IN

Would you like to live in a house that had a flat roof, where you could sit in the fresh air? Houses in the land of Israel had an outside staircase leading to the flat roof.

Sometimes families used the roof as extra living space, even sleeping there in hot weather.

Simon and Andrew's house was in Capernaum. It was probably their house that we read about in Mark chapter 2. The house was crowded with people who wanted to hear Jesus. Some had a special reason for wanting to see Him that day. But when they arrived at the house, they could not get near the door, because so many people were there. They were determined to help a friend who was ill. They had carried him on a sleeping mat because he could not walk.

Mark chapter 2 verses 3-12.

There are some hard words here. 'Paralysed' means unable to move. 'Blasphemy' means to speak in a wrong way about God. Jesus could have told the man to get up straight away. Instead, He spoke to him about his sins.

Only God can forgive us for the wrong things we have done.

When he told the man to get up, He was showing His power to heal. The One who had such power is the Son of God. He has power to heal and to forgive.

How many men carried their friend to the Lord Jesus? How did they manage to bring him into the house?

Day 253: THE TAX COLLECTOR

Do you know what taxes are? Most people who work have to pay tax. This is money that is used to pay for things we all need, like roads, schools and hospitals.

When Jesus lived in Israel, people did not like tax collectors because they collected money for the Romans who ruled Israel.

There was another reason why tax collectors were not liked. Sometimes they took extra money, and kept some for themselves.

One day Jesus saw a man named Matthew at work in the tax office. He asked Matthew to follow Him. Matthew left his work and followed Jesus. After this Matthew invited Jesus to a special meal at his house. The disciples were there and tax collectors and other people came too. Some Pharisees and teachers knew that Jesus had been at Matthew's house. They grumbled about the people that Jesus had been with.

GOD'S WORD

Luke chapter 5 verses 27-32 .

EXTRA INFO

In these verses Matthew is known by another name, Levi.

The Pharisees thought that they were good and that God was pleased with them. They had nothing to do with tax collectors and people they thought were bad.

BY MYSELF

The Lord Jesus came to help those who knew that they were sinful.

Just as sick people need a doctor, so these sinful people knew that Jesus could help them.

ASK ABOUT

Name the pharisee that came to Jesus at night. (John chapter 3 verses 1-2).

Day 254: A LONG ILLNESS

Have you ever had to stay at home because you have not been well? Sometimes even a week seems a long time when we cannot do the things we want to.

John chapter 5 verses 1-9.

This man was made better on the Sabbath day. Some of the Jews said that he should not carry his sleeping mat on the Sabbath day. When he was asked who had told him to pick up his mat, he did not know. Later, the Lord Jesus met the man who had been healed in the temple. The Lord Jesus told him that now that he was well, he must stop doing wrongs things.

The Lord Jesus knew all about the man: He knew the things in his life that needed to change.

Jesus knew that obeying God is even more important than being made well.

After he had seen the Lord Jesus again, the man told the Jews who it was who had made him better. They began to treat the Lord Jesus unkindly and even wanted to kill Him because He had healed someone on the Sabbath day.

God has given us one day each week to rest from our usual work. But that does not mean that we cannot help others and show kindness on that day. The Jews should really have been saying thank-you to God, because a man was well after being ill for thirty-eight years.

What question did the Lord Jesus ask the man at the pool? When the Lord Jesus spoke to the man, how long did it take him to get well?

Day 255: IN THE SYNAGOGUE

Which hand do you write with? Many of us write with our right hand, some with the left. There are many things that really need both hands. Can you think of something that would be very hard to do, if you were not able to use one of your hands?

One day the Lord Jesus saw a man who could not use his right hand. It was a Sabbath day and the man had gone to the synagogue. The Pharisees and some men who were teachers of God's law were there.

GOD'S WORD

Luke chapter 6 verses 6-11.

Once again, instead of being glad to see a man being helped by the Lord Jesus, the Pharisees were angry.

EXTRA INFO

The Pharisees had made so many of their own rules about the Sabbath day, that they had forgotten what the Sabbath day was really for.

The Pharisees and teachers were used to people listening to them. They did not like to see people listening to the Lord Jesus. The miracles that Jesus did all showed that He is the Son of God. The Pharisees did not want to believe this.

BY MYSELF

They watched the Lord Jesus, to see if He would do or say something wrong.

Of course they were never able to find anything wrong in either His words or His actions.

ASK ABOUT

Which verse tells us that the Pharisees were watching the Lord Jesus? Which verse tells us that they were angry?

Day 256: THE TWELVE DISCIPLES

Jesus came into the world as a baby. He grew as we grow, and became a man, but He was also the Son of God. His birth in Bethlehem was the beginning of His life on earth, but before this He had always been with God His Father. It is not surprising that while Jesus was living in this world, He spent many hours praying.

Sometimes Jesus got up very early in the morning and found a quiet place to talk to His Father.

One day He went to a mountain and spent the whole night there praying. The next day He called together His disciples. We do not know how many people followed Jesus at this time. From this group of people He chose twelve men who He also called apostles.

An apostle is someone chosen by the Lord Jesus to tell others about Him.

Luke chapter 6 verses 12-16.

The Lord Jesus chose these twelve men to be with Him. They would see the miracles that He did and they would listen to Him teaching about God. Then He would send them out to teach others. He also gave them power to heal people who were ill.

Crowds of people began to gather around Jesus. They came to listen to Him because no one had ever spoken to them as He did. Many came to be healed. The power of the Lord Jesus healed all of them. It became hard for Jesus and His disciples to find time for meals, so many people crowded around to see Him.

Can you remember the two sets of brothers who were disciples? (Mark chapter 1 verses 16 and 19).

Day 257: ON THE MOUNTAIN

The Lord Jesus had many things to tell His disciples. One day He went up a mountain and sat down and began to speak to them. Probably many other people followed Him there and listened, but He was really teaching His disciples.

First of all He spoke about people who are truly happy. He spoke of those who sorrow because they know they are sinful; people who long to live in a way that pleases God. He spoke of people who are kind, and of people who are ill-treated because they belong to Him. This was different from the way people usually think of happiness.

We often think that if we are rich or famous we will be happy. Jesus taught a different way of thinking.

You will remember the commandments that God gave to His people in the time of Moses. Jesus began to teach His disciples that it is not just the wrong things we do that God sees, but He sees our hearts. The commandment says it is wrong to kill: Jesus said that it is wrong to even feel angry with someone who has done us no harm.

Sometimes people treat us unkindly and we feel like being unkind in return.

Matthew chapter 5 verses 43-48.

God sends sunshine and rain on people who never thank Him for it. Jesus wants His followers to be like that. We are to be kind and helpful to our friends and even to people who make our lives difficult.

What did Jesus say we should do for those who treat us badly?

Day 258: HOW TO PRAY

Sometimes people are well-behaved when someone is watching, but they do wrong things when they think that no one is looking. A person who acts this way is a hypocrite. When Jesus taught His disciples, he said that they should not be like that. He knew that some men stood praying in the synagogue or even in the street. They wanted people to think that they were very good. They were not really praying to God at all.

GOD'S WORD

Matthew chapter 6 verses 5-13.

EXTRA INFO

God is our Creator: the One who made us. If Jesus is our Saviour and Friend, then we can call God, Father.

You may have heard the words of verses 9-13 before. We call these verses 'The Lord's Prayer'. When Christians meet to pray, they sometimes say these words together. We do not have to use these words every time we pray. They are to teach us about the way we should pray. First of all we think about the One we are praying to.

BY MYSELF

God is in Heaven. He is absolutely pure and sinless.

We want the time to come when sin will no longer spoil God's world. When we pray for our 'daily bread' we are asking God to give us what we need for each day. Asking God to forgive us our debts is asking Him to forgive our sins. People who know that God has forgiven them will forgive others. Jesus knows how easily we are tempted to do wrong. We need to ask God to help us to say no to sin.

ASK ABOUT

What do we call people who pretend to be better than they really are? Where does the Lord Jesus say we should go when we pray?

Day 259: THE TWO BUILDERS

Jesus taught that the lives of those who follow Him will be different from others. They were not to spend all their time storing up riches that will not last. They should not be worried about having enough to eat or clothes to wear.

The words that Jesus spoke to His disciples on the mountainside are called 'the sermon on the mount'.

Jesus said that the God who cares for the birds and flowers will look after those who love and obey Him.

Of course this does not mean that Christians should not work hard to earn money to buy food and clothes. It means that the really important thing will be to please God and live for Him.

There were many other things that Jesus spoke to His disciples about that day. But He ended His words with a parable – that is, a story with a meaning.

Matthew chapter 7 verses 24-27.

A house built on the sand is no use at all. Rain would wash the sand away and the house would fall. Building on the rock is hard work, but the house would not fall. We hear what Jesus says when we read our Bibles. If we do not do as He says, then we are like the foolish builder. We need to be like the wise builder. We must trust Jesus to forgive us for the wrong things we have done and ask Him to help us to love and obey Him. If we do this, our lives will begin to show that we belong to the Lord Jesus.

What can happen when we store up treasure for ourselves? (Matthew chapter 6 verse 19).

Day 260: A CENTURION'S SERVANT

I wonder if you have ever seen soldiers in their uniform. You may have seen pictures of the Trooping of the Colour, or of some other parade. The soldiers in the land of Israel were Roman soldiers because Israel was part of the Roman Empire. In the city of Capernaum there lived a man who was a Centurion.

A Centurion was in charge of one hundred soldiers.

This Roman Centurion was kind to the Jewish people. He had helped them to build a synagogue.

Luke chapter 7 verses 1-10.

In verse 8 we read that the Centurion was a man under authority. This means that he had power from the Emperor, so that his soldiers must obey him. So he believed that in the same way, the Lord Jesus had power from God over illness. The Lord Jesus told the people that this Centurion had great faith: he trusted the Lord Jesus completely. Faith in God does not mean hoping that everything will be all right. It means being absolutely certain that God will always do what He says He will do.

God has not promised that He will always make us better when we are ill. He has promised that all who trust the Saviour will be with Him forever.

You have already learned that promise in John chapter 3 verse 16. Make sure that you have remembered it.

Why did the Centurion say that the Lord Jesus need not come to his house? What had happened at the Centurion's house?

Day 261: A WIDOW'S SON

Do you remember what the word 'widow' means? It means a woman whose husband has died. We read in the Bible that we should help those who are widows.

In New Testament times, life was very hard for a widow. It was difficult to earn money for food. She would be very thankful if she had a son to help her.

Luke chapter 7 verses 11-17.

Jesus understood how sad life was for this woman, without her son. When He brought her son back to life, He showed that the Son of God has power over death. The people were amazed, and said that Jesus must be a great prophet. They would have remembered how God answered Elijah's and Elisha's prayers and brought two boys back to life. As the people saw Jesus give a widow's son back to her, it is not surprising that they said He must be a great prophet. The prophets had brought God's messages to the people of Israel. God caused miraculous things to happen through some of them. The people knew that God had sent them. The miracles done by the Lord Jesus reminded the people of the miracles of the prophets.

They realised that only the power of God could bring someone back to life.

They had not understood that the Lord Jesus was greater than the prophets. His power over sickness and death, His power to create and His wonderful teaching, all showed that He is the Son of God.

How many sons did this widow have? What did the Lord Jesus say to her?

Day 262: JOHN IN PRISON

John the Baptist had done the work that God had given him to do. He had told the people to prepare for the coming of the One who God had promised to send into the world. When he knew that Jesus was the promised Saviour, he had told others about Him. John knew that as people began to listen to Jesus, they would no longer need to listen to him. John had told people that they must repent: they must stop doing the things that they knew were wrong. He even spoke to King Herod about wrong things he had done.

King Herod had married a lady named Herodias, but she was his brother's wife. This was against God's commandment.

Herodias would have liked John to be put to death, but King Herod was afraid that this would make the people angry. So John the Baptist was put into prison, because he had spoken the truth. When news about the miracles of the Lord Jesus began to spread, some of John's disciples came to tell him.

Luke chapter 7 verses 18-23.

The Jewish people expected their Messiah to be a great King. They thought that He would free them from the Roman Empire that ruled over them. The Lord Jesus had not done this. John the Baptist wanted to be sure that Jesus was the promised One. John's disciples saw the power Jesus had over all sorts of illness.

Jesus knew that John would understand that only the Son of God could do such things.

What answer to John the Baptist's question were his disciples to give him?

Day 263: A SINNER FORGIVEN

Do you like having visitors? If you do, I am sure that your family likes to make them comfortable.

In Israel, it was often hot and dusty. Visitors were usually given water to wash their feet after a journey.

One day Jesus was invited to the house of Simon the Pharisee. A meal was served, but there was no welcome and no water for Jesus' feet. A woman living nearby had done many wrong things. When she heard that Jesus was in Simon's house, she took a flask of scented oil and came and stood behind Him. She began to cry and her tears fell on the feet of the Lord Jesus. She wiped his feet with her own hair and poured the oil over them. Simon the Pharisee was horrified that Jesus should allow such a woman to even touch Him.

Jesus knew all about the woman and He also knew what Simon was thinking.

He told a story about two men who borrowed money but could not pay it back. The man they had borrowed from was kind and neither of them needed to repay it.

Luke chapter 7 verses 40-47.

The sinful woman was like the man in the story who owed a lot of money. She knew that she had done many wrong things. When she heard that she could be forgiven, she loved the Lord Jesus very much. Simon was like the man who only owed a little. He had forgotten that he was a sinner in need of forgiveness.

What did Jesus say to the woman after He had spoken to Simon? (Luke chapter 7 verse 48).

Day 264: SOWING THE SEED

Do you like listening to stories? Sometimes Jesus used stories to teach people. His stories are called 'parables' because they have a meaning. One day, when Jesus was by the Sea of Galilee, crowds of people gathered round Him. He got in a boat, so He could speak to them without the crowd pressing too closely.

GOD'S WORD

Matthew chapter 13 verses 1-9.

The story was one that people could understand. Later, Jesus explained the meaning to His disciples. People hear of how God sent His Son into the world so that sinful men and women, and boys and girls can be forgiven. That message is called 'the gospel'.

EXTRA INFO

The word gospel means 'good news'.

When people hear the good news, it is like seed that falls on different sorts of soil. Some people do not understand what they have heard. Just as in the parable the birds took the seed, the devil causes people to forget the good news. Then some seem to believe in Jesus. But they find that being a Christian is not easy, and give up. The third sort of soil is like people who listen to the message about God. But they are too busy to become real followers of Jesus.

BY MYSELF

The good soil is like people who understand the good news about the Lord Jesus.

Their lives are changed. Instead of living to please themselves, they now want to live to please God.

ASK ABOUT

What happened to the seed among thorns?
What happened to the seed on good ground?

Day 265: THE STORM

Have you ever been in a boat? It is lovely on a calm day, but it can be frightening in stormy weather. One day there had been crowds of people around the Lord Jesus. They listened to Him, because He spoke to them in a very different way from the Pharisees and the teachers of God's law. The Pharisees made things seem very difficult. The Lord Jesus talked about things that people knew about: seeds and soil, plants and weeds, building a house, catching fish. They could go on thinking about what the parables meant.

The people also knew that Jesus had done many wonderful miracles. They wanted to see Him and hear what He said. But after having many people with Him all day, one evening Jesus decided to go to the other side of the Sea of Galilee. Some of the disciples were fishermen: they were used to the sea. But such a storm arose that even they were frightened.

Mark chapter 4 verses 35-41.

Jesus was not afraid: He was asleep. When the disciples woke Him, He calmed the storm.

Because the Lord Jesus is the Son of God, He has power over the wind and the waves.

Even though the disciples had seen the Lord Jesus make ill people better, they were amazed that He could control the storm. They need not have been afraid while He was with them. If we know the Lord Jesus as our Saviour and Friend, we need never be afraid.

What did the disciples say to the Lord Jesus when they woke Him? What did the Lord Jesus say to them after He had calmed the storm?

Day 266: JAIRUS'S DAUGHTER

One day, a man named Jairus came to see the Lord Jesus. Jairus was in charge of the synagogue. He had one daughter who was about twelve years old. She was very ill: Jairus was afraid that she was going to die. When He met the Lord Jesus, He bowed down to Him and asked Him to come to his house.

Many people were crowding round the Lord Jesus as He set off to Jairus's house. In the crowd was a woman who had been ill for twelve years.

This woman had spent all her money trying to get well, but she only got worse.

She had decided to try to get near enough to the Lord Jesus to touch His clothes. She believed that if she did that, she would get well. The woman came behind the Lord Jesus and touched the edge of His cloak. Straight away, she knew that she was better. Even in the crowd, the Lord Jesus knew that someone had touched Him. He spoke kindly to the woman who had been ill, and told her that her faith in Him had made her well.

While this was happening, Jairus was waiting for the Lord Jesus to see His daughter. Some messengers arrived with bad news for Jairus: it seemed that it was too late to help the little girl.

Luke chapter 8 verses 49-56.

When Jesus arrived at Jairus's house, everyone was sad and crying. But soon all that was changed: the little girl was well again.

How old was Jairus's daughter? How long had the woman who touched Jesus' clothes been ill?

Day 267: KING HEROD'S BIRTHDAY

Jesus went from one village to another teaching the people and healing the sick. One day He decided to send His disciples out in twos to teach and to heal. Before they set out He talked to them about what they would do. Jesus knew that not everyone would listen to them. Sometimes they would be treated unkindly, but they were not to be afraid.

At this time King Herod had a birthday celebration. The daughter of Herodias came and danced to entertain his guests. Herod was so pleased with her that he promised to give her whatever she wanted. She asked her mother what she should ask for. Herodias told her to ask for the head of John the Baptist. She did as her mother said. Herod was very sorry when he heard her request. John had done nothing to deserve such punishment, but Herod's guests had heard his promise. He gave instructions for John to be killed.

The disciples came back to Jesus to tell Him all that they had been doing.

Mark chapter 6 verses 30-32.

The disciples were probably very tired and they would also have heard the sad news about John the Baptist.

So many people wanted to see the Lord Jesus that it was impossible even to find time for meals.

Jesus said that they should be quiet and rest. They got into a boat and set off across the Sea of Galilee.

What did Jesus say that the disciples should do in a quiet place? It was so busy what couldn't they do?

Day 268: A VERY LARGE MEAL

It is good to have a time for rest and quietness when we have been very busy. Some people like to spend a day in the countryside with no telephone to answer and no doorbell to ring. The Lord Jesus set off with His disciples, to a place where there would not usually be many people around. But somehow, news of where the Lord Jesus had gone reached the crowds who wanted to see Him. They followed Him, and He did not send them away. He talked to them and healed those who were ill. The day went on and still the people stayed. The disciples asked the Lord Jesus to send the people away so that they could buy food for themselves. The Lord Jesus told the disciples that they should give the people something to eat.

There were a lot of people there: about five thousand men as well as women and children.

Luke chapter 9 verses 12-17.

Five loaves of bread and two small fish was not very much for such a large crowd, was it? But the Lord Jesus provided enough food for everyone to have plenty.

Once again Jesus had done something that only God could do.

The men and women and boys and girls who were there knew that no ordinary man could perform such a miracle. Jesus was showing quite clearly that He is the Son of God.

Find the name of the place where this miracle happened. (Luke chapter 9 verse 10). What was left over at the end of the meal?

Day 269: WALKING ON THE SEA

We read yesterday about the great crowd of people who enjoyed a meal of bread and fish, which the Lord Jesus provided for them. Although there were more than five thousand people there, this is called 'The Feeding of the five thousand', because the Bible tells us that there were five thousand men present.

After the disciples had collected all the left over food, Jesus told them to cross to the other side of the Sea of Galilee. Then He told the people to go.

 Jesus spent some time on His own and prayed to God, His Father.

During this time, the disciples were finding it very hard to row against the wind.

 ## Matthew chapter 14 verses 25-33.

 The fourth watch of the night would have been between three o'clock and six o'clock in the morning. This is because night-time was counted from six o'clock in the evening until six o'clock in the morning and each watch is three hours.

Just as Jesus was able to calm the storm, He was also able to walk on water without sinking. Peter tried to do this. He looked at the storm and became afraid.

The boat landed at Gennesaret. Wherever Jesus went, people knew that He had made sick people well. The message soon got round that He was at Gennesaret. People brought sick friends and family. Even if they just touched Jesus, they were made better.

 What did the disciples feel like when they saw Jesus walking towards them? What did they say when He got into the boat?

Day 270: FOUR THOUSAND FED

In New Testament times there was no television or radio, but news still spread quickly. Wherever Jesus went, people wanted to see Him. They had heard of the wonderful things He had done. One day He sat down on a mountainside near the Sea of Galilee. Many people were brought to Him: some could not walk, some could not see, some could not speak. Jesus healed them all. The people thanked God!

Matthew chapter 15 verses 32-39.

Once again Jesus provided food for a large crowd of people. But still there were people who did not believe that the Lord Jesus had come from God.

We have already heard of the strict Pharisees. There were also some people called 'Sadducees'.

Sadducees were mainly rich people. Most of them were also priests who had duties at the temple.

The Pharisees and Sadducees did not always agree with each other. But one thing they did agree on: they did not want people to listen to Jesus. They thought that they were the ones to teach people about God.

They tried very hard to think of difficult questions to ask the Lord Jesus.

He knew that they were envious because of the crowds that followed Him. But with great patience He answered all their questions.

How long had the crowd of people been with the Lord Jesus? How many people were there?

When something unusual happens people soon begin to talk to one another about it. It is not surprising that the Lord Jesus was talked about. Twice great crowds of people had been given food by Him. Many who were ill had been made well. Lots of people had listened as Jesus talked to them. Jesus knew that they would be speaking about Him.

GOD'S WORD

Matthew chapter 16 verses 13-17.

Some people thought that Jesus was John the Baptist risen from the dead. Herod thought this, probably because he knew that he had done wrong when he had put John to death. Some people thought that Jesus must be Elijah. God had given Elijah power to perform miracles long ago. They began to say that Elijah had come back to life. There were others who thought that Jeremiah or one of the other prophets had returned.

Jesus was not a prophet who had died and then come back to life. He is the Son of God. Peter knew this. Peter said that Jesus is the Christ. Jesus said that Peter understood because God had helped him.

EXTRA INFO

The word, Christ means that Jesus is the anointed One.

BY MYSELF

Many people talked about the Lord Jesus but did not understand who He was.

After this, the Lord Jesus began to talk to His disciples about how He would die and rise from the dead. They did not understand this: it was not what they expected to happen to the Son of God.

ASK ABOUT

What name did Jesus use for Himself? Who did Peter say that the Lord Jesus is?

Day 272: THE TRANSFIGURATION

Are you good at remembering things? Sometimes things happen which are so special that we feel we would like to remember them always. There was a day which was very special to Peter, James and John. Peter wrote about it in a letter many years later. He had certainly not forgotten what he had seen and heard that day.

GOD'S WORD

Luke chapter 9 verses 28-36.

EXTRA INFO

Your Bible may call these verses 'The Transfiguration'. That long word means 'change': as the disciples looked at the Lord Jesus, His whole appearance was changed.

Moses and Elijah had both lived a long time before the Lord Jesus lived on earth. But they were able to be with Him on the mountain. This reminds us that when a person dies, that is not the end. Either we will be with God forever or we will be shut out of Heaven.

BY MYSELF

It is so important that we ask God to forgive us for the wrong things we have done.

Jesus died in our place so that we can be forgiven and be with Him forever. Moses and Elijah had known long ago that God had promised to send a Saviour. It was wonderful for them to know that He had come.

We have read about the miracles that show that Jesus is the Son of God. Now we have read how Peter, James and John heard God's voice from Heaven telling them that this is true: Jesus is the Son of God.

ASK ABOUT

Which three disciples went up the mountain with the Lord Jesus? Which two men appeared and talked with the Lord Jesus?

I hope that you have never felt jealous of anyone. We can be jealous of someone having more friends than we have, or we can be envious of the things other people have. There were people who were jealous when they saw the crowds following the Lord Jesus. The priests and Pharisees and teachers of the law wanted the people to listen to them.

They knew that the Lord Jesus had done many miracles which made the people wonder if He could be the promised Saviour.

One day the chief priests and Pharisees sent the temple guards to arrest Jesus.

It was the Feast of Tabernacles. Many people were in Jerusalem. Jesus talked to them.

John chapter 7 verses 45-52.

The Pharisees were not pleased, because the guards had not brought Jesus to them. Even the guards had realised that the Lord Jesus spoke differently from the way the Pharisees spoke.

One Pharisee did not like to hear the way the others spoke about Jesus. His name was Nicodemus. (We read about Nicodemus on DAY 247.) Because the Pharisees were jealous of Jesus, they said very unkind things about Him. It must have been hard for Nicodemus to speak in a fair and honest way, but he did.

What did the temple guards say about the Lord Jesus? The Pharisees said that the Lord Jesus came from Galilee. Do you remember where the Lord Jesus was born?

Day 274: SIGHT FOR A BLIND MAN

Isn't it wonderful to be able to see? God has given us eyes to see one another and to see many beautiful things around us.

One day the Lord Jesus met a man who had never been able to see: he had been born blind.

John chapter 9 verses 1-11.

It was a wonderful day for the man who had been blind, but the Pharisees did not think that. Once again they said that it was not right to heal on the Sabbath day. They asked his parents whether it was really true that the man had been blind, and if so, how had he been made to see. The man's parents told the Pharisees that their son had been born blind. But they would not say that it was Jesus who had healed him, because they were afraid of the Pharisees. Then the Pharisees began to question the man himself.

The man did not yet understand who Jesus was. But he did know one thing: he had been blind and now he could see.

Instead of thanking God for sending His Son with power to heal, the Pharisees were angry and jealous. They told the man not come to the synagogue any more. But Jesus met him again, and helped him to understand who it was that had given him his sight. The Pharisees refused to believe that Jesus was the Son of God. The man who had been given his sight, believed in the Lord Jesus.

What did the blind man do to get money to live on? What was the man who had been blind sure of? (John chapter 9 verse 25).

Day 275: SHEPHERDS

If you live in a country area, or if you have had a holiday in the countryside, you will have seen sheep in the fields or on the hillside.

Usually the field has a fence or stone wall around it, so that the sheep cannot wander away and get lost.

In New Testament days, sheep were brought into the sheepfold at night. A stone wall kept out any wild animals. An opening in the sheepfold allowed them to go in and out. At night, a shepherd lay across the opening. If there was danger, he would protect the sheep. In the morning the shepherds would come for their sheep. The sheep knew the voice of their shepherd and followed him. They did not follow a stranger because they did not recognise his voice.

The shepherd would go ahead of his sheep, leading them to fields of good, green grass.

Sometimes a shepherd paid someone to look after his sheep. But they might run away if a wild animal came, because the sheep did not belong to that shepherd.

John chapter 10 verses 7-14.

Jesus talked about being the Good Shepherd. He cares for His people, just as a shepherd cares for his sheep. He also said that He is the gate (or door) for the sheep. The only way into the sheepfold was the opening where the shepherd lay. In the same way, the Lord Jesus is the only way to God.

What does the man who is paid to look after the sheep do when there is danger? What does the good shepherd do?

Day 276: WHO IS MY NEIGHBOUR?

Do you know what the word 'neighbour' means? It usually means someone who lives near us - the person next door or just across the road. One day a man asked Jesus how he could get eternal life.

Eternal life means living with God forever.

Jesus realised that this man knew what God had said in the Old Testament. So He asked him what was written in God's law. Read the man's answer in Luke chapter 10 verse 27. The man gave the right answer. But then he asked who his neighbour was.

Luke chapter 10 verses 30-37.

God's command to love our neighbour, means that we should be as kind to others as we would want them to be to us.

The priest and Levite did not show any kindness to the man who had been hurt. The Samaritans and the Jews did not usually speak to each other. And yet it was the Samaritan who did all that he could to help.

We can see from this story that our neighbour can be anyone we meet. We should care just as much about other people as we do about ourselves. If you think carefully about that, you will realise that it is very hard to do. Read verse 27 again. How many people do you think have done what this verse tells us we should do? Only One: The Lord Jesus Himself. He is the only One who can change us, so that we will learn to love others, as God wants us to.

What happened to the man on his way to Jericho? Who were the three people who saw him?

Day 277: MARY AND MARTHA

Have you got any brothers or sisters? If so, do you like doing the same things, or do you think that you are very different from each other?

Mary and Martha were two sisters who lived in a village called Bethany.

We have read about the Pharisees and teachers of God's law who were jealous of the Lord Jesus. But there were also people who loved the Lord Jesus and knew that He had come from God. Mary and Martha were pleased to welcome the Lord Jesus to their home.

Luke chapter 10 verses 38-42.

These two sisters seem quite different from each other. Martha was busy, Mary quietly listened to Jesus. Perhaps Martha wanted to provide a special meal. This can be hard work, with different foods to prepare. We all need to eat, and it was kind of Martha to invite Jesus to a meal. But a simple meal would have been enough. Then Martha could have listened to Jesus too.

As we grow up, we find that time goes by very quickly. We need to think about how we use our time. We cannot sit listening to Jesus in the way that Mary did. But God does speak to us when we read our Bibles, and when we pray, we are speaking to Him. There are things we need to do: going to school or to work.

We must make sure that each day there is time to talk to God and to listen to Him.

What did Martha say to the Lord Jesus? Ask God to help you to remember that He is with you, even when you are busy.

Day 278: A FOOLISH MAN

Do you know what it means to be greedy? We sometimes say that someone who eats too much is greedy. It can also mean wanting more money, or other things, than we really need.

One day a man spoke to Jesus about some money. He wanted the Lord Jesus to tell his brother to share some money with him. Jesus told the people to be careful that they did not become greedy.

Luke chapter 12 verses 16-21.

The rich man in the parable thought that he had all he needed. He did not think about God. He did not think about helping others. And he never thought at all about what would happen to him when he died. The Lord Jesus continued to talk to His disciples. He told them that they should not spend their time worrying about what to eat or what to wear. They should look at the birds and the flowers that God cares for.

Boys and girls and men and women are more precious to God than the birds.

God our Father knows the things we need. If we live our lives to please Him, He will take care of us. If we love the Lord Jesus, we will not want to spend all our time getting more things for ourselves. We will want to use what we have to help others. We do not want to be like the rich man in the story who lost everything when he died. We want to be like those who Jesus talked about, who have treasure in Heaven.

What does it mean to be greedy? What three things did the rich man say that he would do?

Day 279: A THANKFUL WOMAN

Some things we do so easily that we never think about them at all. If you are fit and healthy you probably never think how good it is to stand up straight. But in the Bible we read about a lady who had been ill for eighteen years. There was something wrong with her back: she could not straighten up. Life must have been very difficult for her with her bent back. She must have longed to be able to stand up straight like other people, instead of always looking down at the ground.

GOD'S WORD

Luke chapter 13 verses 10-17.

What a wonderful day for this lady. How she must have thanked God for making her better. Sadly, there was someone who was not pleased for her. The man in charge of the synagogue was angry because the lady had been healed on the Sabbath day. But Jesus said that even an animal would be led to the water so that it could drink on the Sabbath day. Those who cared for their animals should care even more for this poor lady who had been ill so long.

EXTRA INFO

God has given His people one day each week to rest from their usual work. It was never meant to be a day when people would not help one another.

After Jesus had spoken to the ruler of the synagogue, all the people were glad. They had seen the lady with her bent back. They were happy to see her well again.

BY MYSELF

The people were glad to see the wonderful things that Jesus did.

ASK ABOUT

How long had this lady had a bent back? How long did it take the Lord Jesus to make her well?

Day 280: INVITATIONS AND EXCUSES

One day Jesus was invited to a meal at the home of a Pharisee. As they talked around the table, Jesus spoke about who we should invite to have a meal with us. We should not just ask our friends and relations, who could then ask us back for a meal with them. We should ask poor people who cannot repay us.

GOD'S WORD

Luke chapter 14 verses 16-24.

EXTRA INFO

Some Bibles use the word 'banquet' in verse 16. This is a word we use for a very special meal, with lots of good things to eat.

In this parable, Jesus is teaching us how people treat God's invitation.

BY MYSELF

God is willing to forgive us for the wrong things we have done.

But many people make excuses, like the people in the story. They are just too busy. It is not wrong to buy a field, or animals for the farm. It is not wrong to get married. These are good things to do, just as going to school or visiting friends is good. But these are not the most important things.

Do you remember Mary who lived at Bethany? She knew that the most important thing was to listen to Jesus. We need to understand what God is saying in the Bible. We can thank God for sending Jesus into the world so that we can be with Him in Heaven. Or we can be like those people in the story who were too busy to enjoy the banquet.

ASK ABOUT

What three excuses were made for not going to the banquet? What did the man tell his servant to do to fill his house?

Day 281: A LOST SHEEP

Would you like to live where there were no doctors and nurses to look after sick people, or where the roads were never mended? Not many people would like to live in a place like that.

Roads and hospitals have to be paid for, and that is why people who go to work have to pay taxes.

One of the disciples was a tax collector. In those days, tax collectors did not have many friends. People did not like them because they cheated: they took too much money and kept some for themselves. The Pharisees noticed that the tax collectors gathered around the Lord Jesus, listening to Him.

Other people who had not lived very good lives also came to hear Jesus.

Jesus made these people feel welcome. Jesus knew that the Pharisees were not happy. He told three parables to explain why He welcomed sinful people.

Luke chapter 15 verses 3-10.

A shepherd who lost a sheep would want to go and find it. A lady who lost a silver coin would want to search for it. And yet the Pharisees did not care about men and women who needed someone to show them the way to God. In Heaven there is great joy when someone repents. If the Pharisees had really loved God, they would have been glad to see sinful people listening to the Lord Jesus.

What did the shepherd do when he found the lost sheep? Who is our Good Shepherd?

Day 282: THE LOST SON

The Pharisees thought that they understood God's law but they did not understand God's love for sinners.

After the parables of the lost sheep and the lost coin, the Lord Jesus told a third parable: the lost son.

Luke chapter 15 verses 11-16.

When the younger son was far from home with no money and no food, he began to think about his father. He made up his mind to go home and tell his father that he had done wrong. He would say that he did not deserve to be treated as a son any longer: he would be a servant and work for his father.

Luke chapter 15 verses 20-24.

The father loved his son and welcomed him home, just as God welcomes those who ask for His forgiveness. The older son heard music and dancing, so he asked a servant what was happening. When he knew that there was a celebration for his brother's return, he was angry and would not join in. He was just like the Pharisees. They thought that they were good and that God was pleased with them. They did not realise that they had proud, sinful hearts, and needed God's forgiveness.

It is people who know they are sinful, who find God's love and forgiveness.

What did the younger son do with his father's money? How did the father welcome his son home?

Day 283: LAZARUS

Mary and Martha had a brother called Lazarus. One day the two sisters sent a message to the Lord Jesus, to tell Him that their brother was ill.

Jesus loved Mary and Martha and Lazarus, but He did not hurry to see them.

He stayed two more days in the place where He was. After that, He told His disciples that their friend Lazarus had died. They then set out for Bethany.

John chapter 11 verses 17-27.

Martha thought that if Jesus had come sooner, Lazarus would not have died. She told her sister that Jesus had asked to see her. Mary went to speak to Him. She also said that if He had come sooner, her brother would not have died. She was very sad. Both sisters believed that Jesus could have made Lazarus well again. He asked to see where Lazarus had been laid. The grave was a cave with a stone across the entrance. The Lord Jesus asked for the stone to be taken away. He prayed to God His Father and then He called Lazarus to come out of the grave. Lazarus came out: Jesus had given him life.

Many saw what the Lord Jesus had done, and believed in Him. But the Pharisees were afraid that many more people would believe in the Lord Jesus.

The Pharisees thought that if the people made Jesus king, the Romans would be angry. So the Pharisees decided that the Lord Jesus must be put to death.

What word in verses 24 and 25 means rising from the dead? What did Martha believe about the Lord Jesus?

Day 284: A MAN SAYS THANK-YOU

EXTRA INFO

Some illnesses are infectious: we can catch them from each other. Usually we need not worry about this: we can get over things like chickenpox or a bad cold quite quickly.

The Bible describes a very serious illness called leprosy. This illness could be passed by one person to another. God gave instructions to Moses so that the people would know what to do if anyone had leprosy. The person had to be looked at by the priest. If the priest decided that the illness was leprosy, then the leper would have to leave his home and family. He would have to live away from other people. If someone came towards him, he must shout 'unclean'. All this was done so that others would not catch the illness. Only the priest could decide if a leper was well again, and ready to return to his family. It must have been a very sad day when a man or woman, boy or girl, was found to have leprosy. To be ill and have to leave your home and family was very hard.

GOD'S WORD

Luke chapter 17 verses 11-19.

These men must have heard of the many people who had been healed by the Lord Jesus. They were not allowed to join the crowds who came to see Him. But they did call out to Him. All ten were made well again. To be cured of leprosy was wonderful: you would expect that all of them would have been very thankful. But only one came back to thank the Lord Jesus.

BY MYSELF

We have many things to thank God for: think about some of these things now.

ASK ABOUT

What did the Lord Jesus tell the ten lepers to do?

Day 285: TWO PRAYERS

Some people think that they are better than everyone else. They may be very clever, or have lots of money. They may just be proud of themselves because they think that they are good. The Pharisees believed that they kept God's laws and that God was pleased with them. They did not want to have anything to do with tax collectors and sinful people. The Lord Jesus told a parable about a Pharisee and a tax collector.

Luke chapter 18 verses 9-14.

Do you think that the Pharisee was really praying? Instead of praying, he was telling God how good he was. The tax collector's prayer was quite different. He knew that he had done things that were wrong.

He did not pretend to be better than he was. He just asked for God's mercy.

The word 'mercy' means not getting what we deserve.

When we do wrong, we deserve to be punished. When God is merciful to us, He forgives us and does not punish us. He can do this because the Lord Jesus came to take our punishment for us.

The Pharisee was too proud to realise that he needed a Saviour. The tax collector knew that he could never make himself good enough for God. And yet the Lord Jesus said that he was justified. An easy way to remember what that word means, is to say 'just-as-if-I've-never-sinned'. When God forgives, He promises that He will not remember the wrong things we did.

Can you find God's promise not to remember our sins, in Isaiah chapter 43? What verse is it?

Day 286: A RICH YOUNG MAN

As the Lord Jesus went from place to place He met all sorts of people. He met people who no one wanted to be friends with. He met rich people who had many friends. He met people who were old and people who were very young.

One day some young children were brought to the Lord Jesus. The disciples would have sent them away as if Jesus was too busy to see little children.

Mark chapter 10 verses 13-16.

The Lord Jesus told His disciples not to send the children away. He welcomed them and took them in His arms.

We can be quite sure that the Lord Jesus will always hear when boys and girls pray to Him.

After Jesus had met the children, a rich young man asked Jesus how to get eternal life. Jesus reminded him of God's commandments, but the young man said he obeyed these. Jesus then told him to sell what he owned and give the money to the poor people. Then he should follow the Lord Jesus.

The young man was very sad when he heard this. He did not want to give up his riches, so he turned away from the Lord Jesus. This reminds us that the Lord Jesus knows each one of us. He knows when there is something that we love more than Him.

This young man found that he loved his riches more than he loved God.

Who did Jesus want to come to him?

Day 287: WORKERS IN THE VINEYARD

Do you have a garden with flowers or vegetables in it? If you do, then someone must work hard at gardening. There is plenty of work to do digging and watering and weeding, so that the plants grow well.

Jesus told a story about a man who had a vineyard. He had many vines growing in his field and he would expect a good harvest of grapes. He needed workers to care for the vines so he went out to see who would come and work for him.

Matthew chapter 20 verses 1-7.

A denarius was a Roman coin. It was the usual pay for a day's work.

In the parable, the men were paid in the evening. Each one received the same amount of money. Those who had worked all day grumbled because they thought that they should have been paid more than those who had only worked one hour. The owner of the vineyard said that he had paid them the money they had agreed to work for. He had been very generous to pay others the same amount for less hours of work.

Some people learn to love and obey Jesus while they are very young. Like the men who started work early in the day, they may have many years to work for Him. There are others who never hear about God's love and forgiveness until they are much older. They may not have very much time at all to please God.

All who come to the Lord Jesus are given the same loving welcome.

How many times did the owner of the vineyard go out to find workers?

Day 288: BLIND BARTIMAEUS

Nowadays many blind people are able to work and earn money, but in New Testament days they could not do so. One day Jesus came to the town of Jericho. A blind man sat begging by the side of the road.

To beg means to sit by the roadside and ask people to give you money.

Mark chapter 10 verses 46-52.

Bartimaeus called Jesus 'Son of David'. King David lived a thousand years before Him, but Jesus was born into King David's family. At first the crowd did not like to hear the blind man calling out. But the Lord Jesus was not too busy to stop and talk to him, even though there were a great many people around Him.

Jesus asked Bartimaeus what he wanted. This question gave Bartimaeus the chance to show that he was not asking for money. He was asking for his sight. If anyone else had come along the road, Bartimaeus would have asked for money.

He knew that Jesus was different from other people.

He had faith: he believed that the Lord Jesus could cure his blindness. The Bible tells us that there is another kind of blindness. We may be able to see with our eyes, but God may say that we are blind. We are blind if we do not believe in the Lord Jesus Christ. The Lord Jesus said that the Pharisees were blind: they did not recognise Him as the Son of God.

What was the name of the blind man? What name did he use when he called the Lord Jesus?

Day 289: ZACCHAEUS

Zacchaeus was a tax collector and he was rich. When he heard that Jesus had come to Jericho, he decided that he would like to see Him. But Zacchaeus was not very tall and could not see because of the crowd.

GOD'S WORD

Luke chapter 19 verses 1-10.

Zacchaeus was pleased to welcome Jesus to his house. But the people watching were not pleased. People did not like tax collectors because they knew that the tax collectors cheated them. They took more money than they should have done, so that they could keep some for themselves.

Meeting Jesus brought a big change to Zacchaeus. Instead of wanting to get as much money as he could, Zacchaeus now wanted to give money away. He wanted to help poor people and also to pay back the money he should not have taken. Zacchaeus was truly sorry for the wrong things he had done.

BY MYSELF

The Lord Jesus said that salvation had come to Zacchaeus' house.

EXTRA INFO

Salvation means knowing that our sins are forgiven so that we can one day go to Heaven.

It is no use asking to be forgiven if we want to keep on doing something wrong. Zacchaeus showed that he was sorry, by wanting to change: he did not want to go on cheating. We could say that Zacchaeus had 'repented'. He was sorry for his sin and now wanted to please God.

ASK ABOUT

How did Zacchaeus manage to see the Lord Jesus? Learn verse 10 off by heart.

Day 290: HOSANNA

The Lord Jesus was on the way to Jerusalem. His disciples knew that it was dangerous for Him to go there. Other people who followed Him were afraid. They knew that plans had been made to put Jesus to death. They came to the Mount of Olives, a hill just outside Jerusalem. The Lord Jesus sent two of His disciples to bring Him a young donkey to ride on.

GOD'S WORD

Mark chapter 11 verses 1-10.

EXTRA INFO

More than five hundred years before, a prophet called Zechariah had told the people that their King would come to them, riding on a young donkey.

Many people shouted 'Hosanna', and spread cloaks or branches on the road. They had seen many of Jesus' miracles. Perhaps they thought that He would now become king, and set them free from the Romans.

That night the Lord Jesus and His disciples stayed at Bethany. The next day, He went to the temple. Once again He saw all the buying and selling going on there. He overturned the tables and made those people leave. He reminded them that the temple was a House of Prayer. It was not a place to cheat and charge too much money.

BY MYSELF

Many people listened to the Lord Jesus.

When the chief priests and teachers of the law saw this, they wanted to kill Him. But they were afraid to do so at once because they knew that the people would be angry.

ASK ABOUT

What was the name of the hill just outside Jerusalem? What were the two disciples to bring?

Day 291: THE WIDOW'S GIFT

The Lord Jesus spoke to His disciples on the mountainside one day. He told them that they should not pray so that everyone would see them and think how good they were. They should find a quiet place to pray. The Lord Jesus said the same about being kind to people. If we can help someone, it should be done as quietly as possible.

God sees what we do and He knows when we are kind and helpful.

Near to the temple was a place where people could give money. It was called the Treasury.

One day Jesus watched people putting their gifts into it. People who were very rich could give a lot of money. Sometimes they did this in such a way that others could see that a large gift was being given.

Luke chapter 21 verses 1-4.

The widow only had two small coins (the Bible you are reading may call them 'mites'). They would hardly buy anything. She could not give as much as the rich people did but she gave what she could.

Jesus said that she had given more than anyone else. The rich people had plenty of money left for themselves. The poor widow gave all that she had.

Jesus does not expect boys and girls to be able to do the same things as grown-ups can do. He does not expect poor people to give as much money to help others as rich people can. He does want us all to show that we love Him by the things we do and say.

What did the Lord Jesus say about the poor widow's gift?

One day, as Jesus came out of the temple, His disciples came to Him. They spoke about the wonderful buildings. It must have been a magnificent sight. It was not the temple that the people had built after being captives in Babylon. This was one that King Herod had built to please the Jewish people. Instead of admiring the buildings, Jesus told His disciples that they would be destroyed: every stone would be thrown down.

Jesus sat down on a hillside called the Mount of Olives. The temple could be seen from there, but it was a quiet place where the disciples could talk to Him.

The disciples asked Jesus when the temple would be destroyed and how were they to know when Jesus would come back?

The disciples believed that Jesus would come again.

Matthew chapter 23 verses 37-39 and chapter 24 verses 1-3.

Jesus explained that a terrible time was coming for Jerusalem. A great army would come and the Jewish people would be taken captive. When this happened, the temple with its fine buildings, would be destroyed.

These were sad words for the disciples to hear. God had sent prophets to the Jews, but they did not want to hear God's messages. Now God's own Son had come into the world. Some people had welcomed Him. But most did not want Him. Sad days were ahead.

Which words show how much the Lord Jesus loved the people?

Day 293: COMING AGAIN

People had often crowded around Jesus. They saw Him heal many people. They listened as He talked to them in a way that they had never heard from anyone else.

There were times when He spoke to His disciples away from the crowds.

As Jesus sat on the hillside, He answered the disciples' question about the Temple. He spoke to them about what would happen before He would come back to this world. He knew that there would be men who would pretend to be prophets. Some people would believe them even though they did not bring a true message from God. Some men would pretend to be the Lord Jesus. Jesus told His disciples to take no notice of them.

There will be no mistaking the time when Jesus comes again. God will gather all those who love Him to meet Him.

Matthew chapter 24 verses 36-39.

When Noah was building the ark, no one, except his own family, took any notice of him. Jesus said that it will be like that before He comes again. People all over the world will hear that they can be forgiven for the wrong things they have done. But many will not listen. They will live as though God was not there. Those who know Jesus as Saviour and Friend look forward to seeing Him when He comes again. But those who will not believe, will take the punishment for the wrong they have done.

Do we know when Jesus will come again?

If someone special was coming to your house, you would want everything to be clean and tidy. You would want to be ready for the visit. Thousands of years before Jesus came into the world, God promised that He would come. Some people, like Simeon and Anna, believed God's promises and looked forward to the coming of the Lord Jesus. They made sure that they were ready by living the way God wanted.

When Jesus talked to His disciples about the time when He will come back to this world, He did not say when it would be. But He did say that we must be ready to meet Him. He will come as a great King. The Lord Jesus told some parables about being ready.

GOD'S WORD

Matthew chapter 25 verses 1-13.

EXTRA INFO

There were no electric lights or torches with batteries in New Testament times. Oil lamps were used.

The ten young ladies (or bridesmaids) were waiting for the bridegroom. They would light the way to the house where his bride was. It was too late to buy oil when the bridegroom arrived. The people listening would have understood this story. It described a wedding just as it would have happened in those days.

BY MYSELF

The Lord Jesus told that story to teach us that we should be ready to meet Him.

Many years have gone by since Jesus went back to heaven. But God knows the right time for His return. All who love and obey Him will be ready to meet Him.

What was the difference between the girls who were wise and those who were foolish?

Day 295: THE SERVANTS

The parable we read yesterday was about being ready when the Lord Jesus comes again. He told another story to teach us about being careful what we do until He comes.

Matthew chapter 25 verses 14-18.

The talents that the man gave to his servants were silver and worth a lot of money. Two of the servants worked hard, so that when their master came back, they would have gained more money for him. The third servant did not even try to work for his master.

When the man returned from his long journey he was pleased with the first two servants. They had done well and he rewarded them for their work. The third servant handed back the silver talent he had been given. He made excuses for not working by saying that his master was not a good man. This servant was punished for his laziness. His silver was given to the servant who had ten talents. This story teaches us that all who belong to Jesus have something to use for Him.

God has made us all able to do different things.

Some people are good at teaching others and helping them to understand the Bible. Some are good at talking to people they meet about Jesus. Sometimes boys and girls think that because they cannot do great things, they cannot do anything for the Lord Jesus.

Little things done because we love Jesus, mean that we are using the time well, until He comes.

How many talents of silver did each servant have when the master went away? How many did each have when he came back?

Day 296: THE PRECIOUS PERFUME

Martha's sister Mary had some perfume that was worth a lot of money.

Do you know what perfume is? It is something that has a beautiful smell. It can be made from flowers such as roses or lavender. You will see bottles of perfume at the chemist's shop.

John chapter 12 verses 1-8.

Mary poured her precious perfume on Jesus' feet.

Mary showed her love and gratitude to Jesus. Why do you think Mary was very thankful? Do you remember what happened to her brother, Lazarus?

One disciple complained about what Mary had done. Judas had been with Jesus, listened to Him, and seen the wonderful things He had done. But he did not have a loving heart. He pretended to care about the poor, when he actually wanted the money for himself. Jesus said that there will always be poor people who need help. He understood Mary's generous act.

People heard that the Lord Jesus was in Bethany. Many came to see Him and also to see Lazarus. The chief priests did not like to see so many people coming to the Lord Jesus. They knew that the news of Lazarus being raised from the dead was spreading. They began to make plans to kill Lazarus. The priests should have known that only the power of God could have given life to Lazarus. Like the Pharisees, they wanted the people to listen to them.

What were the names of the brother and two sisters who lived at Bethany? What does the Bible say that Judas was?

Day 297: JUDAS

Jesus had twelve disciples. Which one was a thief? It was the one who complained about Mary pouring her perfume on Jesus. His name was Judas Iscariot.

As the time of the Passover Feast drew near, Judas knew that the chief priests wanted to put Jesus to death. He also knew that they were afraid to take Him away while so many people were around Him. We have read about how jealous the priests and Pharisees were of Jesus. But many of the people wanted to be with Him and listen to His words.

Those who were planning to put the Lord Jesus to death, did not want the people to be angry with them.

Judas went to the chief priests. He asked them how much money they would give him if he helped them. They paid him thirty silver coins. After this, Judas watched for a time when he could hand the Lord Jesus over to His enemies. It is hard for us to understand how a disciple could have done such a terrible thing. Judas had seen and heard the same things as the other disciples. But he had not given up his sinful ways. His heart (the person he really was) had not changed. It is good to be with others who love the Lord Jesus. But that will not make anyone a Christian.

Judas had been with the disciples of the Lord Jesus. But he did not know Jesus as his Saviour.

Matthew chapter 26 verses 14-16 and Luke chapter 22 verses 1-6.

What word means 'hand someone over to their enemies'? (Luke chapter 22 verse 4). How much was Judas given by the priests?

Day 298: THE PASSOVER

Have you ever thought about how much water your family uses every day? It is so easy to turn on the tap whenever water is needed that we seldom think about it at all. It would be quite different if we had to carry all our water from a well.

In New Testament times it was usually the women who did this. So when the Lord Jesus told two of His disciples to follow a man carrying a jar of water, he would have been quite easy to find.

Mark chapter 14 verses 12-16.

Unleavened bread was bread made without yeast. Yeast makes bread rise, so unleavened bread is rather flat and not as soft as normal bread.

In the Book of Exodus, the people of Israel ate bread without yeast when they left Egypt. God said that they should eat unleavened bread for seven days each year after the Passover Feast. The Passover meal was a special time for the Jews. It was a time to give thanks to God for bringing them out of slavery.

They remembered the lamb that died instead of the oldest son in each family.

Jesus knew that soon He would die, in place of sinful men, women, boys and girls. This would be the last meal He would eat with His disciples. He had many things to tell them, to help them understand all that was going to happen.

Which disciples went to prepare the Passover meal? (Luke chapter 22 verse 8). Why was it not difficult to find the man the Lord Jesus told them to follow?

Jesus and His disciples ate the Passover meal together in the evening. Jesus gave thanks for the bread, then broke it and gave it to the disciples. He also gave thanks for the wine and shared it with them. He told them that in future the bread would remind them of His body. The wine would remind them of His blood which would be shed when He died for them.

Jesus had many things to talk to His disciples about, but the disciples were arguing about which one of them was the greatest.

Jesus explained that a really great person would be the one who was ready to help others.

John chapter 13 verses 3-5 and 12-15.

The roads in the land of Israel were hot and dusty. A servant would have the job of washing people's feet when they came into the house.

Peter was surprised when Jesus washed his feet. If we love Jesus, we will want to be like Him. We will want to help others in any way we can.

Jesus then told His disciples that one of them was going to betray Him. They looked at each other, not knowing which one of them He meant. Even though Judas had gone secretly to see the priests, Jesus knew what he was planning to do. When Judas left the room, the other disciples thought he had gone to buy something. They did not know that he was going to help the people who wanted to put Jesus to death.

Which verse tells us that the Lord Jesus was going back to God His Father? Who was surprised that the Lord Jesus would wash his feet?

Day 300: WORDS OF COMFORT

I hope you have never had a friend who turned out not to be a real friend at all. The disciples found it very hard to understand what the Lord Jesus meant when He said that one of them would betray Him. They knew each other well, and did not expect that Judas would do such a dreadful thing. But the Lord Jesus had more to say that was hard to understand. He told the disciples that they would all leave Him. Peter said that he would never do so.

Matthew chapter 26 verses 34-35.

To deny or disown someone means that you pretend not know that person.

The disciples must have felt sad. They did not understand what would happen. Jesus comforted them.

John chapter 14 verses 1-6.

Jesus told them that it was better that He was going back to His Father. When He went back to Heaven, God would send the Holy Spirit to them. While Jesus lived on earth, He was only in one place at a time - like we are. If we belong to the Lord Jesus the Holy Spirit is with us wherever we are, all the time.

After He had talked to His disciples, the Lord Jesus prayed for them.

He asked His Father to watch over them. He prayed for people everywhere who would come to believe in Him.

How many times did Jesus say that Peter would deny him?

Day 301: IN THE GARDEN

After the Passover meal, Jesus and His disciples went to the Garden of Gethsemane near the Mount of Olives. It was a quiet place and Jesus went there to pray to His Father in Heaven. Leaving some of the disciples to wait, He took Peter, James and John with Him.

Jesus knew that He would be put to death the following day. Just as in Old Testament times the lamb died instead of the person who had done wrong, so Jesus had come to die in the place of all who trust Him to forgive them. But Jesus was filled with sorrow, as He thought of all the wrong that we have done being laid on Him. Three times He prayed to His Father, and three times He found His disciples sleeping. They were so sad that they were unable to keep awake. Their eyes would not stay open. However, an angel came to help Him and to strengthen Him.

Jesus told His disciples to get up. He knew who was coming towards them at that very moment.

Luke chapter 22 verses 47-53.

Judas had done what he had been paid to do. He led those who hated Jesus to the place where Jesus was.

The Garden of Gethsemane was a quiet place so people wouldn't see Jesus being arrested by his enemies.

Jesus could have asked God to send angels to rescue Him. But He allowed Himself to be led away. He knew that because of His death, many people would have forgiveness and new life.

Where did Jesus go to pray? How did Judas show the crowd where Jesus was?

Day 302: THE TRIAL

It is easy to say that we will be brave, but it is not easy to be brave, when we are frightened. Peter had said that he would never leave Jesus. The other disciples said the same. But when Jesus was led away from the garden, the disciples ran away. They were afraid of what might happen to them.

Jesus was taken to the High Priest's house. When someone has broken the law - perhaps by stealing, or hurting another person - they are put on trial.

Being put on trial means that someone decides whether a person has done wrong or not. The person who decides is usually called a judge.

Jesus had done nothing wrong. He had lived a perfect life. But He was put on trial. First of all He was questioned by the High Priest. No one could be found who could truthfully say that the Lord Jesus had done wrong. So people were brought to the High Priest's house to tell lies about Him.

The High Priest asked Jesus to tell him if He was the Son of God. The Lord Jesus answered 'yes'. Then all the priests and teachers of the law, who were there, said that He should be put to death. While this was happening, Peter was outside the house in a courtyard.

Luke chapter 22 verses 54-62.

Peter pretended that he did not know the Lord Jesus because he was afraid. But afterwards he was very, very sorry.

How many people said that they knew that Peter had been with the Lord Jesus? When Peter heard the cock crow, what did he remember?

Jesus had done many wonderful things. He healed the sick. He gave sight to the blind. He calmed the storm. He fed the five thousand. He taught people about God. He was kind to people that other people did not care about. Yet the priests and teachers of the law wanted Him to be killed. They were envious, because the people had listened to the Lord Jesus and had seen the miracles He had done.

At this time Israel was part of the Roman Empire. The Jewish leaders could not put the Lord Jesus to death. Only the man that the Emperor had put in charge could do that: his name was Pilate.

The Jewish leaders took Jesus to Pilate. They told Pilate that Jesus had said that he was a King. The Roman Emperor would not allow anyone to make himself a king. When Pilate questioned Jesus, he found no fault in Him. He sent Him to be questioned by King Herod.

Finding nothing wrong, Pilate told the people that Jesus did not deserve to be put to death.

Mark chapter 15 verses 6-15.

At the Feast of the Passover, one prisoner was set free. Barabbas was a prisoner who had done many wrong things. The crowd shouted for Barabbas to be set free and for the Lord Jesus to be put to death. This was what the priests told the crowd to ask for.

Why did the leaders of the Jews hate the Lord Jesus? What did Pilate say about Him?

Day 304: CRUCIFIED

Do you remember that day long, long ago, when Adam and Eve disobeyed God?

God had said that those who sin must die. But God promised that He would send a Saviour.

The Saviour would take the punishment for all the wrong things that His people had done.

In the Book of Revelation chapter 21 verse 27 we read that nothing impure can enter Heaven. To be shut out of Heaven is to be where there is no love, no goodness, no joy: a place the Bible calls 'hell'. God sent Jesus, so that sinful people can be forgiven and be with Him forever. No sin will spoil Heaven: Heaven is for those who have been forgiven and changed by Jesus.

Mark chapter 15 verses 21-32.

Crucifixion was very cruel. The person was nailed to a wooden cross and left to die. But Jesus prayed that God would forgive those who had done this to Him. One of the thieves who was crucified with Jesus was sorry for the wrong things he had done. Jesus forgave him. He promised the man that he would be with Him in Paradise that very day. People laughed at Jesus as they saw Him on the cross. They asked Him why He did not save Himself, if He was really the Son of God. We know that the Lord Jesus did not save Himself because by His death He saved others.

**Who carried the cross for the Lord Jesus?
Who else was crucified at the same time?**

Day 305: THE GOOD SHEPHERD

It was nine o'clock in the morning when Jesus was crucified. In the middle of the day, at about twelve o'clock, the sun stopped shining. It became very dark for three hours. During that time, the curtain in the Temple was torn in two from top to bottom. That curtain had hung between the Holy Place and the Most Holy Place, but it was not needed anymore.

We do not need to be shut out from God's presence because of sin. Jesus is the way to God.

John chapter 19 verses 25-30.

Even though He was on the cross, the Lord Jesus thought of His mother. The disciple who He asked to take care of her was John.

Just before He died the Lord Jesus said 'It is finished'. He had finished the work that He came into the world to do. There was no need for any more animals to be sacrificed. There was no need for any priests to offer sacrifices. In John chapter 10 we read that the Lord Jesus is the Good shepherd who gives His life for the sheep. Just as a good shepherd would face danger for his sheep, the Lord Jesus gave His life for His people.

There was a soldier standing nearby watching the Lord Jesus. After hearing the words that Jesus spoke from the cross he knew that this could not be an ordinary man. Jesus must be the Son of God.

Some of the women who used to help the Lord Jesus, stood at a distance watching all that happened.

Who was to be like a son to Mary? What were Jesus' last three words?

Day 306: A SECRET DISCIPLE

BY MYSELF

Before the Lord Jesus died he was taken prisoner. When he was led away the disciples were afraid and ran off.

GOD'S WORD

Two disciples followed at a distance to see what would happen. One of these disciples was Peter. While Jesus was being questioned, Peter pretended that he did not know Him. But other people did not behave in this way.

John chapter 19 verses 38-42.

Two men cared for the body of Jesus. Joseph of Arimathea was a leader of the Jewish people. He was a secret disciple of Jesus. He had been afraid of what the other Jewish leaders and teachers would say if they knew that he believed in the Lord Jesus. But he had not agreed with those who wanted to put Jesus to death. Now, when others were frightened, he came forward. Nicodemus was the Pharisee who had talked to Jesus at night. He would also have realised that Jesus should not have been killed. He too was willing to help when the friends of Jesus had deserted Him.

EXTRA INFO

Myrrh and aloes were perfumes made from plants, that people used in those days. The tomb or grave in the garden would have been like a small cave. A large stone was placed across the entrance to the tomb.

A group of women stayed to watch where the body of Jesus was laid. Then they went away to prepare the beautiful scented oils and spices that they planned to take to the grave.

ASK ABOUT

Who did Joseph ask to allow him to care for the body of Jesus?

Sometimes things happen that we do not understand: things that make us feel very sad. The day after the Lord Jesus was crucified was the Sabbath day. This must have been a time of great sorrow for His disciples. They had listened to the words of Jesus. They had seen His miracles. They had believed that He was the Saviour who God had promised to send into the world. Now it seemed that they would never see Him again.

The priests and the Pharisees knew that the Lord Jesus had said that He would rise again. They asked Pilate to arrange for His grave to be guarded. This was because they thought that the disciples might steal the body and then tell people that Jesus had risen from the dead.

Pilate told the Jewish leaders to make the grave secure themselves. They did this and put men on guard.

Matthew chapter 28 verses 1-8.

The angel told the women the wonderful news that Jesus had risen.

The guards were terrified by what had happened, but the angel told the women not to be afraid. The women hurried to tell the disciples what they had seen. The disciples could not believe what they heard. Peter and another of the disciples went to the grave to see for themselves. They saw that the grave was empty except for the cloth that the body of Jesus had been wrapped in. They went back to their homes not really understanding what they had seen.

Who told the women that Jesus had risen from the dead?

Day 308: MARY MAGDALENE

One of the women who went out very early on that first Easter morning was Mary Magdalene. The Lord Jesus had helped her when she was in great need. Since that time she had helped to provide food and other things that the Lord Jesus must have needed.

After the two disciples had looked into the grave where the body of Jesus had been, Mary stayed in the garden. She stood near to the grave and she was crying.

GOD'S WORD

John chapter 20 verses 11-17.

Through her tears, Mary did not see that the man standing nearby was Jesus. All she could think of was that someone had moved His body. It was when she heard her name, that she knew who was speaking.

BY MYSELF

All her sadness was over. Mary knew now that Jesus really had risen from the dead.

Jesus warned her that He would not be staying among His followers as He had before. He would soon go to be with His Father in Heaven. Jesus gave Mary a message for the disciples. The One He was going to be with was His Father and their Father. Those who love and obey the Lord Jesus can call God, their Father. The Lord Jesus called the disciples His brothers. Mary told the disciples all that Jesus had said to her.

EXTRA INFO

The Lord Jesus died for everyone who believes in Him. God raised Him from the dead: we call this the resurrection. Now there can be no doubt that Jesus is the Son of God and He is alive for evermore.

ASK ABOUT

Who did Mary think was standing near her in the garden?

Day 309: LIES

I hope that you never tell lies: it is always wrong to do so. After the Lord Jesus had risen, some people were actually paid to tell a lie. The men who had been told to guard the grave where the body of Jesus lay, saw an angel. The angel moved the stone from the entrance to the grave. The guards shook with fear when they saw it. They went to the chief priests to tell them what had happened. The guards were told to say that they had fallen asleep and while they were sleeping, the disciples had come and stolen the body of Jesus.

GOD'S WORD

Matthew chapter 28 verses 11-15.

EXTRA INFO

Usually a guard who fell asleep on duty would have got into trouble. But the priests said they would make sure that everything was all right.

The priests paid money to the guards to stop them telling the truth. They did this because they were afraid that people would believe that Jesus had risen from the dead.

BY MYSELF

The guards had seen the angel. They knew that the disciples had not stolen the body.

The guards told lies because they were paid to do so. Why did the priests not want anyone to believe that Jesus was alive? They had been the very people who wanted to kill Him. If it was true that He was alive, then it must be true that He is the Son of God. This was what the priests did not want to admit.

ASK ABOUT

What happened to the guards when they saw the angel? (Matthew chapter 28 verse 4). What were the guards paid to say?

Day 310: ON THE WAY TO EMMAUS

EXTRA INFO

We sometimes say that something is 'too good to be true'. This is when something so wonderful has happened that we can hardly believe it.

On the day that Jesus rose from the dead, two people were walking from Jerusalem to the village of Emmaus. One of them was named Cleopas: we do not know the name of the other. They were talking about what had happened to the Lord Jesus when a third person began walking with them. He wanted to know what they had been talking about. They told him about how Jesus had been crucified. They described what had happened when the women found the grave empty. They did not realise that it was Jesus Himself who was walking along with them. Jesus began to speak to them about all that was written in the Old Testament about Him.

GOD'S WORD

Luke chapter 24 verses 28-35.

Now that these two friends had seen the Lord Jesus, they hurried back to tell the disciples.

BY MYSELF

As they talked together, Jesus came to them.

They felt afraid when they saw Him. He showed them His hands and His feet, and then asked them for something to eat. This helped them to believe that it was really true that He was alive. Then, He talked about what was written in the Old Testament. They had not understood that the One God had promised to send into the world would die and then rise again. In the Book of Isaiah chapter 53 we read of how the Saviour will die to take the punishment for our sins.

ASK ABOUT

Where were the two friends walking to?
When did they recognise the Lord Jesus?

Day 311: THOMAS

Has anyone ever said 'I don't believe you', when you told them something had happened? One disciple found it very hard to believe that Jesus was alive. Thomas had not been with the others when Jesus came.

John chapter 20 verses 24-29.

Thomas needed to see the Lord Jesus before he could believe that He had risen. We have not seen Him, but we can believe that He died and rose again.

John chapter 20 verses 30-31 and chapter 21 verse 25.

John tells us that Jesus did so many wonderful things that they could not all be written down. But enough has been written for us to know that Jesus is the Son of God.

Only God's sinless Son could die in place of sinful people.

When Adam and Eve disobeyed God, they had to leave Eden. They were not allowed to stay and eat the fruit of the tree of life. Sin spoils God's world. But through the death of the Lord Jesus, we can have life. When we become Christians, we want to please God instead of ourselves. We are still tempted to do wrong. The Bible tells us that one day, when we see the Lord Jesus, we will be like Him. We will no longer be tempted to sin. We will only do what is right and good.

Who did not believe that the others had seen the Lord Jesus? What did he say when he did see the Lord Jesus?

Day 312: ON THE SEA SHORE

Do you remember what Peter did, the night before Jesus was crucified? He meant to stay by Jesus but three times he pretended not to know Him. Now Jesus had risen from the dead. Would He still have work for Peter to do? It may be that Peter thought that the Lord Jesus would not want him now. In any case, he decided to go fishing. Some of the other disciples went with him. But they did not catch any fish that night.

John chapter 21 verses 4-14.

After the long night had gone by without any fish being caught, how different it was when the Lord Jesus came. How much better the disciples must have felt after the meal that He had prepared for them.

Jesus then spoke just to Peter. He asked Peter whether he loved Him.

He asked this question three times. Peter answered each time that he did love the Lord Jesus. Jesus made it clear that He still had work for Peter to do. He asked him to look after His sheep. Jesus was not telling Peter to be a shepherd instead of a fisherman. He was telling Peter to teach and care for people, so that others would come to love God. It was about three years since Jesus had called Peter to follow Him. Now for the second time He said to Peter, 'Follow Me'.

Just as Peter had denied the Lord Jesus three times, now he was able to say three times that he loved Him.

Which verse tells us that the disciples did not recognise Jesus at first? What happened when they did what the Lord told them to?

WITNESSES AT HOME AND ABROAD

The Book of Acts was written by Luke. It begins with the ascension of the Lord Jesus Christ and His charge to His disciples to be His witnesses in Jerusalem, Judea, Samaria and to the ends of the earth.

Crucially, before this widening circle of witness could begin, the disciples were instructed to await the coming of the Holy Spirit. Ten days after the Lord's ascension, the Holy Spirit came. The immediate effect was that Christ was preached and many people were saved.

The first seven chapters of this Book are centred on Jerusalem and include the first imprisonments for the faith, and the first martyr. Chapters eight to twelve are concerned with the taking of the gospel to the regions of Judea and Samaria, the impetus for this being the growing persecution of the church at Jerusalem. Included in this section of the Book is the account of the conversion of Saul of Tarsus who had been zealous in his persecution of the church.

From chapters thirteen to twenty-eight, we read of the gospel being taken to other nations. Saul the persecutor became Paul the apostle, who travelled tirelessly, preaching the gospel wherever he had opportunity. He made three missionary journeys, reaching Europe on the second journey and returning there during the third. Paul was then imprisoned at Caesarea for over two years, during which time he was able to testify to the Governors Felix and Festus as well as to King Agrippa. He appealed to Caesar and was taken to Rome, where he was allowed to rent a house and preach Christ to all who came. Whether this was Paul's final imprisonment or whether he had a further period of freedom, is not recorded. The Book of Acts gives no further details of his life and no account of his death.

Day 313: RETURN TO HEAVEN

Easter Day is when we especially remember the resurrection of the Lord Jesus. For forty days after the first Easter morning, He appeared to His disciples. He did not stay with them, but met with them from time to time. He told them to go all over the world telling people about Him. One day, the disciples went with the Lord Jesus to the Mount of Olives, outside Jerusalem.

GOD'S WORD

Acts chapter 1 verses 6-12.

Jesus explained to the disciples how they were to tell people everywhere about Him. They would be His witnesses.

EXTRA INFO

Witnesses are people who can tell what they have seen or heard.

The disciples had seen all that Jesus had done. He had shown them that He was the Son of God. They had seen Him taken away to be crucified. They had seen Him alive after He rose from the dead. They could tell people about these things. Jesus told them to start in Jerusalem. Then they were to travel through Judea and Samaria. After that, they must go to other lands with the good news that God had sent the Saviour. But before they began their work, they were to wait at Jerusalem. The Lord Jesus knew that they could not do this work on their own. He promised that God would send His Holy Spirit to them.

BY MYSELF

The Holy Spirit would help them to speak about the Lord Jesus.

ASK ABOUT

What is the promise in verse 11? What is the word we use for people who can tell others what they have seen?

Day 314: THE HOLY SPIRIT COMES

Fifty days had passed since that wonderful day when Jesus rose from the dead. Ten days had passed since the disciples had watched Jesus go up into heaven. Now, on the Day of Pentecost, they were together waiting in Jerusalem as Jesus told them to.

Pentecost was a special day for the people of Israel and many people had travelled to Jerusalem for it.

Acts chapter 2 verses 1-8.

To understand these verses we must think about who God is. Because God is so much greater than we are, you will not be surprised that some things about God are not easy to understand. We can only know as much as God has told us about Himself in the Bible. The Bible tells us that there is one God who exists in three persons: God the Father, God the Son and God the Holy Spirit. We know that the Lord Jesus taught us to pray to His Father in Heaven. We also know that Jesus, God the Son, became a man on earth. The Bible tells us that God the Father and God the Son send the Holy Spirit to those who become Christians. Jesus said that the Holy Spirit is our teacher, our comforter and our helper. When someone becomes a Christian it is because the Holy Spirit has shown them that they need a Saviour.

For those who love and trust the Lord Jesus it is the Holy Spirit who helps us to understand the Bible so that we can grow into strong Christians.

How many countries had people come to Jerusalem from? (Acts chapter 2 verses 9-11).

Day 315: PETER SPEAKS

People from different countries speak different languages. If we want to talk to someone from another land we need to learn their language. On the Day of Pentecost, people from many different lands were surprised to hear the disciples speaking their languages. The coming of the Holy Spirit made this possible, although the crowd did not realise it at first.

GOD'S WORD

Acts chapter 2 verses 22-24 and 36-39.

When Peter told them that they had crucified God's Son, the people wondered what they should do. When it was explained that they should repent, about three thousand people became Christians.

EXTRA INFO

To repent means to stop doing what is wrong, and to trust in Jesus to forgive us and teach us what is right.

On the night before Jesus was crucified, Peter was so frightened that he said he did not even know the Lord Jesus. What a difference the coming of the Holy Spirit had made. Now Peter was able to stand up in front of a great crowd of people and talk about Jesus.

When God gives the Holy Spirit to us, we do not expect to talk in different languages. Pentecost was a very special time when God made sure that people from many lands heard about the Lord Jesus.

BY MYSELF

The Holy Spirit helps us not to be afraid to speak about the Lord Jesus.

ASK ABOUT

Find three places where the disciples would tell people about the Lord Jesus. (Acts chapter 1 verse 8).

Day 316: NO LONGER LAME

We have read about blind men who had to beg because they could not work. One day Peter and John met a man who had to beg because he could not walk.

Acts chapter 3 verses 1-8.

The people who knew the lame man were amazed. After he had been healed, the man held on to Peter and John, and a crowd soon gathered.

Peter explained that it was not his power that had healed the lame man, but faith in the Lord Jesus.

Peter spoke about how Jesus had died and risen from the dead. He told the people to repent so that their sins could be forgiven. Many who heard what Peter said believed in the Lord Jesus. But some of the priests and leaders of the people did not like to hear Peter teaching about Jesus. As it was getting late, they put Peter and John into prison for the night so that they could question them the next day.

As we read the Book of Acts you will find another word for disciples. The word is 'Apostles' and it means people who are sent to do a special job. Jesus had already told them what their work would be: telling people about Him. The Apostles were men who had seen the Lord Jesus after He rose from the dead. They were able to tell others what they had seen.

The New Testament was written by the apostles and their helpers. The Holy Spirit helped them to do this and He also helps us to understand what they wrote.

What was the name of the gate of the Temple where the lame man was laid? How often was he brought there?

Day 317: QUESTIONED

When we do something wrong, we expect to be punished in some way. Peter and John had not done anything wrong, and yet they had been held in prison for the night. When the next day came, they were taken out of prison to a place where the priests and leaders of the people were waiting to see them.

These men knew that the lame man had been healed. They asked Peter and John how they had done this. Of course the Apostles told them that it was not their power, but the power of the Lord Jesus that had caused the lame man to get up and walk.

GOD'S WORD

Acts chapter 4 verse 13-20.

The leaders of the people did not thank God that a lame man had been healed. They told Peter and John to stop telling people about Jesus.

EXTRA INFO

The Bible teaches us that we should obey those who rule over us, unless what they tell us to do is different from what God has said.

BY MYSELF

The Apostles had been told by Jesus to tell people about Him. They knew that they must obey God.

Why do you think it is so important for people to be told that Jesus has been crucified and has risen from the dead? It is because our sins can only be forgiven when we trust in Jesus. He took the punishment for our sins when He died on the cross. When He rose from the dead, He showed that He is the Son of God, who is able to forgive us for the wrong things we have done.

ASK ABOUT

How old was the lame man who had been healed? (Acts chapter 4 verse 22).

Day 318: ANANIAS AND SAPPHIRA

Are you good at sharing? It is not always easy to share your favourite toys with others.

Some of the first Christians were rich and some were poor. The rich Christians sold their land and their houses so that the Apostles could share it with the poor.

GOD'S WORD

Acts chapter 4 verses 34-37 and chapter 5 verses 1-4.

No one told Ananias and Sapphira to sell their land. They did this when they saw what others had done. When the land was sold, they did not have to give all the money to the Apostles. It was not wrong to keep some money for themselves, although it would have been generous to give it all. It was the lie that Ananias told that was wrong. He wanted to seem more generous than he really was. When Peter told Ananias that he had lied to God, Ananias died. Later on Peter spoke to Sapphira and she also lied about the money. When Peter told her how wrong this was, she died as her husband had done. This true story of Ananias and Sapphira reminds us that God knows all about us.

BY MYSELF

If we do wrong we should tell God about it and ask for His forgiveness.

EXTRA INFO

It is foolish to pretend we are better than we really are.

ASK ABOUT

What does God promise to do when we confess our sins? (1 John chapter 1 verse 9).

Day 319: GAMALIEL'S ADVICE

Do you remember how jealous the priests and leaders were of Jesus? They saw great crowds listening to Him and following Him. Now the apostles were the ones that the leaders became jealous of. Many sick people were brought to the apostles and were healed. Instead of being thankful that people had been made well, the High Priest had the apostles put into prison.

Acts chapter 5 verses 19-26.

Again the apostles were brought to the High Priest. He reminded them that they had been told not to teach about Jesus. But Peter said that they must obey God.

When the priests and leaders of the people met together, this was called a council.

One member of the council was a man named Gamaliel. He asked for the apostles to be put outside for a while. Then he spoke to the council. He advised that they should let the apostles go. In time it would be clear whether God was with them or not. If God was not with the apostles, they would soon be forgotten. But Gamaliel knew that if the apostles were sent by God, no one would be able to stop their work.

The council agreed with Gamaliel. The apostles were beaten, told not to speak about Jesus and then set free.

They did not stop speaking about Jesus, but continued to do so every day, as He had told them to.

Why did the council try to stop the apostles telling people about Jesus?

Day 320: HELP FOR THE NEEDY

We have already read about how the first Christians shared what they had with each other. Some of those who were poor were the widows.

Widows are ladies whose husbands have died.

They received special help each day so that they would have enough food and other things that they needed. But it was said that some of the widows did not receive as much help as others. The apostles knew that their time must be used in teaching people about the Lord Jesus. They decided that men should be chosen to make sure that help was given to those who needed it.

Acts chapter 6 verses 2-8.

Stephen was one of the seven men who were chosen. He helped to look after the poor people and spoke to people about the Lord Jesus.

Stephen was brought before the priests and leaders of the people as Peter and the other apostles had been. Men were brought in to tell lies about Stephen.

Stephen spoke about all that God had done for the people of Israel in Old Testament times.

And yet he said that when God sent His Son to them, they had killed Him. The council was very angry with Stephen. They did not like to hear that they had done wrong when they put the Lord Jesus to death.

Find the names of some of the people Stephen talked about. (Acts chapter 7 verses 2, 8, 9 and 20).

Day 321: STEPHEN

It must be very frightening to stand up in front of men who are really angry. Stephen knew that he had not done anything wrong. He knew that lies had been told about him.

Acts chapter 7 verses 55-60.

The Lord Jesus had promised that He would never leave those who belong to Him. Instead of being afraid, Stephen saw Jesus in heaven and knew that he was going to be with Him.

A young man named Saul was present when Stephen was stoned. Saul thought that it was wrong to tell people that Jesus is the Son of God. He was not sorry about Stephen's death. Saul knew God's laws. He believed that he could keep them all and that God would be pleased with him.

Saul did not understand that he needed the Saviour who God had promised to send.

A difficult time began for Christians. Saul threw them into prison. Whenever the leaders of the people saw a Christian who they thought should be killed, Saul agreed with them. This was a time of persecution.

Persecution means ill-treatment or cruelty.

Many Christians from Jerusalem went to live in other places rather than be taken to prison. Wherever they went they told people about the Lord Jesus. No one was able to stop the good news from spreading.

Who did not leave Jerusalem? (Acts chapter 8 verse 1).

Day 322: THE MAN FROM ETHIOPIA

One of the men chosen to help those in need was Philip. Philip went to Samaria and told the people there about Jesus. Then one day an angel spoke to him.

Acts chapter 8 verses 26-31.

The man in the chariot was an Ethiopian. That means he was from the country of Ethiopia. Ethiopia is a country in Africa.

The Ethiopian was reading some words from chapter 53 of the Book of Isaiah. He read about someone who would suffer and die because of the wrong that other people had done. He wanted to know who this had been written about. Philip was able to tell the Ethiopian that Isaiah was writing about the Lord Jesus.

Philip told him who Jesus was and what He had done. The man understood what Philip said.

The Ethiopian saw some water near the road and asked if he could be baptised. Philip asked him whether he truly believed in the Lord Jesus. He told Philip that he believed that Jesus is the Son of God. Both of them got out of the chariot and went down into the water. There at the roadside the treasurer to the Queen of Ethiopia was baptised as a follower of the Lord Jesus. Philip left him to continue his journey.

We do not read about him again in the Bible but no doubt this man from Ethiopia took the good news about the Lord Jesus back to his own country.

What did the Ethiopian do as he continued his journey? (Acts chapter 8 verse 39).

Day 323: THE DAMASCUS ROAD

Have you noticed that people are all different and do their work in different ways? Some people are inclined to be lazy: they do not like to work at all. Some people work quite hard but do not put much effort into their work. Others put all their energy into whatever they do: Saul was like this.

He thought it was wrong to teach about Jesus. He continued to work really hard to stop this happening.

Acts chapter 9 verses 1-8.

Saul was on his way to Damascus, so that he could take the Christians there as prisoners. It was while he was travelling that the Lord Jesus spoke to him. After the brightness of the light which he had seen, Saul was unable to see anything. He had to be helped into the city of Damascus.

Saul stayed in the house of a man named Judas who lived in Straight Street.

For three days Saul remained blind and did not eat or drink. He knew that while he was in Damascus he would be told what to do, and so he waited.

Saul was a Pharisee: one of the men who were careful to keep God's commandments. He had been so sure that the Christians were wrong to believe that Jesus is the Son of God. He thought that he was right to try to stop them telling others about the Lord Jesus. Suddenly all this had changed.

Saul now knew that Jesus was alive and had spoken to him.

What two questions did Saul ask the Lord Jesus?

Day 324: A CHANGED LIFE

In the city of Damascus there lived a man whose name was Ananias and he was a Christian. One day the Lord Jesus told Ananias to go to the house where Saul was staying.

Acts chapter 9 verses 13-20.

Ananias did as he was asked even though he knew how badly Saul had treated those who were Christians. Saul began to tell people that Jesus is the Son of God. Everyone who heard him was amazed. He had been well known as one who persecuted Christians.

Now Saul was a Christian and his life had completely changed.

For a time the Jews in Damascus listened to Saul as he explained that Jesus is the Saviour God promised. Then they began to plot how to kill him. They kept watch at the city gates, but Saul knew what they were doing.

One night the Christians let Saul down over the city wall in a basket.

Safely out of Damascus, he went to Jerusalem. When he arrived Saul had another difficulty to face. The Christians there were afraid of him. They did not believe that Saul was a Christian too. But one of them, named Barnabas, believed Saul and took him to the apostles.

How did Saul escape from Damascus? (Acts chapter 9 verse 25). Who took Saul to the Apostles? (Acts chapter 7 verse 27).

Day 325: DORCAS

In New Testament times rich people might travel by chariot: the poor people often had to walk. Donkeys could carry heavy loads and in the desert camels were used.

The apostles travelled to visit Christians and to speak to others about Jesus even though it wasn't easy.

One day Peter came to a place called Lydda. A man named Aeneas lived there. He was paralysed and had been in bed for eight years.

EXTRA INFO

Someone who is paralysed is unable to move.

Peter told him to get up and he was able to: the Lord Jesus had healed him. The people believed in Jesus when they saw what had happened.

BY MYSELF

Not far from Lydda was the town of Joppa where a lady called Dorcas lived.

GOD'S WORD

Acts chapter 9 verses 36-43.

The people who Dorcas had been kind to were sad when she died. They must have been amazed when Peter's prayer was answered and they saw Dorcas alive again.

People listened to the apostles when they saw the power of Jesus to heal and to give life. The apostles had the important job of telling people about Jesus. God worked miracles through them so that people would believe that He had sent them.

ASK ABOUT

Someone in the Book of Exodus performed miracles so that people would know that God had sent him. Who was it? (Exodus chapter 4 verses 1-5).

Day 326: PETER'S VISION

God had promised Abraham that a great nation would come from his family.

This nation was called Israel and its people have been called different things over the years: Israelites, Hebrews, Jews. They called other people Gentiles.

Israel should have shown other nations how good life is for a nation that obeys God. But the people of Israel copied the nations around them who worshipped idols. To stop this happening, Jews decided not to have anything to do with people from other lands.

In the town of Caesarea there lived a Roman soldier named Cornelius. He was in charge of one hundred soldiers but he was kind and generous and wanted to please God.

One day an angel told him that God had heard his prayers. The angel said that he should send for Peter who was in Joppa. Cornelius called for two servants and a soldier. He told them what had happened and sent then to find Peter. The next day as they came to Joppa, Peter was on the roof of the house praying.

Acts chapter 10 verses 9-17.

The Jewish people had been taught that some animals must not be eaten. They were 'unclean'. Peter did not understand at first what this vision meant. Tomorrow we will see how it helped him when he met Cornelius.

How many times did Peter see the sheet coming down?

Day 327: CORNELIUS'S HOUSE

Peter came down from the housetop and met the men Cornelius had sent to Joppa. They explained why they had come and Peter invited them to stay with him that day. The next day Peter set out with them for Caesarea.

GOD'S WORD

Acts chapter 10 verses 24-29.

EXTRA INFO

Just as the Jews had been taught that some animals were 'unclean', they had thought that people who were not Jews were unclean as well.

BY MYSELF

Now God was teaching Peter that the good news about the Lord Jesus was for everyone, not just the people of Israel.

Jesus had told the apostles to be His witnesses everywhere. Peter talked to Cornelius, his family and his friends about Jesus, the wonderful things He had done, and how He had been crucified. Then he spoke about the resurrection and how their sins would be forgiven if they believed in Jesus.

While Peter was speaking, the Holy Spirit came to those who were listening, just as he had come to the apostles on the day of Pentecost. Some men were amazed that God had given the Holy Spirit to Gentiles. But Peter said that those who had received the Holy Spirit should be baptised. Cornelius, his family and his friends had become Christians. They asked Peter to stay for a few days. No doubt they wanted him to tell them more about the Lord Jesus before he went away.

ASK ABOUT

Where did the Lord Jesus tell His disciples to take the good news about Him? (Mark chapter 16 verse 15).

Day 328: SET FREE

When Jesus was with His disciples, He warned them that following Him would not be easy. As we read through the Book of Acts we see how true that was.

King Herod had James (John's brother) put to death. This pleased the Jews who did not believe in Jesus, so Herod put Peter into prison.

Day and night, Peter was guarded by soldiers so that he could not escape.

Acts chapter 12 verses 6-10.

Peter realised that he was not dreaming, and that God had sent His angel to rescue him. He went to the house of a lady named Mary, the mother of John Mark. As Peter was knocking at the door, people were in the house praying for him. A girl called Rhoda came to the door. She was so overjoyed to hear Peter's voice that she forgot to open the door.

Rhoda hurried in to say that Peter was there, but at first no one believed her.

At last because he kept on knocking, someone opened the door. Everyone was astonished that he was free. He told them what had happened and then went away to another place.

The next day the soldiers could not understand where Peter could have gone. King Herod gave orders that the guards should be put to death for letting him escape. But it was God who had set Peter free.

What two things happened when the angel came into the prison?

Do you know what a Church is? I expect you have seen Church buildings where people meet to worship God and learn about Him from the Bible. When we read about the Church in the New Testament, the word does not mean a building: it means people.

When someone becomes a Christian they become a member of the Church. They will then want to meet with others who love the Lord Jesus.

When Christians were cruelly treated in Jerusalem, they moved to other places. Churches began when the apostles travelled around telling people about Jesus.

In the New Testament there are two letters that Peter wrote to help the Churches. The Christians still had a lot to learn about God and about how God wanted them to live. Peter wrote to them because he still had a lot to teach them. God's Holy Spirit helped him to write the words that God wanted Him to write.

Peter reminded the Churches that what they had heard about the Lord Jesus was really true.

2 Peter chapter 1 verses 16-18.

There are some difficult words in these verses but you may remember the day Peter is talking about. He is remembering the time on the mountain when even Jesus' clothes became bright. Peter never forgot that wonderful day.

The letters that Peter wrote so long ago are still helping Christians today.

Look at 1 Peter chapter 1 verse 1 and count how many places Peter was writing to.

Day 330: A JOURNEY BEGINS

Do you remember how God told Ananias that He had chosen Saul to tell people about the Lord Jesus. Some time after this, Saul was with the Church in the city of Antioch. The Christians there knew that the Holy Spirit was telling them to send Saul and Barnabas away, to begin their work.

Saul and Barnabas took John Mark with them and set out on their journey. From this time Saul used his Roman name, Paul. First of all they sailed to Cyprus and preached to the Jews in Salamis. After this they travelled through the island as far as Paphos. From there they sailed to the country we call Turkey.

EXTRA INFO

John Mark went back home to Jerusalem, but Paul and Barnabas continued on their way, visiting cities in Turkey.

Paul usually spoke to the Jewish people first when he arrived at a city. He knew that he could meet with them on the Sabbath day in the synagogue. The Jews knew the Old Testament with God's promise to send a Saviour.

BY MYSELF

Paul wanted to tell them that the Saviour had come.

GOD'S WORD

Acts chapter 13 verses 26-33.

By the next Sabbath day, many people came together to hear Paul and Barnabas. The Jews were jealous and began to cause trouble. Paul and Barnabas were sent away. But wherever they went, some people became Christians.

ASK ABOUT

Name two places that Paul and Barnabus went to. (Acts chapter 13 verse 4 and 13).

Day 331: MISSIONARIES

A missionary is someone who tells others about the Lord Jesus. If we love Jesus we can be missionaries just where we are. But often missionaries travel to other lands to tell people that the Saviour has come.

Paul and Barnabas were missionaries who travelled from place to place. In the city of Lystra they met a man who had never been able to walk.

Acts chapter 14 verses 8-12.

The people who lived at Lystra worshipped idols: false gods which could not help them. They called Paul and Barnabas by the names of their gods because of the miracle of healing. Paul quickly told them not to do this.

Paul explained that they had come to tell them about the true God, who made the heavens, earth and sea.

Paul and Barnabas had to leave Lystra when some of the Jews from other towns came and stirred up trouble. They then visited those who had become Christians in the places they had been to already. Finally they returned by boat to Antioch. The church there met together to hear about all that God had done. Peter had learned that Gentiles as well as Jews could become Christians when he met Cornelius. Now the church at Antioch heard how Gentiles had become Christians in the towns that Paul and Barnabas had visited.

What had a man at Lystra never been able to do?

Day 332: GOOD NEWS FOR ALL

The first Christians were the disciples and friends of Jesus. These Jewish Christians already knew the books of the Old Testament. They were used to thinking of God as their God: not the God of the other nations. Gradually they were learning that God wants people from every land to believe in the Lord Jesus.

While Paul and Barnabas were in Antioch, some men arrived from the church at Jerusalem. They taught the Christians who were not Jewish that they must keep all the Old Testament laws. Paul and Barnabas thought that this was wrong and went to meet the other apostles and leaders of the church at Jerusalem.

Paul and Barnabas told the Jerusalem church about their journey and about the Gentiles who became Christians.

Acts chapter 15 verses 7-12.

Peter knew that the Jewish people had never been able to do all that God's law told them to. That was why they needed a Saviour.

Both Jews and Gentiles are saved from sin by repenting and trusting in the Lord Jesus.

After listening to Peter, Paul, Barnabas and James, the church decided to send a letter to the Christians at Antioch. Two men, Judas and Silas, took the letter. The church at Antioch was grateful for the letter. Jews and Gentiles were learning to understand one another.

Who stayed in Antioch? (Acts chapter 15 verse 35).

Day 333: JOHN MARK

John Mark left Paul and Barnabas after their visit to Cyprus. The Bible does not tell us why. But a life of travelling must have been hard.

It was also dangerous when people were angry with them for telling people about Jesus.

After spending some time in Antioch, Paul suggested to Barnabas that they should set off on another journey.

Acts chapter 15 verses 36-41.

Paul wanted to see how the people who had become Christians were getting on. John Mark and Barnabas were cousins. Paul did not think it wise to take someone with them who had turned back on their first journey. The Bible is always honest: even Christians sometimes cannot agree. However, the result was that two sets of missionaries set off: Paul and Silas; Barnabas and John Mark.

We do not read any more about Barnabas in the Book of Acts.

It seems likely that Barnabas helped John Mark by taking him with him. Some years after this, Paul asked for John Mark to come to him. Paul was in prison in Rome and he said that John Mark would be useful to him. It is good to know that Paul felt that he could now trust John Mark to help him.

God can still make us useful and helpful to others even after we have failed.

Where did Barnabas and John Mark travel to?

In the city of Lystra there lived a boy whose name was Timothy. His mother was Jewish and his father was Greek. While he was still a child his mother and his grandmother read to him from the Old Testament.

They did not have the New Testament: that was written later by the apostles and their helpers. The Holy Spirit helped those who wrote both the Old and New Testaments, which we now have as our Bible.

When Paul arrived at Lystra on his second journey, he met Timothy, who had become a Christian. Paul heard what the other Christians at Lystra said about Timothy. He knew that Timothy really loved Jesus. He asked him to join with him and Silas on their journey.

Timothy agreed and become a trusted helper.

Sometimes Paul wanted to know how a group of Christians were, so he sent Timothy to them. He also helped the church at Ephesus for a time.

Paul wrote two letters to Timothy which are in the New Testament. The letters were written to help Timothy in his work of teaching and caring for those who had become Christians.

2 Timothy chapter 1 verses 1-7.

Timothy was a younger man than Paul and Paul calls him his son. Paul understood that Timothy's life would not be easy. He wanted him to know that he prayed for him often.

What were the names of Timothy's mother and grandmother?

Day 335: LYDIA

If you look at old maps, you will find that some of the place-names have changed over the years.

It is now nearly two thousand years since Paul and the other apostles were travelling. So you will not be surprised to discover that some places they visited are no longer called by the names they knew.

Paul sailed to a part of Macedonia which we now call Greece.

Someone else had now joined the travellers: the writer of the Book of Acts, whose name was Luke. We know when Luke was with Paul because he uses the word 'we' instead of 'they'.

Acts chapter 16 verses 11-15.

Philippi was an important city in that part of Macedonia. 'Purple' was a well-known dye which came from that country. Lydia was a seller of purple clothe. God helped Lydia to understand when Paul spoke about the Lord Jesus. She became a Christian and was baptised. Lydia then invited Paul and those who were with him to stay at her house. Lydia's kindness must have been a great comfort to the travellers.

She was grateful to them for bringing the good news about the Lord Jesus.

In Philippi where did the women meet to pray? Name one of the women who was baptised? Who asked Paul and his friends to stay at her house?

Day 336: IN PRISON AT PHILIPPI

Have you noticed how no two days are the same? One day everything goes well and then on another day everything seems to go wrong.

Paul and his friends had seen people in Philippi become Christians. But after a time some men became angry with them. Things were said that were not true. Paul and Silas were beaten and put into prison, although they had not done anything wrong.

GOD'S WORD

Acts chapter 16 verses 23-32.

The jailor had been told to make sure that Paul and Silas could not escape. When the doors of the prison opened, the jailor knew that he would be punished if the prisoners had gone. After they had listened to Paul and Silas, the jailor and his family became Christians.

EXTRA INFO

The jailor cared for Paul and Silas and brought them some food. The next day orders were given that Paul and Silas could go free.

Before they left Philippi they visited Lydia and the others who had become Christians.

When Paul and Silas were put in prison, it did seem that everything was going wrong. No one would have thought that the jailor and his family would become Christians after meeting them.

BY MYSELF

If we love the Lord Jesus, even when things seem to go wrong, God is still with us, just as He was with Paul and Silas.

ASK ABOUT

What were Paul and Silas doing at midnight in the prison?

We have read about the visit of Paul and his friends to Philippi. Lydia and her family, and the jailor and his family became Christians.

EXTRA INFO

It is most likely that some time later, Paul made a second visit to the Christians in Philippi. In Acts chapter 20 we read that he went through Macedonia and then sailed from Philippi.

Paul wanted to be sure that the Christians went on to become strong Christians. He prayed for them, and travelled to see them. Then there came a time when Paul was kept in prison. He was no longer free to travel, but he was able to write letters. One of the letters he wrote was to the church at Philippi. In our New Testament it is called Paul's letter to the Philippians. In it Paul tells the Christians at Philippi that he is praying for them. He also asks them to care for one another as true followers of the Lord Jesus.

GOD'S WORD

Philippians chapter 4 verses 4-9.

There are some hard words in these verses that you will understand better when you are older. But you can see that in verse 6 Paul is telling us that we should pray about everything, instead of worrying about everything. In verse 8 he tells us to think about things that are true and good and lovely.

BY MYSELF

Because Paul wrote a letter, he did not just help the Philippians. This letter has helped Christians everywhere for nearly two thousand years.

ASK ABOUT

Who else was with Paul when he wrote this letter? (Philippians chapter 1 verse 1).

When Paul and his friends arrived at a city they usually went to the Jewish people first. Paul would meet them at the synagogue on the Sabbath day.

Paul, Silas and Timothy came to Thessalonica after they left Philippi. Paul spent three Sabbath days there talking to the Jews in the synagogue. He explained that Jesus was the One who God had promised in Old Testament days.

Paul told them that the promised Saviour had to die and rise again from the dead.

Some of the Jews in Thessalonica believed in the Lord Jesus after Paul had spoken to them. Some of the Greeks also became Christians.

Acts chapter 17 verses 5-9.

Some Jews, who did not believe Paul, became angry. They caused so much trouble that Paul and Silas left Thessalonica and travelled to the next town which was called Berea.

The Jews at Berea were quite happy to listen to Paul as he spoke about the Lord Jesus. They looked in the Old Testament to find out whether what Paul said was true. Many became Christians, as well as some of the Greeks who lived there. But men came from Thessalonica to stir up trouble in Berea. The Christians there helped Paul to get safely away by sea. Timothy and Silas stayed in Berea, but Paul sailed to Athens.

There are two letters in the New Testament that Paul wrote to the Christians at Thessalonica.

What three things did Paul tell the Christians at Thessalonica to do? (1 Thessalonians chapter 5 verses 16-18).

Day 339: IDOL WORSHIPPERS

Athens was an important city in the land which we now call Greece. The people of Athens worshipped many false gods and goddesses. There were many idols and temples in Athens. There was even an altar that had 'to the unknown god' written on it.

Paul was sad to see so many idols. The people of Athens did not know about the God who made them.

While Paul waited for Silas and Timothy to come, he began to talk to the people. He spoke to Jews in the synagogue and to other people in the market place. He told them about the resurrection of the Lord Jesus.

The people of Athens liked listening to new ideas. They did not understand what Paul was saying. They brought him to a place called Mars Hill and waited to hear what he would say.

The Areopagus is another name for Mars Hill.

Acts chapter 17 verses 22-27.

Paul wanted the people to know the God who made the world. He told them that they should not think of God as an idol made by men. When he spoke about Jesus rising from the dead, some people laughed at him. Others said that they would listen to him again. But there were some who believed Paul's words about the Lord Jesus

Name two people who became Christians in Athens. (Acts chapter 17 verse 34).

Day 340: A LONG STAY AT CORINTH

When he left Athens, Paul travelled about forty miles to the city of Corinth. There he met a man named Aquila and his wife Priscilla. They were tent makers, as Paul himself had been. Paul stayed with them and joined them in their work. In this way Paul could earn money to buy the things he needed. On the Sabbath days he went to the synagogue to talk to the people there.

Silas and Timothy had stayed longer in Berea than Paul had done. They were not with Paul in Athens, but travelled to Corinth and met him there.

Acts chapter 18 verses 8-11.

Paul knew that God wanted him to be in Corinth. God knew that many people there would become Christians.

Some of the Jews tried to get Paul into trouble. They went to see Gallio who was in charge of that area. But Gallio would not listen to them. He knew that Paul had not done anything wrong. As God had promised, no one was able to hurt Paul at Corinth.

When people become Christians they begin a new life. Instead of wanting to please themselves, they want to please God. But Paul knew that they had a lot to learn. He wanted to help the Christians at Corinth.

Two of Paul's letters to Corinth are in the New Testament, and are called the first and second letters of Paul to the Corinthians.

Who went with Paul when he left Corinth? (Acts chapter 18 verse 18).

Day 341: THE SILVERSMITHS

Travelling from place to place can be tiring. Sometimes it is good to spend some time back at home. After Paul left Corinth he visited Ephesus. He did not stay there as he was on his way to Jerusalem. He promised that he would come back. After he talked with the Christians in Jerusalem, he went to Antioch. Antioch was the place he had first set out from. He spent some time there, before setting out on a third journey.

Paul's third journey brought him back to Ephesus and he stayed there for more than two years. Many people in Ephesus worshipped idols.

There was a temple there for the statue of the goddess Diana. A number of people made their living by making copies of this statue and selling them.

While Paul stayed in Ephesus he told the people about Jesus. Many became Christians.

The people realised that idols and statues were of no use. The silversmiths who made the statues could not sell as many as they used to.

Acts chapter 19 verses 24-27.

People became very angry and rushed to a building called the theatre. A lot of people joined in without knowing what it was all about. For about two hours the crowd kept shouting, 'Great is Diana of the Ephesians'. At last the city clerk managed to quieten the people. He told them that there was no excuse for such a noisy gathering and he sent them to their homes.

Which silversmith started all the trouble at Ephesus?

Day 342: PAUL SAYS GOOD-BYE

An angry crowd can be very frightening. Paul was not afraid but wanted to go in and talk to the people. The other Christians would not let him go into such danger. When the riot was over, Paul said good-bye to the Christians in Ephesus. He began his journey again stopping at the towns he had visited before. He wanted to see how those who had become Christians were getting on.

When Paul reached a town called Miletus, he sent a messenger to the church at Ephesus. He asked the elders of the church to come and meet him at Miletus.

The elders were the leaders and teachers of the church.

When they met Paul, he spoke to them about the years he had been with them in Ephesus.

Paul reminded them of what he had taught them. He knew that he would never see them again.

He warned them that others would come and teach things that were wrong. Some people want to be important and persuade people to follow them. They would not care for the church as Paul had done.

Acts chapter 20 verses 33-38.

These Christians from Ephesus were sad. They did not like to think that they would never see Paul again. But Paul wanted to go to Jerusalem in time for Pentecost.

In Paul's letter to Ephesus what did he tell husbands to do and what did he tell children to do? (Ephesians chapter 5 verse 25 and chapter 6 verse 1).

Day 343: RESCUED BY SOLDIERS

When someone becomes a Christian, the Lord Jesus makes a great change in their life. In Acts chapter 9 we read about Saul who treated Christians very cruelly. But Saul became Paul, the man who travelled thousands of miles to tell people about Jesus.

It was not the change in his name that was most important. It was the change from Saul the proud Pharisee, to Paul the loving follower of the Lord Jesus.

He was now loved by Christian people in the many places he had visited. Some warned Paul that it was most dangerous for him to go to Jerusalem. They were afraid that he would be taken prisoner there.

Paul continued his journey. He was sure that he should go to Jerusalem whatever happened.

Just as his friends had feared Paul did become a prisoner. Lies were told about him which the people believed. An angry crowd took hold of Paul. He was badly hurt, but was rescued by Roman soldiers. The Commander of the soldiers tried to find out what Paul had done. People shouted different things and so the commander could not find out what was true. As Paul was led away by the soldiers, the crowd followed, still shouting. Paul had not done anything wrong. Lies had been told by those who did not want him to tell people about Jesus.

Acts chapter 21 verses 30-34.

Name one other place where Paul was a prisoner. (Acts chapter 16 verse 12).

Day 344: PAUL THE PRISONER

Roman soldiers had rescued Paul from the angry crowd. Paul had been badly treated by the people and yet he asked permission to speak to them. The Commander of the soldiers said that he could do so. At last the crowd became quiet, when they realised that Paul had something to say to them. Paul began to tell the story of his own life, especially of how he became a Christian.

GOD'S WORD

Acts chapter 22 verses 6-13.

Paul went on to explain that God had sent him to teach the Gentiles about Jesus.

EXTRA INFO

The Jews called people from other lands 'Gentiles'.

BY MYSELF

The crowd became angry again. They did not understand that God wanted people in every land to hear about the Lord Jesus.

The Commander of the soldiers did not understand why the people were so angry with Paul. He gave orders that Paul should be beaten. Paul asked one of the soldiers whether it was right that he should be beaten. He explained that he was a Roman citizen. The soldier knew that to be a Roman citizen was something special. Roman citizens must not be tied up or beaten unless is was proved that they had done wrong. The soldiers were afraid because they had already tied Paul up. Those who were going to question him went away. Paul was kept as a prisoner that night.

ASK ABOUT

Who had been Paul's teacher? (Acts chapter 22 verse 3).

A person caught stealing, will be accused of being a thief. A person caught hurting someone will be accused of causing harm to them. If the police are called they will soon know about what happened. The soldiers who were keeping Paul as a prisoner did not know what he had done. They thought that he must have done something very wrong to make the crowd so angry. They needed to find out the truth.

The Commander of the soldiers sent for the priests and leaders of the Jews. Paul was brought in. There was such an argument among the Jewish leaders, that the soldiers had to take Paul away. That night, God spoke to Paul. God told Paul that one day he would be able to tell people in Rome about the Lord Jesus.

Rome was the most important city in the Empire.

Paul knew that no one would be able to stop him doing the work that God had given him to do.

The next day some Jews made a plan to kill Paul. But one of Paul's relations heard about it and told Paul.

Acts chapter 23 verses 16-22.

The Commander of the soldiers knew that it was not safe to keep Paul in Jerusalem. He gave orders to take Paul away during the night. Soldiers took him to the town of Caesarea, where Felix the Governor lived. Felix was in charge of Judea. He would now have to find out whether Paul had done anything wrong.

What was the name of the Commander who wrote a letter about Paul? Who did he write the letter to? (Acts chapter 23 verses 26).

Day 346: FELIX LISTENS TO PAUL

Felix the Governor waited five days for the priests and leaders of the Jews to come to Caesarea. They brought with them a man named Tertullus who was good at making speeches. He told Felix that Paul caused trouble among the Jews wherever he went. He also said that Lysias the commander of the soldiers took Paul away from the Jews in a rough way. But it was the soldiers who rescued Paul from the angry crowd! The men who came with Tertullus agreed with him that Paul was a troublemaker.

It was then Paul's turn to speak. He spoke about what he had been doing. He explained that he had not done anything to anger the people. Felix knew quite a lot about those who believed in the Lord Jesus. He decided to wait for the commander of the soldiers to come, before making up his mind about Paul.

Acts chapter 24 verses 22-27.

Felix kept Paul as a prisoner for two years.

Felix sent for Paul sometimes and Paul was able to talk to him about the Lord Jesus.

Felix hoped that he would be given money to set Paul free, but Paul would not do this. Festus took Felix's place as Governor. So Felix never did decide whether Paul had really done anything wrong. He did not want to make the Jews angry by setting him free. However Paul's friends were allowed to visit him and he was not treated badly.

What was the name of Felix's wife? What was the name of the new Governor who took Felix's place?

Day 347: PAUL SPEAKS TO A KING

Paul's imprisonment brought his years of travelling to an end. His journeys had taken him many miles across land and sea. He had taken the good news about the Lord Jesus to many places. However, even as a prisoner, God still had work for Paul to do.

Paul was now able to tell some of the most important people in the land what it means to be a Christian.

Paul had spoken to Felix the Governor and his wife Drusilla. He was yet to speak to the new Governor and the king. Festus visited Jerusalem and the priests there talked to him about Paul.

Acts chapter 25 verses 1-7.

Once again the Jewish leaders accused Paul of many things. Festus asked Paul if he was willing to go back to Jerusalem. Paul would not have been safe there. He decided that he would rather go to Rome. The emperor would decide what to do. Paul told Festus this and it was agreed that he would be sent to Rome.

While Paul was still at Caesarea, King Agrippa came to visit Festus. Paul was brought in to speak to King Agrippa. Festus and many of the important men of the city were there. Paul told them about how the Lord Jesus had met with him on the road to Damascus. He explained how this had changed his life. King Agrippa was very interested in all Paul said.

All those who heard Paul that day agreed that he had done nothing wrong.

What three important men did Paul speak to about Jesus?

Day 348: SHIPWRECKED

Do you like travelling? It is certainly exciting seeing new places and meeting different people. But travelling in New Testament days could be very dangerous.

The journey from Caesarea to Rome was two thousand miles. In a sailing ship this could take a long time.

Paul was taken to a ship along with some other prisoners. A man named Julius took charge of them. He was a centurion which means he was an officer in charge of a hundred soldiers.

There were several stops on the way. The third place the ship stopped at was the island of Crete. So much time was spent there that Paul said that they should stay for the winter. But it was decided that they should sail a little further. The centurion and the owner of the ship wanted to reach Phoenix and winter there. However, a strong wind soon blew the ship off course. A great storm arose and the sailors were afraid that everyone would be drowned.

Acts chapter 27 verses 20-26.

Paul was not afraid in the storm because God promised that no lives would be lost.

The ship stuck fast on a sand bank. The waves began to break the ship up. Everyone on board either swam ashore or floated towards land on bits of wood from the ship. All two hundred and seventy-six were saved from the shipwreck. When they reached the shore they found that they were on the Island of Malta.

Who was Julius? (Acts chapter 27 verse 1).

Day 349: PAUL IN ROME

The people of Malta were very kind to those who had been shipwrecked. It was wet and cold, so a fire was made to help everyone to dry out. After two weeks in a storm it must have been good to be safe on land.

Paul spent three months on the island of Malta and then set sail for Italy. The ship took him to a town called Puteoli. There he met Christian people who looked after him for a week. Other Christians who lived in towns between Puteoli and Rome came to meet him.

Being with people who loved the Lord Jesus as he did, was a great help to Paul at this time. When he arrived at Rome he was kindly treated.

Acts chapter 28 verses 16 and 30-31.

Paul was a prisoner and yet he was still able to teach people about the Lord Jesus. We do not read any more about his life in the New Testament.

We do know that Paul used all his energy to tell others about the gospel.

Do you remember what the word 'gospel' means? It means 'good news' – the good news that God sent the Lord Jesus to die on the cross so that our sin can be forgiven. Many people thanked God that Paul had travelled to their towns bringing this good news.

What was the name of the island where Paul was shipwrecked? (Acts chapter 28 verse 1). How long did he stay there? (Verse 11).

PAUL'S LETTERS FROM PRISON

The New Testament contains twenty-one letters. The next thirteen days readings introduce four of them. Paul's letters to the Ephesians, Colossians, Philippians and Philemon all mention the fact that he was a prisoner. The verses from Colossians chapter three are given as an example of Paul's teaching on how the Christian faith is to be lived out. The short letter to Philemon contains much practical teaching for a difficult situation: how a run-a-way now converted slave should behave and how his Christian master should receive him. We also see the gracious way in which the apostle deals with both.

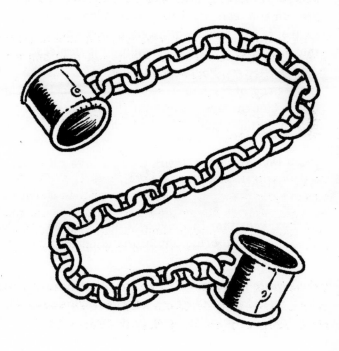

Day 350: LETTERS FROM PRISON

Paul wrote letters to help Christians to understand more about what the Lord Jesus had done for them. He also wanted them to know how Christians should live, at home, at work, or when they met together.

GOD'S WORD

Colossians chapter 3 verses 18-25.

In these verses Paul tells us what life should be like for a Christian family. God has given to men the task of caring for the family. The father should treat his children kindly and love his wife. The wife should respect her husband because he is the head of the family. Children should be obedient to their parents.

In verse 22 we read about bondservants or slaves. In New Testament times many people were slaves. We can still learn from this verse. When we work for someone, we should work well. In fact Paul tells us that whatever we do, we should do it to please God.

In his letters, Paul reminds us that just as the father is the head of the house, so the Lord Jesus is the head of the Church. Jesus said that His people would be known by their love for one another.

BY MYSELF

If we love the Lord Jesus we will love all those who belong to Him.

Paul explains that this love will be shown by care for one another, by being unselfish and uncomplaining.

EXTRA INFO

Paul wrote his letters nearly two thousand years ago. They have helped Christian people ever since, because it was God who helped him to write them.

ASK ABOUT

Can you find something else that Paul did for Christians? (Colossians chapter 1 verse 3).

Day 351: THE RUNAWAY SLAVE

Do you remember what a slave was? A slave had to work for the person who had bought him and do whatever he was told to do. Slaves were not free to go wherever they wanted to.

At the time that Paul was travelling from place to place, there were many slaves. Some were quite well treated and trusted by their owners. Some people even arranged for their slaves to be set free.

We read about a slave in a letter that Paul wrote to a man named Philemon. We know that Philemon was a Christian who was helpful to other people, because of what Paul says about him.

Philemon verses 3-7.

Philemon had a slave named Onesimus. One day Onesimus ran away from his master. He may have stolen some of Philemon's money to take with him. Paul was in prison at this time, but Onesimus met him and became a Christian. Being a Christian made a difference to Onesimus's life.

He became a great help to Paul. Paul was not free to come and go himself.

It must have been very useful to have someone willing to carry messages or bring things that were needed. Paul felt that he would like to keep Onesimus with him. However, he knew that Onesimus still belonged to Philemon. Although he was now a Christian, he was still a runaway slave. Paul thought about what would be the right thing to do.

What did Paul do for Philemon?

Day 352: A LETTER TO PHILEMON

Paul decided that Onesimus should return to Philemon. He had a letter to send to the Christians in Colosse, where Philemon lived. A man named Tychicus was going to deliver that letter, and Onesimus could go with him.

A slave who had run away could be punished if he was returned to his master.

Paul wrote the letter to Philemon for Onesimus to take with him. Paul explained all that had happened to Onesimus: how he had become a Christian and how helpful he had been while Paul was a prisoner.

Philemon verses 10-16.

When Paul calls Onesimus his son, he means that Onesimus became a Christian through their meeting. He cared for him as a father would care for his son. Paul went on to tell Philemon how much he would like to keep Onesimus with him. But he would not do this without Philemon's permission. His main reason for writing was to make sure that Onesimus was treated kindly. He even asked Philemon to welcome him just as he would welcome Paul himself.

We do not know what happened when Onesimus arrived back at Colosse. We can be quite sure that Philemon would be willing to take advice from Paul.

The Christians were learning that when you belonged to God's family you must care for one another whether slaves or free.

What do you think Paul was hoping to be able to do? (Verse 22).

A LETTER TO JEWISH CHRISTI

Many believe that the apostle Paul was the author
to the Hebrews, but this cannot be proved. The Jew
addressed in this letter may well have been tempted
to the ceremony and ritual of Judaism. The writer em
the superiority of Christ and of the Christian faith. Th
from chapter eleven not only give the opportunity to
at some Old Testament characters, they also reinforce
Biblical view of these men and women of faith.

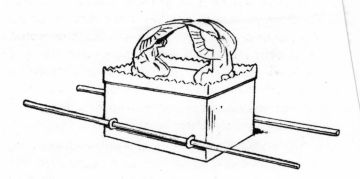

In The New Testament there are twenty-one letters that were written to people who had become Christians. Thirteen were written by Paul, one by James, two by Peter, three by John and one by Jude. The other letter may have been written by Paul, but we cannot be quite sure. It is called the letter to the Hebrews.

EXTRA INFO

Hebrews is another name for the Jewish people.

The first people to become Christians were Jews. Peter spoke to many Jews on the day of Pentecost. They knew about God's promises in the Old Testament. The Holy Spirit helped Peter to show that Jesus was the One who God had promised.

BY MYSELF

Three thousand people became Christians that day. Other Jews became Christians when Paul spoke to them about Jesus.

As time went by, Jewish Christians found that a lot of Jews did not believe in Jesus. They expected the Messiah to be a great king who would set them free from Rome. They did not believe that Jesus is the Son of God who rose from the dead. The letter to the Hebrews was written to help Jewish Christians understand that Jesus really is the Son of God.

GOD'S WORD

Hebrews chapter 1 verses 1-3.

Some Bibles use the word 'purged' in verse 3. That word means, 'made us clean'

ASK ABOUT

God spoke first by sending prophets, but now He has spoken in a different way. Who did he send?

Day 354: NO MORE SACRIFICES

We often call the building where Christians meet a church, but the word really means people who belong to the Lord Jesus. The church included Jews and people from other nations.

When they met together they read the Bible and prayed, and they learned to care for one other.

Their leaders were called pastors, teachers or elders. These were men who God had chosen to help Christians understand how God wanted them to live.

It may be that some Jewish Christians looked back to the time when they took their offerings to the Temple. There they would see the High Priest in his beautiful clothing. In their Christian meetings there were no priests and no sacrifices. The letter to the Hebrews would have helped them not to want the old days back. The priests had offered sacrifices for themselves as well as for the people. Even the High Priest was sinful and needed to be forgiven. But our High Priest is the Lord Jesus. He had no sin and He offered His own life as a perfect sacrifice for the sins of others.

The writer of this letter wanted the Jewish Christians to remember that from the time of Moses and Aaron, many, many sacrifices were offered. But when the Lord Jesus gave His life, no other sacrifice would ever be needed. These Christians could be quite sure that they could come to God because of the better sacrifice that was made by their Great High Priest.

Hebrews chapter 7 verses 26-28.

How often did the priests in Old Testament times offer sacrifices? What sacrifice did the Lord Jesus offer?

Day 355: OLD TESTAMENT PICTURES

In the Book of Exodus, God's special tent was called the tabernacle. Moses set up the tabernacle exactly as God commanded. The letter to the Hebrews helps us to understand why it was so important that the tabernacle was exactly as God said it should be. Behind a curtain there was a room in the tabernacle that could only be entered once a year by one person. This was the Most Holy Place.

EXTRA INFO

On the Day of Atonement, the High Priest offered sacrifices for himself and the people, then he went in to the Most Holy Place.

When Jesus was crucified He gave His life as a perfect sacrifice for the sins of others. What happened in the Temple that day? There was a curtain in the Temple just as there had been in the tabernacle.

BY MYSELF

When Jesus died, that curtain was torn from top to bottom.

The opening of the Most Holy Place was like a picture of a door being opened into Heaven. The Lord Jesus did not go into the Temple after He rose from the dead: He went into Heaven. The tabernacle was a picture of what God's Son would do. The Jewish Christians did not need the picture anymore. What Jesus did was better than anything the Old Testament priests did. They had looked forward to the coming Saviour: now He had come. The Old Testament Books are there to help us understand why Jesus came.

GOD'S WORD

Hebrews chapter 9 verses 24-26.

ASK ABOUT

How many times did the Lord Jesus need to give His life to take away our sins?

Day 356: ABEL, ENOCH AND NOAH

EXTRA INFO

The word 'faith' means believing that God will always do what He says He will do.

We cannot be sure that people will keep their promises. Even if someone really means what they say, something might happen to stop them doing as they said. God is not like that. Nothing can stop God doing what He has promised. If we believe that, then we have faith in God.

We cannot see faith, but we can see the things that people are able to do because of their faith. In the letter to the Hebrews chapter 11 we can read about the faith of some of those who lived in Old Testament times. The first person named in this chapter is Abel. God accepted the sacrifice that he brought but God did not accept his brother Cain's offering. This was because Abel had faith that God would forgive the wrong he had done if he brought the sacrifice God asked for. He was not giving God a present. He believed God and so he obeyed God.

Enoch is the next person in this list of people. He is one of the two people in the Bible who did not die. He believed God and he lived in a way that pleased God

This chapter tells us that Noah built the ark by faith. When God told Noah about the flood, Noah believed God. Even though no one had ever seen such a flood before, Noah obeyed God and built the ark.

BY MYSELF

Those who believe God, show that they do by obeying God.

GOD'S WORD

Hebrews chapter 11 verses 4-7.

ASK ABOUT

Can you remember the name of the man, besides Enoch, who did not die? (2 Kings chapter 2 verse 11).

Day 357: ABRAHAM'S FAMILY

In the Book of Genesis we read about Abraham. He left the place where he lived because God told him to, even though he did not know where he was to go. He waited twenty-five years for the son God promised, and then he was ready to offer Isaac to God as a sacrifice. The letter to the Hebrews tells us that Abraham did this because of his faith. He believed God's promises and he obeyed God. Sarah also had faith: she believed that even though she was old, she would have the baby boy that God had promised.

Isaac, Jacob and Joseph each have a place in this list of men and women of faith.

Hebrews chapter 11 verses 20-22

It did not seem as though Isaac had faith in what God had said about Jacob and Esau before they were born. But when Isaac sent Jacob to visit his Uncle Laban, he was certain that God's promises were for Jacob. Isaac believed what God had said.

Jacob lived for twenty years with Laban and then he moved with his large family back to Canaan. When he was one hundred and thirty years old he made the journey to Egypt to be near his son Joseph. In the letter to the Hebrews it is Jacob's faith, just before he died, that we read about. God helped him to understand that Joseph's two sons would each become the head of a tribe. He also knew that Ephraim's tribe would be the larger one.

Jacob worshipped. The faith that helped him through life, strengthened him at his death.

What were the names of Joseph's two sons? (Genesis chapter 41 verses 51 and 52).

Day 358: JOSEPH AND MOSES

Jacob's life was eventful. Joseph's was too. Hated by his brothers, rescued from a pit, sold as a slave in Egypt, then put in prison. These were terrible events and yet Joseph became the most important man in Egypt apart from the king.

The writer of the letter to the Hebrews was helped by the Holy Spirit to write about Joseph at the end of his life.

Joseph looked forward to the time when God would bring His people into their own land. He was so sure of this, that he wanted what was left of his body to be taken to that land.

Hebrews chapter 11 verses 23-30.

Why did Moses choose to help his people when he could have gone on living as the son of a princess? How was he brave enough to speak to the King of Egypt? How was it that he was not afraid to lead the Israelites through the Red Sea? The answer is that Moses did all these things by faith.

Moses believed that God would do what He promised, so he obeyed God.

When the Israelites marched round Jericho it did not seem a likely way to make walls fall down, but God told Joshua that they would. Joshua believed God and God caused the walls to fall on the seventh day.

Did the people of Israel remember what Joseph had asked them to do? (Exodus chapter 13 verse 19).

Day 359: MORE PEOPLE OF FAITH

EXTRA INFO

There are just two women who are named in Hebrews chapter 11. The first one is Abraham's wife Sarah the other one is Rahab.

Rahab lived among the Canaanites who worshipped idols, but when she heard about the true God, she believed. Because she believed, she helped the two men who Joshua had sent and she was saved when Jericho was destroyed.

BY MYSELF

Rahab was saved because of her faith.

After Joshua died, the Israelites had leaders called judges. Five judges are named in Hebrews chapter 11.

GOD'S WORD

Judges chapter 6 verses 11-16.

Gideon was sent by God to save Israel from the Midianites. God said that Gideon's army of thirty-two thousand was too big. The people needed to trust in God not in soldiers. God promised to save Israel with just three hundred men. Gideon believed God's promise. Israel was set free from the Midianites.

Barak lived when the Canaanite King Jabin treated the Israelites harshly. The prophetess Deborah told him to take ten thousand men to fight Sisera who was in charge of King Jabin's army. Barak did so. Deborah went too. Israel had a great victory. Barak obeyed God because he believed God.

God gave Samson great strength to fight the Philistines. He had faith in God at a time when people around him were afraid.

ASK ABOUT

Can you find what Gideon thought about himself, from the verses you read today?

We often remember Jephath because of the promise he made to sacrifice whoever met him when he came home from the battle. The letter to the Hebrews reminds us that he was a man of faith.

David was Israel's second king. He learned to trust God while he was young. He was not afraid to fight Goliath. He trusted in God through the years when King Saul wanted to kill him. When he became king, he won many battles against the enemies of Israel.

David believed God's promise that it would be from his family that the Saviour would come.

The Psalms that David wrote show how he trusted God to help him whenever he was in trouble or danger.

Psalm 27 verse 1-5.

Samuel was the last of the judges of Israel. As a child he learned to help Eli the priest. While he was still young God spoke to Him. As he grew older, whenever God spoke to him, Samuel obeyed God. He was not afraid to tell King Saul when he did something that was wrong. He anointed David as God's chosen king. Samuel believed God and obeyed God throughout his life.

Some people's names are not given in Hebrews chapter 11. The writer just says – 'and the prophets'. These men brought God's words to the people. They were often in great danger. Some were put in prison or treated in other cruel ways. They believed that God had spoken and they were obedient to what He said.

How many of the names in Hebrews chapter 11 verse 32 were judges and how many were kings?

FAITH IN PRACTICE

James was a leader in the early church. He made no claim to family relationship with Christ although he was mentioned in Paul's letter to the Galatians as the Lord's brother. Some have seen a problem in his letter, as he emphasises works whereas Paul emphasises faith. There is in fact no contradiction: saving faith always produces evidence in the life. James wanted us to know that if we claim to have faith, this must be seen in the way we live.

Day 361: A MIRROR

We have read about men and women of Old Testament times who had faith in God. We know this because of the things they were able to do.

James, who was one of the leaders in the church in Jerusalem, wrote a letter about faith. His letter teachers us that faith includes obeying God.

James wanted those who said they were Christians to know that believing in the Lord Jesus means living to please Him. People who become Christians have God's Holy Spirit to help them to obey God.

James tells us that reading the Bible is like looking in a mirror. If you looked in the mirror and saw that your face was dirty, would you try to forget what you had seen and go out with your friends?

James chapter 1 verses 22-25.

When we read the Bible we see what we are like, and we also see what we should be like.

If we believe the Bible, we will do what it says. Jesus told a story about two builders. He said that a man who heard His words and did not do them was like the foolish builder. The man who heard the words of Jesus and did as He said was like the wise builder. The Lord Jesus wants us to be kind and truthful, to love Him and to love other people. These are some of the things that show that we belong to Him.

What does James say it is like when someone hears what God says, but does not do it?

Day 362: SMALL BUT POWERFUL

Did you know that there is a part of your body that is very small, but it can hurt someone without touching them? Can you think what it is? It is that little thing you use when you speak: your tongue.

James warns us that a lot of trouble can be caused by the things we say. Small things can be very powerful. A big strong horse will obey its owner because of the small metal 'bit' placed in its mouth. A large ship can be turned by a small rudder. The tongue is small but it has the power to do a lot of harm.

James chapter 3 verses 7-12.

Wild animals are exciting and frightening at the same time. We are not allowed to stroke lions or put our fingers near the beaks and claws of large birds. But some people have been able to tame all kinds of wild creatures. James says that it is easier to do that, than to tame our own tongue. It is so easy to speak angrily or unkindly or to tell a lie. It is more difficult to speak to others as we would like them to speak to us.

God made us able to speak to Him and to one another. Speech is a wonderful gift from God.

How can we use our tongues to say words that will do good and not harm? No one can tame (or control) their tongue. But we can ask God to help us. Three thousand years ago King David asked God to guard his mouth. We can ask Him to do this for us today.

What is David asking God to help him with in Psalm 141 verse 3?

THE REVELATION OF JESUS CHRIST

If we are afraid to read the Book of Revelation because of its symbolic nature, we will miss much encouragement. Suffering exile for the faith, John was granted a vision of the ascended Lord Jesus Christ. The messages to the seven churches in chapters two and three contain instruction for churches at all times and in all places. Through the symbolism of the remaining chapters we are made aware of great and terrible events which will take place during the time before the Lord Jesus Christ returns. It is emphasised that judgement will come upon the unrepentant. The promise of Christ's coming is found in the first and last chapters of this Book. The message is clear: God is in control of events – the outcome is not in doubt. There is great encouragement here for the Christian living through times of trial and perplexity. The final chapters remind us that we need to keep in view the day when we will see the Lord Jesus Christ and be forever with Him.

Day 363: JOHN'S VISION

James and John were brothers and disciples of Jesus. King Herod had James put to death for being a Christian. But John lived to be an old man. He wrote the fourth book of the New Testament as well as three letters and the very last book of the Bible which is called 'The Revelation of Jesus Christ'.

EXTRA INFO

A revelation is something that we are told or shown that we did not know before.

John tells us that this revelation came from the Lord Jesus. He was told to write down what he saw, and send what he wrote to seven churches. At the time he heard Jesus speaking to him, John was living on the island of Patmos. He had been sent there by those who did not want him to teach others about Jesus.

GOD'S WORD

Revelation chapter 1 verses 9-13.

The Lord's Day was the day when Christians met together, the day we call Sunday. John may not have been allowed to meet with other Christians, but no one could stop him hearing what Jesus said to him.

The Book of Revelation is full of 'picture language'. Even grown-ups find parts of it hard to understand.

BY MYSELF

At the beginning of this book John tells us that he saw the Lord Jesus.

We would say that he had a vision of Jesus. This was not his imagination or a dream. He was not in heaven with Jesus, but he saw Jesus and heard His voice.

ASK ABOUT

Can you find the names of the seven places in today's Bible reading?

410

Day 364: SEVEN CHURCHES

When the Lord Jesus was on earth, John had been with him and talked with Him. When John was on the island of Patmos and had a vision of Jesus, he fell down at His feet. John saw the Lord Jesus in all His splendour. This reminds us that when Jesus came into the world as a man, He left the splendour of Heaven.

The Lord Jesus told John not to be afraid.

John saw Jesus standing among seven lamptstands. He told John that the lampstands meant churches. You have already found the names of the places where the seven churches were. The Lord Jesus knew all about them and He had a message for each of them.

We can read these messages in the second and third chapters of the Book of the Revelation.

To five churches Jesus gives a warning that they are not doing everything in the way they should. There is just one of the seven churches that the Lord Jesus has nothing good to say about. Yet His message to that church is that He loves them and asks them to change their ways.

Revelation chapter 3 verses 20-22.

It is good for us to know that the Lord Jesus loves and watches over His people. He knows those who love and obey Him. He is very patient in teaching us how we should live.

How many churches was John given messages for? Who is standing at the door and knocking?

DAY 365: AN INVITATION

After Jesus had given John His messages, it was as if John was allowed to see right into Heaven. John saw many things and heard many voices praising God. He learned what would happen before Jesus came to earth again. There would be times of great trouble, but God would be in control. John saw a new heaven and a new earth. This world which has been spoilt by sin will end and God will make everything new.

John looked forward to a wonderful time when there will be no more sin or sorrow, pain or death.

Revelation chapter 21 verses 3-7.

Those who refuse to ask God to forgive their sins, will be shut out of heaven. Jesus died so that all who believe in Him can be forgiven. If we refuse to believe, we will have to take the punishment that we deserve.

There are many verses in the Bible where we read words of invitation. God, our great Creator, invites us to come to Him. We do not have to travel to a special place to do this. We simply need to believe what the Bible tells us about the Lord Jesus.

Jesus will forgive all our sins and teach us how we should live to please Him, if we ask Him.

The last chapter of the Bible has its last invitation. The invitation is not for those who are especially good or clever, it is for those who are thirsty. This does not mean being thirsty for a drink. It means wanting to know the Lord Jesus as Saviour and Friend.

Find four things that will not be there when God makes everything new. (Revelation chapter 21 verse 4).

Author: Jean Stapleton

Jean Stapleton made nursing her career before she became a wife and mother. She has been involved in beach missions since 1988, and has experience of working with children of various ages and backgrounds.

Jean says that over the years she has found that there have been many opportunities for the simple, direct teaching of the Word of God to children of varying ages.

"During one period of about five years, children came to our home. Eventually we had to divide these children into two groups as the numbers rose beyond the capacity of our modestly sized living-room. Many of these children knew nothing of the Bible, referring to it as 'the Bible Book' as we introduced it to them."

Wanting to make sure that these children knew the source of all that they were being told, Jean and others soon began handing out Bibles. These children were keen to learn how to 'find the place' and to read these words of God for themselves.

It was sometime, during those years of teaching in Sunday School and week-night activities, that the desire to put pen to paper was born. At last, changes to the family circle meant that time could be found to write. The result was many happy hours spent in the preparation of this book.

Jean and the others involved in the production of this book hope that you too will have many happy hours reading it and that God will bless you through His word.

We'll let Jean finish this with her own words: "It has often been in my times of preparation that I have gained much benefit from the Scriptures. I am a very ordinary wife and Mum with a very wonderful Saviour."

Our Bible Reading Progress Chart

 Genesis: Days 1-42 We've Done It!

 Exodus: Days 43-68 We've Done It!

 Leviticus: Days 69-75 We've Done It!

 Numbers: Days 76-86 We've Done It!

 Deuteronomy: Days 87-89, We've Done It!

 Joshua: Days 90-102 We've Done It!

Judges: Days 103-112

We've Done It!

Ruth: Days 113-118

We've Done It!

1&2 Samuel: Days 119-145

We've Done It!

Kings and Chronicles:
Days 146-182

We've Done It!

Daniel: Days 186-192

We've Done It!

Jonah: Days 183-185

We've Done It!

Ezra: Days 193-198

We've Done It!

Nehemiah: Days 199-204

We've Done It!

Esther: Days 205-211

We've Done It!

Job: Days 212-214

We've Done It!

Psalms: Days 215-219,

We've Done It!

Proverbs: Days 220-224

 We've Done It!

 Ecclesiastes: Days 225

 We've Done It!

 Isaiah: Days 226-228

 We've Done It!

 Jeremiah: Days 229-231

 We've Done It!

 Malachi: Days 232-234

 We've Done It!

Matthew/Mark/Luke/John: Days 235-312

We've
Done It!

 Acts: Days 313-349

We've
Done It!

 Colossians: Day 350

We've
Done It!

 Philemon: Days 351-352

We've
Done It!

 Hebrews: Days 353-360

We've
Done It!

James: Days 361-362

We've
Done It!

 Revelation: Days 363-365

We've
Done It!

NOTES

NOTES

NOTES

NOTES

NOTES

NOTES

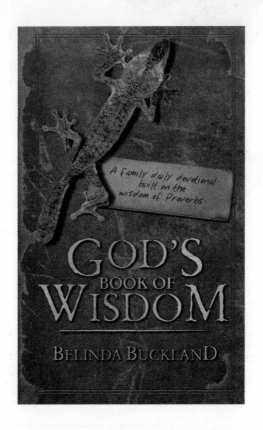

GOD'S BOOK OF WISDOM
BELINDA BUCKLAND

A daily devotional built on the wisdom of Proverbs. The book of Proverbs is a wonderful part of the bible that has loads of wisdom and handy trips in it for life. It is a must read for anyone who wants their family to follow God and avoid the pitfalls.

ISBN: 185792 9632

432 pages, Large Trade Paperback

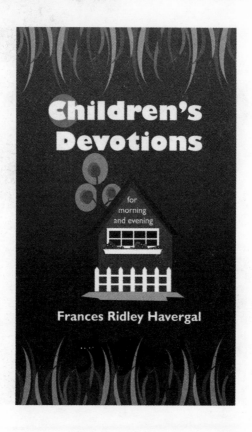

CHILDREN'S DEVOTIONS
FRANCES RIDLEY HAVERGAL

Previously published as "Morning Bells, Evening Pillows" Frances Ridley Havergal was a famous hymn writer who also wrote gospel stories for children. Here are sixty-two of her best! Each devotional story has a scripture and a short poem to think about. They are just right for first thing in the morning and last thing at night.

Age: 6-10 years.

ISBN: 185792 973X

208 pages, Trade Paperback

THE BIG BOOK OF QUESTIONS AND ANSWERS

A FAMILY DEVOTIONAL GUIDE TO THE CHRISTIAN FAITH

SINCLAIR B. FERGUSON

This is a book for families to help them discover the key doctrines of Christianity in a way that stimulates discussion and helps children want to know more. Parents can sigh with relief - their dreams have come true.

Winner of Christian Children's Book of the Year.

ISBN: 185792 2956

96 pages, Large Format Paperback

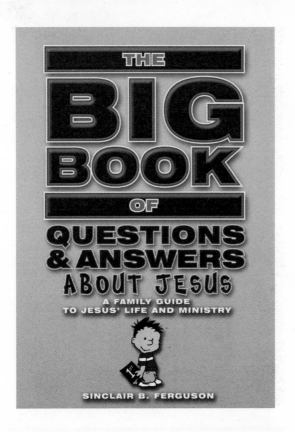

THE BIG BOOK OF QUESTIONS
AND ANSWERS ABOUT JESUS
A FAMILY GUIDE TO JESUS' LIFE AND MINISTRY
SINCLAIR B. FERGUSON

This book focuses on the person and work of Jesus Christ. A great rescource for parents and teachers.

Shortlisted for Christian Children's Book of the Year.

ISBN: 185792 5599

96 pages, Large Format, Paperback

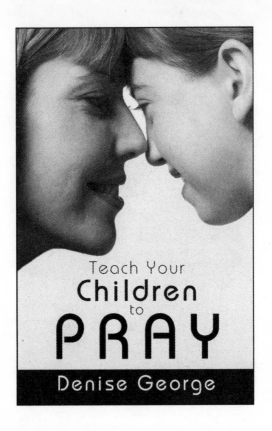

TEACH YOUR CHILDREN TO PRAY
DENISE GEORGE

This is a non-judgmental, practical, spiritual, hands-on, "I've been there" approach to Christian parenting … with a wonderful, inspiring, "get me started" focus on prayer. You will be itching to try out these ideas with your own family. You'll be encouraged by the honest approach of the author. You'll be inspired by the activities and ideas sections. And those really difficult questions that you've wanted to ask someone but haven't dared … have a look at the question section. Someone has probably asked the question before you.

ISBN: 185792 9411

304 pages, Trade, Paperback

...of such is the kingdom

nurturing children in the light of scripture • Dr. Timothy A. Sisemore

OF SUCH IS THE KINGDOM
DR. TIMOTHY SISEMORE

Are you, and your church, bringing up children the way God wants you to? Sisemore re-examines the tasks of parenting and the care of children in the church from a Biblical and theological point of view. Subjects include: Christian parenting in a hostile world, educating children spiritually and academically, disciplining and discipling, honoring parents, how are children saved?, the church's responsibility towards its children, children's involvement in worship.

ISBN: 185792 5149

192 pages, Large Trade, Paperback

CHRISTIAN FOCUS

Christian Focus Publications publishes books for adults and children under its three main imprints: Christian Focus, Mentor and Christian Heritage. Our books reflect that God's word is reliable and Jesus is the way to know him, and live for ever with him. Our children's publication list includes a Sunday school curriculum that covers pre-school to early teens; puzzle and activity books. We also publish personal and family devotional titles, biographics and inspirational stories that children will love. If you are looking for quality Bible teaching for children then we have an excellent range of Bible story and age specific theological books. From pre-school to teenage fiction, we have it covered! Find us at our webpage: www.christianfocus.com